MEMORIAL ADDRESSES ON SIR WINSTON CHURCHILL

© KARSH, OTTAWA

Winston S. Churchill

89TH CONGRESS, 1ST SESSION . . . . HOUSE DOCUMENT NO. 209

Memorial Addresses

In The

Congress of the United States

And Tributes In Eulogy of

Sir Winston Churchill

Soldier – Statesman
Author – Orator – Leader

UNITED STATES GOVERNMENT PRINTING OFFICE
WASHINGTON : 1965

Compiled Under the Direction

of the

Joint Committee on Printing

Contents

CONTENTS

CONTENTS

CONTENTS

CONTENTS

CONTENTS

H. Con. Res. 153 PASSED MARCH 29, 1965

[BY MR. FLYNT]

Eighty-ninth Congress of the United States of America

AT THE FIRST SESSION

Begun and held at the City of Washington on Monday, the fourth day of January, one thousand nine hundred and sixty-five

Concurrent Resolution

Resolved by the House of Representatives (the Senate concurring), That there be printed with illustrations as a House document all remarks by Members of the Senate and House of Representatives in the Halls of Congress which constitute tributes to the life, character, and public service of the late Sir Winston Churchill. The copy for such House document shall be prepared under the supervision of the Joint Committee on Printing.

SEC. 2. In addition to the usual number, there shall be printed five thousand eight hundred and sixty additional copies of such House document, of which one thousand and five hundred copies shall be for the use of the Senate, and four thousand three hundred and sixty copies shall be for the use of the House of Representatives.

Attest:

RALPH R. ROBERTS,
Clerk of the House of Representatives.

Attest:

FELTON M. JOHNSTON,
Secretary of the Senate.

Biography

Sir Winston Spencer Churchill, former Prime Minister of Great Britain, Honorary Citizen of the United States of America, was born November 30, 1874; son of Lord Randolph Churchill, third son of the seventh Duke of Marlborough, and American-born Jennie Jerome, daughter of Leonard Jerome, proprietor and editor of the New York Times; married Clementine Hozier, September 12, 1908; entered Army, 1895; served as Lieutenant with South African Light Horse, also as correspondent for Morning Post, South Africa, during Boer War; Lieutenant Colonel, commanding 6th Royal Fusiliers, France, 1916; retired from military career, 1916; Under Secretary of State for Colonies, 1906–08; President, Board of Trade, 1908–10; Home Secretary, 1910–11; First Lord of the Admiralty, 1911–15; Chancellor of Duchy of Lancaster, 1915; Minister of Munitions, 1917; Secretary of State for War, 1918–21, for Air, 1916–21, for the Colonies, 1921–22; Chancellor of the Exchequer, 1924–29; First Lord of the Admiralty, 1939–40; Member of Parliament as a Conservative, Oldham, 1900–1904, and a Liberal, 1904–06; a Liberal, N. W. Manchester, 1906–08; a Liberal, Dundee, 1908–22; a Constitutionalist, Epping Division of Essex, 1924–31, and a Conservative, 1931–45; and finally a Conservative, Woodford, 1945–64; Prime Minister, First Lord of the Treasury and Minister of Defense, 1940–45; Leader of Opposition, 1945–51; Prime Minister and First Lord of Treasury, 1951–55; and also Minister of Defense, 1951–52; resigned, 1955; Lord Warden of the Cinque Ports, 1941–45; Lord Rector of University of Edinburgh, 1929–31; Chancellor of Bristol University, 1930; an Elder Brother of Trinity House; Privy Councillor, 1907; Companion of Honor, 1922; decorated Order of Military Merit (Spain), several medals and clasps (British); recipient Order of the Garter, 1953; recipient Nobel Prize for Literature, 1953; Variety Clubs International Humanitarian Award; Charlemagne Prize; Fellow Royal Society; author; American awards including: Benjamin Franklin Medal, Freedom House Award, Pilgrims of U.S. Medal, New York Board of Trade Gold Award; Honorary Citizen of the States of West Virginia, Tennessee, Hawaii, New Hampshire, Nebraska, North

Carolina, and Maryland; first foreigner to be declared an Honorary Citizen of the United States of America by an act of the full Congress, April 9, 1963; conferral ceremony held at the White House, April 9, 1963, with President Kennedy reading the Proclamation of Citizenship; died January 24, 1965, and after a State Funeral was laid to rest in the yard of St. Martin's Church at Bladon, England.

Sir Winston Churchill at an early age with his American mother, Jennie Jerome Churchill

Preface

Remarks by the Honorable John J. Flynt, Jr., of Georgia, in the House of Representatives, February 3, 1965

Mr. Speaker, on Monday, February 1, I introduced a House concurrent resolution which calls for the printing as a House document remarks by Members of the House of Representatives and the Senate in the Congress of the United States, which constitute tributes to the late Sir Winston Churchill.

These remarks would be printed and bound as directed by the Joint Committee on Printing, 10 copies of such document for use by each Member of the House of Representatives and 15 copies for use by each Member of the Senate.

This House document would become a tangible symbol of the gratitude of the American people for the life of Winston Churchill and the contributions which he made during that life of four score years and ten. It will also be a reminder to us that more than that of any single person, his courage, his faith, and his indomitable will provided the leadership which led the United States, Great Britain, and our Allies to victory in World War II.

As the outstanding Briton of this century, as an honorary citizen of the United States, and as an outstanding leader of the free world, Winston Churchill merits this last tribute which we, the Congress, can bestow upon him.

I hope that this resolution will be favorably considered by the House of Representatives.

Memorial to Sir Winston Churchill from the English Speaking Union of the United States and his American admirers. The statue, by William M. McVey, will stand in front of the British Embassy Gardens in Washington, D.C., with one foot resting on British soil (the British Embassy grounds) and the other on American soil.

Head of Sir Winston Churchill by Sir Jacob Epstein. Given to the White House by war-time friends of Winston Spencer Churchill in 1965

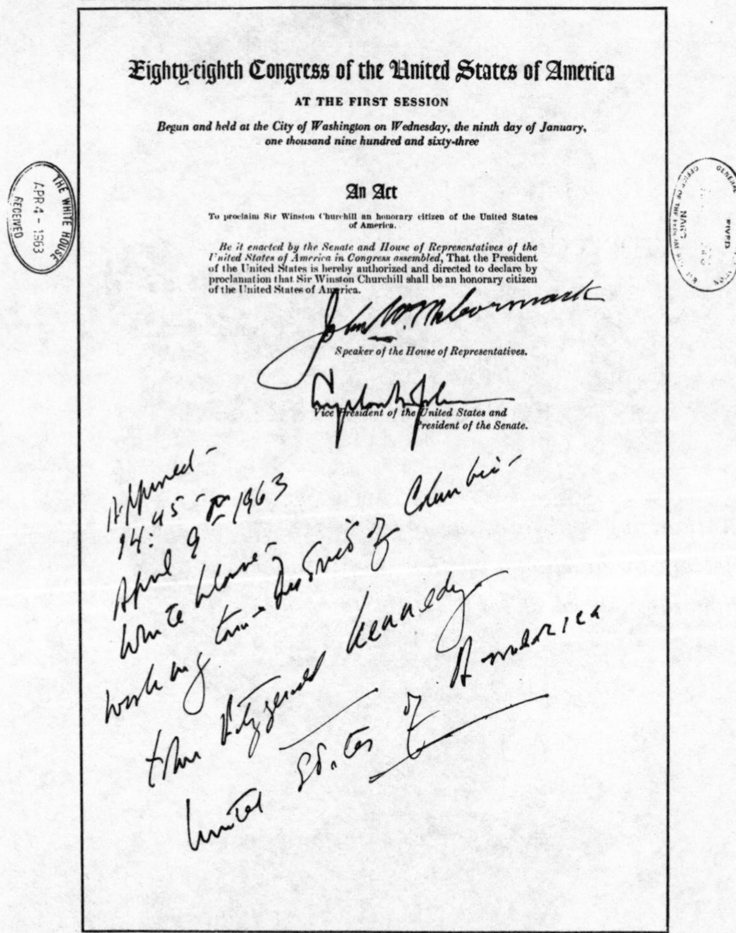

H. R. 4374

Eighty-eighth Congress of the United States of America

AT THE FIRST SESSION

Begun and held at the City of Washington on Wednesday, the ninth day of January, one thousand nine hundred and sixty-three

An Act

To proclaim Sir Winston Churchill an honorary citizen of the United States of America.

Be it enacted by the Senate and House of Representatives of the United States of America in Congress assembled, That the President of the United States is hereby authorized and directed to declare by proclamation that Sir Winston Churchill shall be an honorary citizen of the United States of America.

Speaker of the House of Representatives.

Vice President of the United States and President of the Senate.

Signed Act of Congress proclaiming Sir Winston Churchill an honorary citizen of the United States of America

Proceedings in the Congress of the United States

On Passage of H.R. 4374

Authorizing and directing the President of the United States to declare by proclamation that Sir Winston Churchill shall be an honorary citizen of the United States of America.

In the House of Representatives
of the United States

March 12, 1963

Mr. CELLER. Mr. Speaker, I ask unanimous consent for the immediate consideration of the bill (H.R. 4374) to proclaim Sir Winston Churchill an honorary citizen of the United States of America.

The Clerk read the bill as follows:

Be it enacted by the Senate and House of Representatives of the United States of America in Congress assembled, That the President of the United States is hereby authorized and directed to declare by proclamation that Sir Winston Churchill shall be an honorary citizen of the United States of America.

Mr. CELLER. Mr. Speaker, I say of Winston Spencer Churchill that I know of no individual possessed of so many facets to his life and character and personality, with so many wondrous achievements in so many fields.

He is a giant in world history.

He is a man for all seasons.

His biography is like a fascinating novel.

He inspired controversy, but not without affection and respect.

His is a dazzling, stormy, but inspired career.

His public life has stretched for more than half a century from the staid and solid Victorian era to the present hopeful second Elizabethan Age.

He is a man for the ages—statesman, soldier, author and historian, artist, philosopher, naval chief, orator and raconteur, parliamentarian, war correspondent, and humorist.

The key to his character is courage, with strategic insight coming second. He is never controlled, save by himself. Generosity, candor, openness of mind come next. He has no reserves and no shams.

He scorned concealment.

He has a passion for humanity.

He wants justice done though the heavens fall and he be buried in the ruins..

He is keenly responsive to noble impulses.

His is a life and career beyond the conventional bounds of a great statesman.

He is one of the greatest Englishmen known to history—and at that, he is half American.

Historians will speak of him as the statesman to whom the whole world looked for guidance when the very skies were about to fall upon civilization. They will recount his mastery of the written and spoken word. Lord Justice Birkett said that he ever spoke with the orator's true instinct, and that he had the "sympathy and concurrence of his time." This is especially true of the speech he made after Dunkirk when we all feared the worst. He said in the House of Commons:

> We shall not flag or fail. We shall go on to the end, we shall fight in France, we shall fight on the seas and oceans, we shall fight with growing confidence and growing strength in the air, we shall defend our island whatever the cost may be, we shall fight on the beaches, we shall fight on the landing grounds, we shall fight in the fields and in the streets, we shall fight in the hills; we shall never surrender.

Note his prescience and wisdom in describing the actions of Russia as early as 1939—as they seemed to him as First Lord of the Admiralty—as "a riddle wrapped in mystery inside an enigma."

An incisive humor always accompanied him. He could create laughter with never a fault of tact or taste.

Had his father been American and his mother English, he would undoubtedly have made American history. As it was, his mother was American and his father British and he ascended to the premiership of Great Britain.

In honoring Winston Churchill, we do not confer citizenship in any technical sense. Rather, we give concrete expression of our affection for the man.

Mr. POFF. Mr. Speaker, today, the American people are speaking their respect for Sir Winston Churchill through their chosen Representatives. But we recognize that the quantity and the quality of that respect are unspeakable dimensions. So, ours is not a tribute by word; ours is a tribute by deed. What we say here is and forever will remain inadequate. What we do here, men will always remember. The richest gift is that dearest to the giver. The gift we make is the greatest treasure in the people's storehouse. It is a gift which cannot be embellished in a fancy verbal package. The gift is its own glory, untarnished by much giving. The donee is honored in the receipt and the donor is honored in the acceptance.

Mr. HALLECK. Mr. Speaker, I take pleasure in supporting this bill to confer honorary American citizenship on Sir Winston Churchill.

His magnificent contributions to the cause of freemen assure him a place in history as one of the truly great leaders of this or any other age.

As the son of an American mother he has always been a part of us, and we are, with this action, proclaiming our pride in that fact.

This legislation, I understand, is without precedent. Possibly, too, this is the first time in the record of the Congress of the United States that unique legislation of this sort has met with such unprecedented support from both sides of the aisle.

Possibly, because of his achievements, he has been instrumental in bringing about such a broad area of agreement between the Democrats and Republicans, which would not be the least of his manifold accomplishments. Certainly it is clear evidence of the widespread esteem in which this distinguished gentleman is held by our countrymen.

Beyond that, I trust Sir Winston will recognize in this gesture our admiration for his courage, our high regard for his talents, and our gratitude for his leadership of a gallant ally through one of the most severe ordeals any nation has ever faced.

Mr. WALTER. Mr. Speaker, in adopting this legislation today, the House, speaking in behalf of the American people, will bestow upon Sir Winston S. Churchill, in an unprecedented way, the highest honor this land has ever bestowed upon any person, not an American, living or dead.

I shall not endeavor to recite what Sir Winston has done for his own country, for the unity of the English-speaking world, for the great Atlantic community, and for all the peoples of the West who were and are determined to remain free and never to succumb to a dictatorial or totalitarian rule. It would take a Plutarch to express in words Sir Winston's service to humanity:

> It is not the oratory of a statesman that deserves respect, nor the quality of his voice, said the great Greek philosopher Demosthenes, but his support of the policy willed by the people, and the fact that his country's friends and enemies are his own.

It could be, as Sir Winston wrote me back in 1958 when I suggested to him that I might introduce this type of legislation, that—to quote him—"the high regard and affection" in which he holds our country does not need "an official seal," as he expressed it.

It could be that it is indeed difficult to find an appropriate way of expressing our Nation's reciprocal feelings of esteem, high regard, and admiration for Sir Winston.

Nevertheless, as this Republic does not grant titles of nobility nor civil honors or decorations, this is the best, the most appropriate, and certainly unique way in which we as a nation can honor Sir Winston by adding to all his glory the title of honorary citizen of the United States, the first honorary citizen of the United States in our history. No less can we do to proclaim officially our feelings for the man who always stood for all that we stand for and who has led his country and with it the free world in hours of the gravest trials and tribulations.

It is most gratifying to me personally that I was given the privilege of introducing this legislation and having it brought before the House.

Mr. COLMER. Mr. Speaker, the action being taken here today in honoring this outstanding world citizen, Sir Winston Churchill, by conferring upon him honorary American citizenship is most gratifying to me, as I am sure it is to all American citizens.

This action on the part of the Congress of the United States is an unprecedented one. In all the history of this young Republic no other citizen of a foreign government has been so honored—not even the great Lafayette, the splendid friend of this young Nation. But, I can conceive of no one who is more entitled to this signal honor than Sir Winston Churchill. Surely, no world figure who strode across the stage of history throughout the memory of man contributed more to the democratic ideals of the free people than has Sir Winston Churchill. His striking and effective leadership of the Allied cause in the recent tragedy of World War II will be recorded in the annals of history as possibly the greatest factor in the victory of free peoples over nazism and its philosophy of oppression of the liberties of mankind.

Again, Mr. Speaker, being the son of an American mother and an English father, Sir Winston, more than any other, truly epitomize the union between the two great English-speaking peoples. In fact, when he addressed a joint session of the Congress on December 26, 1941, in this very Chamber, he referred to his birth in this humorous vein:

> The fact that my American forebears have for so many generations played their part in the life of the United States, and that here I am, an Englishman, welcomed in your midst, makes this experience one of the most moving and thrilling in my life, which is already long and has not been entirely uneventful.
>
> I wish indeed that my mother, whose memory I cherish across the vale of years, could have been here to see. By the way, I cannot help reflecting that if my father had been American and my mother British, instead of the other way around, I might have got here on my own. In that case, this would not have been the first time you would have heard my voice. In that case, I should not have needed any invitation; but, if I had, it is hardly likely that it would have been unanimous. So perhaps things are better as they are.

Nature seldoms grants to any one mortal being so many talents as she has so bountifully bestowed upon this great world figure. Certainly, he is one of the most versatile characters recorded in the annals of the history of the human race. As a writer, historian, painter, orator, warrior, and statesman, he excels.

Mr. Speaker, if I may be pardoned a personal reference in order to emphasize my own personal admiration for this truly great man, I should like to relate my own personal experience as chairman of the Postwar Economic Policy and Planning Committee during the late war. I had the unusual privilege of interviewing a substantial number of world leaders, including the late, but not lamented, Joseph Stalin. Included in this group was this most unusual and talented statesman, Sir Winston, himself. I can truthfully say that the highlight of this humble Member's existence was the high privilege of being his guest at a family dinner. The memory of that eventful occasion as well as the benefit of his thinking in reference to the necessity for a firm policy in dealing with the Kremlin masters will ever remain with me.

Mr. Speaker, I introduced a resolution in August 1962 to carry out the purposes of this resolution. But, because there was some question raised at that time as to whether this met with Sir Winston's approval, I did not press the matter. However, at the beginning of this new Congress, I reintroduced the resolution, after first corresponding with him and receiving his confidential reply to my letter. I am, I repeat, very happy that the Judiciary Committee, under the leadership of my distinguished colleague the gentleman from Pennsylvania, Francis Walter, and the gentleman from New York, Chairman Emanuel Celler, has finally brought this timely and appropriate action to the attention of the House. I am confident that it will pass both Houses of the Congress without marked or substantial dissent and that the President of the United States will exercise the mandate of the Congress with pleasure and alacrity.

Mr. CHELF. Mr. Speaker, those of you who have served with me in this Chamber for the past 18 years know that I rarely take the floor to speak and that when I do, I must needs feel very deeply and sincerely about the subject matter at hand. The legislation before us now not only interests me greatly but it is an honor and a privilege for me to urge all of you wholeheartedly to support this bill which would bestow honorary American citizenship upon that great, worldwide statesman, the very honorable Sir Winston Churchill.

This legislation unanimously passed our Immigration and Nationality Subcommittee and, within hours thereafter, it unanimously passed the full Judiciary Committee. I sincerely trust, therefore, that it will pass the House of Representatives unanimously today.

Every American and all free people the world over have a vast store of love, affection, and admiration for this magnificent Englishman whose blood coursing through his veins is one-half American through his mother, the former Jennie Jerome, of New York.

During his 88 wonderful years, he has given unstintingly in loyal service to his beloved country. However, his admiration for the United States is well known. He has visited our Nation 16 times. Upon being made a member of the Society of the Cincinnati, composed of descendants of the officers who fought in the American Revolution, he said here in January 1952:

I am deeply grateful and proud of my American ancestry and think it is a wonderful thing that I have the honor to rejoice in that fact, while at the same time I have never failed in the proper observance of correct constitutional duties to my own country.

His "blood, toil, tears, and sweat" speech delivered in the House of Commons on May 13, 1940, sounded the alert which stirred the hearts and inspired to action all people committed to the cause of freedom. This speech stands as a monumental challenge to liberty lovers, which may remain unmatched in brilliance and appeal "forever and a day, till these walls shall crumble in ruins and molder in dust away."

He continued not only to lead the British people but, also, was a constant source of inspiration to all of our allies during the long, anguished years of World War II. As long as any of us shall live we shall carry the memory of the resolute, valiant Churchill pictured on land and on sea, emerging even from the ashes of destruction and human misery, but always holding his hand aloft, with his fingers forming his famous V-for-victory sign, standing as a shining symbol of hope and man's determination to remain free. God willing the young men and women of our own beloved country, including my own son, Frank, Junior, would try to emulate this world-renowned and famous leader.

As you may recall, the British general elections were held in July 1945, and the Conservative Government headed by Mr. Churchill unfortunately was defeated. I was in England during that campaign and it made me sick at heart to hear him criticized and to learn at that time that his own people did not really appreciate him.

At a private gathering at a home in England, during that visit I made a little speech with an impassioned plea. I told them how wrong I knew them to be in taking such an attitude toward him, that as an ally and a friend, I could most certainly understand their bitter disappointment over the lack of food, housing, and clothing, but that they knew in their hearts that these shortages were brought about by the war. I also told them that while they might be lacking in some material things, they had their honor, their integrity, and their very heads on their shoulders because of the leadership of this wonderful man. I quoted to them from the Bible:

> A prophet is not without honor, save in his own country and in his own house.

Oh, how glad I was to get a favorable reaction during my talk when they gave me several rousing "hear, hears." Later on, as I knew they would, the British people rallied around Sir Winston again and took him back into their confidence and their hearts where he has remained ever since and shall forevermore—actually, they had never let him out of their hearts.

While we in America cannot properly honor this well-loved man any more than he has already been honored, nevertheless, this action taken today by the U.S. House of Representatives is without precedent in all of our glorious history and will resound as a 21-gun salute, from those of us here who represent the 190 million Americans who love, respect, admire, and revere this extraordinary Englishman for his successful fight to preserve the peace of the world.

To find words adequate to describe properly this distinguished man is comparable to gilding the lily, bringing cotton to Alabama, the derby to England, and good bourbon to my native Kentucky.

His bravery, his fortitude, his tenacity of purpose, and his unyielding desire to win shall never be forgotten.

In my opinion, his achievements shall stand out forever like the Washington Monument, Big Ben, the Eiffel Tower, and the Pyramids. By his unselfish service to mankind, he has emblazoned his name with honor and everlasting distinction in huge letters of gold in the silver pages of world history. Why? Because during war, travail, "blood and tears and sweat," fear, want, privation, devastation, chaos, and despair—at a time when it seemed all was lost—this incomparable leader was the epitome of hope, the very embodiment of courage, the preserver of time, the protector of faith, the guardian of destiny, the inspiration for victory, and the successful negotiator of the peace.

These and many other attributes have endeared him not only to America, the native land of his sweet and gentle mother, but to all creeds and colors, the rich and the poor, in every nation of the free world, who love liberty, decency, and Christianity.

To paraphrase one of his own famous statements: "Never in the field of human conflict was so much owed by so many to one man."

May he have a full fruition of his dreams and a happy realization of all of his endeavors. "May his leaf never wither and whatsoever he doeth, may it prosper." May God in His infinite wisdom spare and protect our beloved friend, Sir Winston, for many years to come and may He who reigns as the King of Kings, the master of all lodges, nations, and men, smile graciously, abundantly, beautifully, and everlastingly from His wide blue canopy of heaven upon this, our worthy candidate for the position of the world's most honored peacemaker since that lowly Man walked the shores of Galilee many centuries ago.

It is said in the fifth chapter of Matthew:

Blessed are the peacemakers for they shall be called the children of God.

Sir Winston was a peacemaker but only on honorable terms. And here, my colleagues, I am reminded of those beautiful lines in the wartime song "The White Cliffs of Dover"—remember?

There will be blue birds over
The white cliffs of Dover
Tomorrow—just you wait and see;
And there will be love and laughter
And peace forever after
Tomorrow—when the world is free.

Sir Winston helped to make these words come true.

Thank the Lord, he did not place his light "under a bushel, but on a candlestick and it giveth light unto all in the house."

I trust that Sir Winston will forgive my inadequate words of praise—and I say this from a humble heart, unfortunately, not in America or England or anyplace else, on the face of the globe, is there another Churchill with the command of the King's English which he alone possesses.

May he live to be over 100 years of age and then, God willing, may we be permitted to turn the wheels of the speedometer of time back and start all over with him again.

Hail—noble Englishman!

Hail—great American!

Mr. WHITENER. Mr. Speaker, the legislation we have under consideration today in the House of Representatives to authorize the President of the United States to proclaim Sir Winston Churchill an honorary citizen of the United States of America marks a milestone in the legislative history of our country. Never before has the Congress conferred American citizenship on a citizen of another nation.

It is altogether fitting and proper that the first great figure in world history to be honored with the priceless mantle of American citizenship should be Sir Winston Leonard Spencer Churchill. No other living person is more respected, esteemed, and venerated by our people than is Sir Winston.

He was born November 30, 1874, the son of Lord Randolph Churchill and Jenny Jerome, a vivacious, young, American girl from New York City. Sir Winston has always been proud of his American heritage. The American people have shared this pride, and Sir Winston's background has been a tie that has bound him and our people together in a bond of mutual affection.

In the course of American history there has been only one other person who has captured the hearts, the admiration, and the love of the American people as has Sir Winston Churchill. He can take his place in history along with the beloved Lafayette whose life and character have left a profound and lasting impact on the American people.

The unexcelled genius of Sir Winston has made itself felt in journalism, statesmanship, diplomacy, literature, and in the science of war. In each of these fields he has been a remarkable success.

Soon after his graduation in 1894 from Sandhurst, the English West Point, as number 8 in a class of 150, Sir Winston entered the British Army. He combined the talents of a soldier with that of a journalist, and the books and articles he wrote during the late 1890's and early 1900's form a wonderful part of our heritage of English literature.

In time of crisis the English people have always turned to Sir Winston Churchill for leadership. In 1911 he was made First Lord of the British Admiralty, and with foresight and vigor he went to work to make the British Navy ready for the war he felt certain was coming with the Germans. When the fury of World War I broke over England in 1914, the British Navy was ready to defend the island kingdom, thanks to Sir Winston.

In 1916 he went to the front as a lieutenant colonel in command of the Sixth Royal Fusiliers of the British Army. The same year he was recalled from the front and made Minister of Munitions. From 1918 to 1921 Sir Winston was Secretary of State for War and Air.

Following World War I, Sir Winston combined service in the House of Commons with his literary pursuits. As the approaching storm of World War II appeared on the horizon he called upon the British people in dynamic speech after speech to prepare themselves to meet the scourge of nazism. His was a voice in the wilderness, however, and after Munich he stood in the House of Commons and uttered these words:

> You were given the choice between war and dishonor. You chose dishonor, and you will have war.

When the storm that Sir Winston had predicted broke over the English people he was again called to a position of great leadership in his nation. He was reappointed First Lord of the Admiralty on September 3, 1939. The following year he became chairman of the Armed Services Committee and in the same year assumed the awesome responsibility of Prime Minister.

It was during World War II that Sir Winston reached the zenith of his long and illustrious career. Through his indomitable courage, his inspired oratory, and his unfailing faith in ultimate victory, he led his people, and indeed the people of the free world, to victory.

Throughout his long career Sir Winston Churchill has been an implacable foe of communism. He was one of the first world statesmen after World War II to point out the dangers lurking behind the Iron and Bamboo Curtains. He has consistently urged a strong stand against communism and has never failed to speak out against the Communist conspiracy.

Mr. Speaker, Sir Winston has demonstrated his friendship for the United States time and again in speeches, in the books and articles he has written, and in actions. I think a statement that he made on December 10, 1948, conveys the feelings of this great man toward the United States. In speaking of foreign policy he said:

What are those major themes in foreign policy? The first is an ever closer and more effective relationship, or as I like to call it, fraternal association, with the United States. In the ever closer unity of the English-speaking world lies the main hope of human freedom and a great part of the hope of our own survival.

Again on May 12, 1949, Sir Winston said:

We give our thanks to the United States for the splendid part they are playing in the world.

Mr. Speaker, the American people heartily approve of the action we are taking today in this House to authorize the President of the United States to confer honorary American citizenship upon Sir Winston Churchill. Sir Winston is possibly the greatest living person of our age. His accomplishments and the things for which he stands tower above the ordinary events of our day.

In the broad panorama of human history Sir Winston Churchill will be numbered among the greatest men of all time. It is certain that he will be described as the greatest Englishman.

Let us pass this bill, then, and welcome Sir Winston into the inner circle of American citizenship. In so doing we will have the sure knowledge that posterity will say that England's greatest son was also an American.

Mr. PEPPER. Mr. Speaker, I am proud to have the privilege of joining the Members of this House today in speaking the sentiment of the American people to pay token tribute to one of the colossal figures of history, a man whose striding in seven league boots through the pages and the record of history is one of the great stories of mankind.

Those of us who have been privileged to have some public or private contacts with this unique, this eminent man, shall cherish those as highlights of our lives, because they were the occasions when we approached near the summit of human personality. His intrepid courage, his indomitable will, his unfaltering faith in the presence of danger and difficulty not only tended to save a good old world but were largely the foundation for the building of a nobler and a grander new.

As long as men in their hearts are thrilled by the epic deeds of heroic men, as long as gallantry and courage shall be emulated by aspiring men, women, and youth, the name of Winston Churchill shall be kept warm in the hearts of men, women, and children everywhere.

Mr. Speaker, if this Republic shall last a decade or a thousand years, its glory and its grandeur shall ever be enhanced by the action of this Congress and our President and this country in our time in adding to the roster of our citizens the imperishable, the magnificent name of Winston Churchill.

Mr. CUNNINGHAM. Mr. Speaker, I am honored to be able to participate in these activities in which the House of Representatives offers honorary citizenship to one of the world's living legends and a man who holds a place of esteem in the hearts of Americans.

Sir Winston Churchill was given a fitting tribute by the Nebraska Legislature on February 12 of this year, when by a unanimous vote citizenship in the State of Nebraska was conferred on him. Nebraska was the first State to so honor Sir Winston.

The resolution of the Nebraska Legislature reads in part:

Whereas Sir Winston Churchill has, by his courage, tenacity, wisdom, and leadership both in war and in peace, assured for himself a place of eminence among the great men of history—

Certainly these words sum up the characteristics which the world has come to know in Sir Winston—courage, tenacity, wisdom, and leadership. In his long career of service to his government and the free world, Sir Winston has been a guest in this country on several occasions. They have been occasions on which history was made—wartime conferences, his Iron Curtain speech, or his appearance before the Congress.

He will always have a prominent place in history, not only for his achievements, but because of his writings which will give to future generations an appreciation of the events of today and yesterday.

I am pleased to offer now the resolution passed by the Nebraska Legislature.

LEGISLATIVE RESOLUTION 12

Whereas Sir Winston Churchill has, by his courage, tenacity, wisdom, and leadership both in war and in peace, assured for himself a place of eminence among the great men of history; and

Whereas it is proper that the highest honor and acclaim be accorded Sir Winston Churchill during his lifetime; and

Whereas the greatest honor that this legislature can confer is the grant of citizenship in the great State of Nebraska: Now, therefore, be it

Resolved by the members of the Nebraska Legislature in 73d session assembled:

1. That full citizenship in the great State of Nebraska, with all rights and privileges appertaining thereto, is hereby granted Sir Winston Churchill.
2. That a copy of this resolution, suitably engrossed and signed by the president of the legislature be transmited by the clerk of the legislature to Sir Winston Churchill, Vice President Johnson, Senator Young, Senator Javits, Senator Magnuson, Senator Roman Hruska, Senator Curtis, Congressmen Cunningham, Martin, and Beermann.

DWIGHT W. BURNEY,
President of the Legislature.
HUGO F. SRB,
Clerk of the Legislature.

Mr. BEERMANN. Mr. Speaker, of course, I wish to concur in the remarks made by the senior Member from Nebraska in the House of Representatives [Mr. Cunningham], and add that I, too, will welcome the Honorable Winston Churchill as an honorary citizen of the United States.

As my distinguished colleague has pointed out, Mr.. Churchill is already an honorary citizen of my home State, Nebraska, by virtue of Legislative Resolution 12 passed by the 73d current session of the Nebraska unicameral.

It is my belief that many Nebraskans, particularly those of us who took part in World War II, have a great deal of respect and admiration for Mr. Churchill's strength of character. I think it can be said that it was his hand on the ship of state in England during the 1942 and 1943 bombings that was the prime reason for England's heroic defense of her perimeter.

In addition, Mr.. Churchill's indomitable will and his unyielding defiance gave the English people the strength of purpose necessary to carry them successfully through this conflict. I might also add that probably as a result of Mr. Churchill's tenacity, the United States gained a measure of time, time which was used to prepare for and later win an all-out victory.

In conclusion, I earnestly commend Mr. Churchill's strength of character and purpose to this body and urge that it confer on him the greatest honor that it can possibly bestow; namely, citizenship in the United States.

Mr. MOORE. Mr. Speaker, I rise in support of the legislation before the House today. In March the Legislature of West Virginia conferred honorary citizenship of our State on Sir Winston Churchill. I am well aware of the apprehension in some minds here today about the wisdom of what we are doing. I can only say, as a member of the subcommittee that recommended this legislation, that this action today does not confer upon Sir Winston United States citizenship as we know it and as it is referred to in the statutes. There will be no oath of allegiance to the laws of this Nation. This is a token of recognition, by Presidential proclamation solely. What we do today is to authorize by this declaration the bestowing of an honorary title on Sir Winston, rather than an act that would be an obligation, if he were to appear in a court and assume the rights and obligations of U.S. citizenship.

However, Mr Speaker, it might be appropriate to add just a little footnote to what I have just said. Sir Winston is 88 years old now. But if he were born after May 24, 1934, he would have had a choice to become either a U.S. citizen at birth, or a citizen of Great Britain. Why? When he was born section 1933 of the Revised Statutes of the United States was still in effect and U.S. citizenship could be conferred upon a child born abroad only by his father, if he was a U.S. citizen. No mother, although born in the United States, could then have conferred U.S. citizenship upon her child born abroad. This is why Sir Winston had no claim to U.S. citizenship. That law was changed on May 24, 1934, and the change under which both a father or a mother, a U.S. citizen, could confer citizenship upon a child born abroad is in effect today.

Since we are writing history today rather than passing a bill, I believe that this short explanatory note might be in order, and perhaps interesting for those who seem to nurse qualms or worries about what we are doing today.

Mr. FLOOD. Mr. Speaker, were Sir Winston Leonard Spencer Churchill to accept the offer to become an honorary citizen of the United States—for which there is now pending a bill in Congress—the honor would become a two-way street. This honor is the highest which we in the United States can offer. All this we feel for Sir Winston.

In the opposite direction, it would be difficult to exaggerate the honor which would accrue to the United States in the acquisition of so outstanding a citizen. A mere listing of the professions in which he has served is a source of astonishment. Yet not just in one but in many he has occupied a foremost position. Furthermore, he has served with such distinction that in a variety of fields he has received the highest honors. His tremendous versatility makes even a listing difficult. Where to begin? Statesman, soldier, author, artist, journalist, politician par excellence, lecturer, editor, chancellor or rector in three universities, bricklayer and—less professionally, but nonetheless competently—prophet and soothsayer; all these professions in one man's life, and all creditably performed.

To explain the "prophet and soothsayer" and to take the latter first, there are volumes upon the library shelves around the world consisting of excerpts from his wise remarks, quotations abounding in "The Wit and Wisdom of Winston Churchill"—as one title reads. As prophet, Winston Churchill has foreseen and advised the world abount many things good and bad that have been of immense importance recognized only later by others. During World War I, from having been actually in it he retired in 1916 to become the Minister of Munitions. In that capacity he was in a position to promote the use of the tank as a weapon of war. According to Ludendorff, the latter course of the war was decided in no small measure by the development of the tank.

As early as 1925, Churchill had written an essay entitled "Shall We Commit Suicide?" in which he called attention to the potential danger of Germany. During the thirties he continually warned against German armament and aggression. He also argued both in Parliament and on the lecture platform for a powerful air force.

As statesman, Winston Churchill has been three times Prime Minister of the United Kingdom. During the first of these terms he led the coalition government through World War II, 1940–45. Through the darkest days in England's history, when the threat of Hitler's invasion was very real and there were no allies to help, it was largely the spirit of Prime Minister Churchill, a giant of faith, of courage, and of inspiration, which led his countrymen through their "finest hour."

As a soldier and Cabinet minister he had had outstanding preparation for the highest post in government in such a crisis. His soldiering had begun at an early age. Entering the British Army when he was 21 he had served with distinction in India, won an award of Military Merit from Spain when serving with the Spanish forces in Cuba, and taken part in the Nile Expeditionary Force, writing a book about this African experience.

As author, Sir Winston Churchill was awarded the Nobel Prize for literature in 1953. His histories of both World Wars are practically unrivaled in importance. Four volumes of the first, six of the second are only a few among the total of his literary productions. Memoirs, fiction, biography, history, political studies have flowed from his pen. His speeches alone fill volumes. So prolific is his output that it is the more amazing that he is a master of style; his writings are a literary delight.

We have mentioned but a few of his accomplishments. As you are aware, the doings of this talented and energetic personage already have filled various books. By 1945 he was considered by many as the greatest man in the world; and he never rested upon his laurels. His activities have been noteworthy, however, even more for their quality than for their quantity. The phrases that characterize him and his work are manifold and, withal, highly complimentary. He is known as a man who had the ability to do what he advocated; and he advocated patience and firmness; magnanimity to the defeated enemy in war. He said:

We must look through other people's eyes as well as our own.

He has ever been a man of humanity, of courage, intelligence of the highest order, generosity, loyalty, geniality, humor—yes, and impudence. It is safe to say that no one has delighted more people as well as inspired them.

Among the many facets of this man of apparently limitless ability, that for which we in America may be the most thankful is his interest in the promotion of the Anglo-American alliance. He has said:

Let us be united and let our hopes lie in our unity because we understand each other. We understand when things go wrong, or things are said, or anything like that, we really can afford to pass them by.

Sir Winston has here expressed the core of the Anglo-American alliance. Our countries need statesmen with magnanimity to carry us over the rough places. We need such vision and tolerance and geniality as he has ever exhibited to keep the Anglo-American alliance as a living reality, to keep family quarrels on the small squabble level, never letting them undermine the basic friendship so valuable to us and to the world. Sir Winston in his person has made vast contributions to that friendship. What he has done will stand as a bond forever.

Mr. BENNETT of Florida. Mr. Speaker, luck is being prepared for opportunity. By such definition, Hon. Winston Churchill was a lucky man. He had prepared himself for great leadership and when world events required a man of colossal stature he was available and gave this opportunity a magnificent fruition. America, England, and all of the free world are and will always be debtors to the courage, wisdom, and superlative character of this noble man. With the enactment of this measure today there will go forward to him and his beloved wife and family the love, affection, and gratitude of every true American.

Mr. RHODES of Arizona. Mr. Speaker, I was pleased to note recent remarks attributed to Sir Winston Churchill expressing his desire to accept honorary citizenship should it be tendered to him by the United States. And I support the bill before the House today which proposes a proclamation of honorary citizenship for this great statesman.

Mankind was in one of its darkest hours when Sir Winston Churchill spoke elegant words about "their finest hour." Mankind stood close to a new dark age when Sir Winston Churchill faced a tyrannical enemy poised on the shores of the English Channel and vowed to "fight on the beaches, fight on the landing fields, fight in the fields and in the streets, in the hills; we shall never surrender."

But Sir Winston did more than speak—he acted. He transmitted the required "blood, toil, tears, and sweat" to the reality of a positive strategy and strength for victory.

Winston Churchill was among the first to warn that "an Iron Curtain has descended across the Continent" as early as March 5, 1946. Today we realize that we, like the British Empire during World War II, are in a precarious position requiring the leadership of a Churchill—combining words with deeds and necessitating a will to win. For, as Churchill himself once said:

> No one can guarantee success in war, but only deserve it.

The lesson of Sir Winston Churchill to us today should give rise to policies deserving success for the entire free world now and in the future.

Mr. Speaker, I gladly support legislation tendering honorary American citizenship to Sir Winston Churchill. He said that:

> Never in the field of human conflict was so much owed by so many to so few.

One of the most valiant and gallant of those few was Churchill himself.

Mr. BARRY. Mr. Speaker, I rise in support of this bill to bestow honorary citizenship to one of America's most cherished and respected friends. Mr. Winston Churchill, who so often expresses pride in his American heritage, was the symbol of leadership in the free world during the darkest moments of our time. It seems fittingly appropriate that during the twilight years of this variegated and abundant career that the Congress of the United States, reflecting the will of the people, extend America's highest gift—that of honorary citizenship.

When captain of the ship of state his indomitable spirit narrowed the broad expanse of an ocean that separated freedom loving people, and through his example of courage and leadership he created a bond of unity for the peoples of the Atlantic upon which our future survival depends. Winston Churchill belongs not only to Great Britain, but to the whole world, to each man who reveres liberty and the dignity of the individual. Above all he cherished the rights of the individual. I know that we shall add to a long list this honor as an expression of gratitude and respect from an aware and appreciative Nation.

Mr. VAN DEERLIN. Mr. Speaker, with thousands of other Americans, I am gratified that Congress is about to extend honorary citizenship to Sir Winston Churchill.

No American who served overseas during the war years, and observed the gallant manner in which the British people endured not only the flaring moments of tragedy but the long, grinding years of make-do and do-without could fail to realize how their load was lightened by the never-failing confidence of "Winnie."

On behalf of the people of California, it is with pride that I welcome this great man into fellow citizenship, even though it be but honorary.

Mr. ROOSEVELT. Mr. Speaker, rarely in the history of civilization has there appeared a man of the stature and caliber of Sir Winston Churchill. During his entire lifetime he has demonstrated a selfless devotion to his fellow man. His distinguished career in his own country includes service as a warrior and as a statesman. By his courageous and honorable deeds, he is revered as the inspiration and the moving force which rallied freedom-loving peoples of the world during their most perilous period. World over, Sir Winston is known as a man of peace, a statesman of international repute, philosopher, political leader, artist, and a man of letters. And there is no person who has done so much, to the benefit of so many, in promoting and developing the bonds of strength which hold together the union of English-speaking peoples.

President Kennedy, when a U.S. Senator, stated:

> I believe now that Sir Winston has left active political office, that a grant of honorary U.S. citizenship to him would be a worthy and fully deserved gesture.

The President has reaffirmed that statement only recently.

Including my joint resolution, five bills were introduced in this session of Congress, both in the House and in the Senate, to honor Sir Winston by declaring him to be a citizen of the United States. A precedent for such action has been established by the granting of honorary citizenship to that great French nobleman, the Marquis de Lafayette, for his invaluable service to our cause. Only in this way is it possible for us to demonstrate formally the affection and high regard the American people hold for this grand old man of our time.

As the world's most honored man, Sir Winston already holds a number of American awards. These include honorary citizenship of Jacksonville, Fla.; the Gold Medal of the city of New York; the Franklin Medal of the city of Philadelphia; the American Freedom House Award; the Distinguished Service Medal; the right to wear a pilot's wings of the U.S. Air Force. In addition, Sir Winston has been decorated by 11 foreign countries as well as his own, and is an honorary citizen of 10 other cities.

It is indeed fitting that we bestow this added honor to illustrate our respect and admiration.

Mr. SCHADEBERG. Mr. Speaker, I will cast my vote for granting honorary citizenship to Sir Winston Churchill, fully realizing that one could justifiably oppose this bill.

In conferring honorary citizenship upon Sir Winston, we honor a man, a leader, who by his example inspired in his people the will, the determination, to bring to a successful conclusion, the struggle in which they were engaged against the kind of tyranny which we in our Nation have consistently opposed.

Sir Winston did not vacillate in his determination to keep his nation free, nor did he accept any appeasement-type diplomacy that could be interpreted by others to mean that freemen lack the will to win or are unwilling to make the sacrifice for that which they believe to be right and honorable.

The tyranny of communism today is the same as the tyranny of nazism against which Sir Winston and the great people of his country, of America, and indeed of all the Allied Nations, so valiantly fought. To be sure, it bears a different name. But it is marked with the same kind of ruthless authoritarianism.

Sir Winston symbolized the truth that only he can effectively lead others to sacrifice, no matter how noble the cause, who is himself willing to share in making that sacrifice.

May I add that no nation can lead other nations to sacrifice for the noble ideal of the preservation and extension of freedom and human dignity unless that nation is willing to take the lead in that sacrifice.

We are well reminded that freedom does not come cheap. It is bought—to use the classic words of Sir Winston himself—with "blood, sweat, and tears." And no generation can ever live secure in the false belief that freedom is not its responsibility.

I feel privileged to share in conferring upon this great man of history, Sir Winston Churchill, honorary citizenship in the United States of America. I so cast my vote only after soberly weighing the proposal; after deliberating long on the responsibilities that accompany U.S. citizenship, honorary or otherwise; and after seriously considering all implications inherent in the act. I am certain Sir Winston would have it on no other grounds.

Mr. HORTON. Mr. Speaker, I rise to commend the action of our colleagues in voting to proclaim Sir Winston Churchill an honorary citizen of the United States of America.

Because of his outstanding and distinguished record in world public life, I think we are inclined to forget the close personal ties Sir Winston has to the United States. This bond, of course, extends to his own parentage, for his maternal ancestors were citizens of this Nation.

My home community of Rochester, N.Y., is particularly proud of the fact that Sir Winston's grandmother, Clara Hall, grew up in Rochester. She later married Leonard Jerome, who came to Rochester from New York City.

While in Rochester, Leonard Jerome played an important role in the development of the Native American, a daily newspaper. In 1857, his publication combined with another to become the Democrat and American, a direct forerunner of today's Rochester Democrat & Chronicle.

For these and many other reasons, I regard my opportunity to vote in favor of this bill proclaiming Sir Winston an honorary citizen as a great privilege in behalf of a great man.

In the United States Senate

APRIL 2, 1963

Mr. DIRKSEN. Mr. President, by direction and by authority of the Senate Committee on the Judiciary, I ask unanimous consent that out of order I may call up for immediate consideration H.R. 4374, which is a bill to proclaim Sir Winston Churchill an honorary citizen of the United States of America.

Mr. YOUNG of Ohio. Mr. President, the action of the Congress of the United States in authorizing the President of the United States to issue a proclamation declaring Winston Churchill to be an honorary citizen of the United States of America will be greeted with acclaim throughout the free world, and by the governing officials of all countries of the world which are now engaged in the grim struggle against Communist aggression.

In the entire history of mankind, very few individuals have made as many notable contributions to their times as has Winston Churchill in the 20th century. The entire world is indebted to him for his leadership in the struggle of freemen and women, first against nazism and fascism, and then against communism. He is one of those honored few whose names themselves speak for their achievements.

As a writer, a historian, and an orator, he is, indeed, one of the great masters of all time in the use of the English language. He has earned for himself a place among the literary giants of the English-speaking world.

In addition, Winston Churchill has manifested his greatness and his patriotism in such a manner that a thousand years from now people in far places will recall his life and say of him that, in the dark hour of Nazi aggression, under his leadership, the peoples of the world were restored to their simple dignity as creatures of God.

Many years ago—in fact, in the latter part of December 1941, following Pearl Harbor—as Representative at Large from the State of Ohio, I sat within a few feet of Mr. Churchill and heard him tell a joint meeting of the Members of the Senate and the House of Representatives that his father was an Englishman and his mother an American and had that situation been reversed and had his father been an American and his mother an Englishwoman—he hoped and believed he would be sitting there in his own right as an American citizen.

I remember also on that occasion when he was denouncing that day of infamy, December 7, 1941, he said:

We Anglo-Saxons will teach them a lesson that they and the world will never forget.

He fulfilled that pledge.

Mr. President, on August 9, 1962, I introduced a joint resolution which would have authorized the President to issue a proclamation declaring Winston Churchill an honorary citizen of the United States. This was the first resolution introduced for this purpose. My distinguished colleague, the senior Senator from Ohio [Mr. Lausche] and other Senators joined me as coauthors. That joint resolution was reintroduced on the opening day for receiving resolutions and bills in the present Congress.

Mr. President, the facts are that on July 23, 1962, only a short time before the joint resolution was introduced in this Chamber by me and cosponsored by my colleague [Mr. Lausche] and other Senators, the Plain Dealer, a great newspaper in Cleveland, Ohio, and in our Nation, published an excellent article on Winston Churchill. The article was entitled, "Hero of Two Nations." Its author was Kay Halle.

Miss Halle is one of the outstanding women in the United States. She is a personable television and radio commentator, a journalist, an author, and a world traveler of note. Not only is she at the present time one of the world's outstanding women, but also during World War II she served her country in an executive capacity in the Office of Strategic Services. In recent years she has been serving the administration as a member of President Kennedy's Advisory Committee on the Arts.

Miss Halle, of Cleveland, Ohio, first met Winston Churchill in 1931. At that time she was writing a column from London for the Cleveland News. During her stay in England in the following years, she spent many weekends at Chartwell with the Churchill family. She recalled those years, 30 years later, in her article published in the Plain Dealer.

In that article she wrote of the contribution and the service which Winston Churchill had rendered to his nation, to the United States, and, in fact, to all the nations of the free world. She suggested that it would be fitting if the President of the United States, under an act of Congress, should bestow upon Winston Churchill honorary citizenship of this country.

When the word goes out from Washington that the President of the United States has issued such a proclamation—and it will be issued very shortly, due to the authorization by both bodies of the Congress—it will be a fitting honor, and, I fear, one of the final honors which will come to this great citizen of the world.

I invite attention, Mr. President, to the fact that although many resolutions have been introduced in both bodies to confer honorary citizenship upon Winston Churchill, we should recall at this time that Kay Halle of Ohio was the person who first suggested that this be done.

We can all take some satisfaction that this action, without precedent in the history of our country, has taken place; and that, in his final days on this earth, Winston Churchill, former Prime Minister of England, former leader of the free world, is an honorary citizen of the United States.

Mr. LAUSCHE. Mr. President, I merely wish to commend my colleague for the beautiful remarks he has made with respect to Sir Winston Churchill. I was glad to join him in sponsorship of the measure. I am prouder now, knowing that the objective is reaching its achievement, to be a sponsor along with him of this very fine measure. I commend him for the remarks he has made.

Mr. DIRKSEN. I should afford full credit to the distinguished Senators from Ohio and West Virginia for having introduced the measures in the Senate.

I was directed by the Committee on the Judiciary this morning to report the House bill and ask for its passage, because the Senate bill carried a preamble. Since there was a variance as between texts, the Senate bill would have had to go to conference. Time was of the essence. Therefore, we submitted the House version, and the bill was passed today.

I am deeply grateful to my friend from Ohio for having taken cognizance of this matter quite some time ago.

Mr. YOUNG of Ohio. The distinguished minority leader has, from the beginning, been enthusiastic in his support of this measure, and all Americans can be grateful to him for the fact that, largely due to his leadership, this action was taken today.

The bill will go immediately to the White House, and very shortly Winston Churchill will be made an honorary citizen of the United States.

Mr. RANDOLPH. Mr. President, I am gratified by the overwhelming response to the proposals presented by the distinguished junior Senator from Ohio [Mr. Young] and other members of the Congress to accord honorary citizenship on Sir Winston Churchill, of Great Britain. It was a genuine privilege to have joined in the cosponsorship of legislation to bring this deserved honor to a gallant gentleman and an esteemed leader of freemen.

It is pleasing to recall, too, that the West Virginia Legislature, on February 22, 1963, adopted a resolution bestowing on Sir Winston Churchill the title of "Honorary Citizen of the State of West Virginia."

Sir Winston Churchill is not only a most distinguished elder statesman and citizen of Great Britain, but, indeed, he is now about to become officially an honorary citizen of the United States. In a larger sense we can honor this courageous and inspiring leader during the strife and turmoil of two World Wars as truly a citizen of the world.

TUESDAY, APRIL 9, 1963

Mr. MANSFIELD. Mr. President, in the midst of legislative debate last Tuesday, the Senate paused for a moment to vote U.S. citizenship for an Englishman. The occasion was duly noted by several of our colleagues and all wished the recipient well. However, the demands of duty pressed upon us, and shortly we were compelled to return to the consideration of our business.

Too often these moments go by here without warning and without time for savored meditation. But these past few days of spring have been warm and sunny, conducive to meditation, and their pleasantness disturbed my resting memories of a time some 20 years ago, a time C. P. Snow has called, "the beautiful, shining, desperate summer of 1940."

It was after Dunkirk, and the final fall of France with its accompanying bitter disappointments was only 3 weeks away.

The stubborn resistance of civilization seemed narrowing down to that small island in the North Atlantic; but the voice of that resistance growled out across the airwaves that England would never surrender. We remember those words clearly:

> We shall defend our island, whatever the cost may be. We shall fight on the beaches, we shall fight on the landing grounds, we shall fight in the fields and in the streets, we shall fight in the hills; we shall never surrender, and even if, which I do not for a moment believe, this island or a large part of it were subjugated and starving, then our empire beyond the seas * * * would carry on the struggle, until, in God's good time, the New World, with all its power and might, steps forth to the rescue and the liberation of the Old.

With pride, Winston Churchill addressed his own people, and with patience the people of a sister nation across the Atlantic. It was clear to him that the medieval darkness which was then gathering on the Continent threatened not just the west of Europe, but all of Western civilization. It had been clear to him all along.

Two years before, on October 16, 1938, while the visionaries and the defeatists still believed that Germany had satisfied its last territorial claims and that war could be avoided by giving to the Fuhrer what he otherwise would take by force, Mr. Churchill addressed the people of America:

> I avail myself with relief of the opportunity of speaking to the people of the United States. I do not know how long such liberties will be allowed. The stations of uncensored expression are closing down; the lights are going out; but there is still time for those to whom freedom and parliamentary government mean something, to consult together. Let me, then, speak in truth and earnestness while time remains.

Mr. Churchill restated the development of the philosophy common to our two nations:

As we look back over the long story of the nations, we must see * * * their glory has been founded upon the spirit of resistance to tyranny and injustice. Since the dawn of the Christian Era a certain way of life has slowly been shaping itself among the Western peoples, and certain standards of conduct and government have come to be esteemed. After many miseries and prolonged confusion, there arose into the broad light of day the conception of the right of the individual; his right to be consulted in the government of his country; his right to invoke the law even against the state itself.

Mr. Churchill would not be forced by the fate that threatened his island to compromise reality with expediency. He pointed out then in precise terms the similarity of principle that rules all totalitarian states though his words might have offended a possible ally:

Like the Communists, the Nazis tolerate no opinion but their own. Like the Communists, they feed on hatred. Like the Communists, they must seek from time to time, and always at shorter intervals, a new target, a new prize, a new victim. The dictator, in all his pride, is held in the grip of his party machine. He can go forward: he cannot go back. He must blood his hounds and show them sport, or else, like Actaeon of old, be devoured by them. All-strong without, he is all-weak within.

Mr. Churchill had spoken to us long before that summer of 1940 and patiently warned us of the events which were later to forcefully eject us from the deceptive security of our retirement.

But that was still before us in the summer of 1940. Then England stood alone and the stillness of the fragrant Dover evenings was broken by wave after wave of German planes heavy with bombs for the British heartland. We and the world held our breath awaiting the inevitable, for the island to be engulfed by the irresistible Nazi blitzkrieg.

The English survived that summer, "God's good time" soon came, and the United States entered the war. After an undisturbed and generous youth, history decreed that the time had come for our Nation to take up the burden which the rest of the free world was no longer strong enough to carry. We still bear the heavy part of those burdens and there is not, and will not soon be, opportunity to set them down.

Such are the affairs of men that the years find our old enemies now our stanchest allies, and some among those allies have become our present adversaries. Governments change, friendships change, and the temptation sometimes is to ask why the battles have been fought, where lies the sense to all the bloody sacrifice?

I know of no more compelling proof that our real enemy is not other nations, or other peoples, but tyranny, which rises like a weed in lands that are not tended, to choke off the dignity of man. The struggle since the beginning of history has been, in larger terms, not so much the struggle of nations as a struggle between that dignity and those who deny man's dignity. That war has grown in scope and in intensity until today the world is divided into two great parts, representing those two opposing beliefs.

Some say democracy is outmoded, a thought of the past, and that other "modern" philosophies will rule in times to come. The statement contains its own lie, for tyranny has been the overriding fate of man since his forgotten beginnings. Indeed it is the concept of dignity and freedom that is new, that has been slowly nurtured in the breasts of men, and that has grown stronger in spite of repeated assaults by man's dark lawless past. Our conflict today is but the latest, perhaps the final great battle between tyranny and dignity, and I ask which of those two concepts is new to the history of men.

I hear it said that loss of empire has deprived England of its place among great nations of the world. I believe this is not true and will never be so. For it was England that served as mankind's school of freedom. It was there that our concepts of responsibility and right were painstakingly developed and it is to England that America will forever owe its greatest debt.

That which we have desired to bestow on one of her great statesmen is intended not only as the gift of our highest honor to him, but also as recognition of the debt we owe to the proud nation that he led.

Mr. KEFAUVER. Mr. President, as one of the original cosponsors of Senate Joint Resolution 5, conferring U.S. honorary citizenship upon the Honorable Winston Churchill, I wish to associate myself wholeheartedly with the remarks of the distinguished majority leader, the Senator from Montana [Mr. Mansfield], on the occasion of the signing of this resolution by the President today.

I wish it were within the power of this body to go beyond that and confer upon Mr. Churchill the title, "Honorary Citizen of the World," because, Mr. President, that is truly the title he deserves. He deserves it because the fight he has carried on for the good and decent life for his people is of the kind that all human beings in their hearts, believe in and admire.

Who can ever forget his sonorous voice as he rallied the people of his beloved, sceptered isles against the hated Hitler hordes? Who can ever forget the pledge which he made on behalf of his beleaguered people: to fight the invader on the beaches, in the streets or wherever he might appear?

Who can forget the redoubtable figure of this marvelous man, smiling through the blood, sweat, and tears of his nation's agony, puffing on his familiar cigar and holding aloft two fingers in a promise of victory that, God willing, did come true?

And who can forget the omniscience of this man as he stood in the quiet of a hall at the University of Zurich after the tumult of war had died away, and described his vision of a United States of Europe, a vision that now lies so near the grasp of those of us who believe in a united community of Atlantic nations, dedicated to the peace and freedom and dignity of all men of good will?

Mr. President, the world will long remember this man, Winston Churchill, whom we honor with our simple tribute today. He is one of those of whom it can truly be said, "He is a great man."

Mr. HUMPHREY. Mr. President, today the President of the United States signed the resolution giving to Sir Winston Churchill the first honorary citizenship of the United States and thus making him an honorary citizen of our great Republic.

Mr. President, Winston Churchill is known by every American. The Associated Press, in a remarkable article about this great world citizen, has reminded us of Sir Winston's visit to the Congress. I shall read part of the article, because it tells a little of the story of this great man's capacity and ability, almost with the incisiveness of the great man's rhetoric, to present his views:

For Congress he rolled out a display of this renowned oratory. He looked around the Senate Chamber and remarked impishly:

"I cannot help reflecting that if my father had been an American and my mother British, instead of the other way 'round, I might have got here on my own."

And, you know, I do believe he would have.

During this visit to the Capital Sir Winston addressed a joint meeting of the House and the Senate. All of us remember it. It was a most exciting chapter in the history of the United States.

Mr. President, today is another great chapter in the history of the United States and in the history of Great Britain, our faithful, loyal, and strong ally. When President Kennedy signed the resolution giving honorary United States citizenship to Sir Winston Churchill, I am sure the President was speaking for every American, because our Nation loves, admires, and respects Mr. Churchill. We respect him as a great warrior, as a great wartime leader, as a great statesman, as a great Englishman, and, above all, as a great citizen of the free world.

I think his willingness to accept the title of honorary citizen of the United States is an honor to the American people. We can embrace him as one of our own; he becomes a citizen of this Republic, as well as a citizen of the United Kingdom.

As my colleagues know, Sir Winston's mother was an American. The bond of friendship between this country and the great English leader is all the more enduring because of this parental bond. His steadfast courage and loyalty throughout the war will remain as a constant reminder with all Americans who can recall those grave and fateful days.

What better way than by this act of Congress and this act by the President of the United States to perpetuate for the ages the wonderful relationships existing between the United States and Great Britain.

The United Kingdom and the United States now have a common bond that goes far beyond diplomatic niceties or far beyond the alliances that arise through treaties. We now have the common bond of citizenship in common with Sir Winston.

Mr. MONRONEY. Mr. President, I should like to associate myself with the remarks made by the assistant majority leader, the distinguished Senator from Minnesota, who has so eloquently described his happiness at the designation of citizenship for Sir Winston Churchill.

Many of us remember the day when he spoke at the joint session of the Congress during the bleak days of World War II, when his great leadership of England, matched with that of Franklin Delano Roosevelt, stood guard against the conquering of most of the world by the forces of Hitler. I remember that he remarked to the assembled Senate and the House that his mother was an American and his father was a Britisher. Had it been the other way around, he might have been here in his own right.

I am certain we all agree that, had his father been an American, with his great statesmanship, he would eventually have been a leader in the Senate or in the House of Representatives. His great strength of character, his grasp of strategy, and his great talent of leadership for the British people through hopeless conditions following the fall of France, will stand out as a burning torch for men who desire to maintain their freedom everywhere.

Tributes in Congress

To

Sir Winston Churchill

On Citizenship

TRIBUTE BY

REPRESENTATIVE TORBERT H. MACDONALD

OF MASSACHUSETTS

Mr. Speaker, it is indeed fitting that the Congress of the United States honor Sir Winston Churchill, a statesman and historian whom we admire as a citizen of the United Kingdom and as a citizen of the world.

I wish to call to the attention of my colleagues a poem entitled "Winston Churchill—Flowers for the Living," written by Howard R. Hodson of Wakefield, Mass., which is befitting of the high esteem with which the American public places this distinguished statesman.

The poem follows:

WINSTON CHURCHILL—FLOWERS FOR THE LIVING

As the sun goes down and the curtain falls
On those tremendous days,
And the words won't come to mind or tongue
To form the fitting phrase
For the one whose voice left the world no choice
In the time of blood and tears,
For his leadership and statesmanship
In England's desperate years.
And no one is forgetting
In the eulogistic setting
Of lines devoted to the one,
The many thousand others
And those no record covers
Many a worthy father
And many a splendid son.
Here, in the Great Republic
Are those of English strain
Who respond with admiration
And then, enthuse again.
And may this modest tribute
To one who needs it not
Be added to the many
From far and wide, unsought.

The Armada, Blenheim, Waterloo
Eclipsed, it may be thought
By the fateful Battle of Britain
Where the ominous trial was wrought.
And the Captain and Commander
In fact, if not in name
Was the Gentleman from Downing Street
Who would not quit the game.
The frightened world watched anxiously
Despair yields to surprise,
And on the Day of Victory
It was the Reich's demise.
The great old man is with us
Declining, to be sure,
But his presence still reminds us
What his country could endure.
Those days of dire adversity
Of achievement and acclaim;
The man who named "Their Finest Hour,"
Will leave its greatest name.
They will lay him in the Abbey
Where else does he belong?
They will surpass encomiums
They will exhaust all song.
All honor and all tribute
That the grateful Nation knows
Will be bestowed upon him
In poetry and prose.
But if they want a tribute
The final and the best,
Take it from the vanquished foe
Who put him to the test,
For if someone would ask him
Hitler, in Hell, will say
That 'twas only Winston Churchill
Who made it end that way.
What satisfaction there must be
To envision at life's end
The Pageantry, prepared for few,
With all it does portend.
The impressive pomp and circumstance
Of funereal panoply,
The muffled drum—the cadence slow
The throngs in sympathy.
And all of those who knew him then,

In that former time
When he was not as other men,
And saw the unseen sign.
The Roll is long, and graven there
In honor and in pride
Are England's great, who in their time
Each crisis took in stride,
And measured by the task he faced
To odds to overcome,
Who, in all that Galaxy
Has higher honor won?
The mightiest military power
The world had even known
In vain against him hurled its force,
Withstood by him alone.
Let well his name remembered be
Forever by the free,
And make his best citation this
For Time and History,
"He was the Nazi's Nemesis
And his V was Victory."

—H.R.H.

TRIBUTE BY

REPRESENTATIVE FRANCES P. BOLTON

OF OHIO

Mr. Speaker, on January 9, the opening day of the 88th Congress, I introduced House Joint Resolution 109, authorizing the President of the United States to issue a proclamation declaring Sir Winston Churchill to be an honorary citizen of the United States of America. As the son of an American mother and an English father, Winston Churchill, more than any other, truly epitomizes the union between the two great English-speaking peoples. His courage and devotion to the cause of freedom and human dignity have served to challenge and inspire our Nation as well as his own to victory in war and to achievement in peace.

The gift of honorary citizenship of the United States of America is one honor, one token of rare esteem and love which is within this Nation's power to bestow, and which is worthy of Winston Churchill's place in history.

The Washington Post carried a letter to the editor from Miss Kay Halle of Cleveland, Ohio, and Washington, to whom much credit must be given for making the suggestion that we honor Sir Winston Churchill in this way. I include Miss Halle's letter as part of my remarks.

ONE OF US

When Sir Winston Churchill cut into his 15-pound birthday cake last November celebrating his 88 years, he found the most heartfelt of his memorable utterances inscribed on its icing. "I am an English speaking union." One of his proudest boasts is, "Among Englishmen I have a special qualification, I am directly descended through my mother from an officer who served in Washington's Army. And as such I have been made a member of your strictly selected Society of the Cincinnati. I have my pedigree supported by affidavits at every stage if it is challenged * * * I feel on both sides of the Atlantic. In my mother's birth city of Rochester, N.Y., I hold the latch key to American hearts."

Not long ago I spent a day with Sir Winston at his beloved Chartwell in the beautiful countryside of Kent. During lunch I watched him rise from the anesthesia of his great age, lift his glass of hock and propose a "toast to the good health of your leader and ours." He spoke often that day of "undying fraternal association of your great country and mine." He said that if we are together nothing is impossible as a special relationship exists between the British Commonwealth and the United States. He mused on the eventuality of common citizenship but was "content to leave that to destiny whose outstretched arm so many of us can clearly see. I feel eventually this will come."

The 88th Congress has just begun. It could perform no more rewarding or auspicious first act than to pass with unanimity Senate Joint Resolution 215 already introduced into the Senate by Senator Stephen Young, Democrat, and House Joint Resolution 866 by Congresswoman Frances Bolton, Republican, into the House proposing honorary American citizenship for Sir Winston Churchill.

Some might consider this setting a precedent. If it were anyone but Sir Winston the point could be argued. Sir Winston is a precedent. Once before we so honored a Frenchman, the Marquis de Lafayette who fought by our side to help us win freedom. There is little time to lose if we are to make one of the greatest of our blood brothers, Sir Winston Churchill, truly one of us.

KAY HALLE.

WASHINGTON.

TRIBUTE BY

SENATOR RALPH W. YARBOROUGH

OF TEXAS

Mr. President, I share the pleasure of the Senate at its having been able to complete action on the resolution granting honorary American citizenship to Winston Churchill. As a cosponsor of one of these resolutions, I am proud to have been associated with this fitting recognition for one of the greatest men in the world in this century. None of us who were adults at the time of World War II can ever forget what this man meant to the world in rallying the forces of democracy. It is entirely fitting that we grant him an honor that is unique, for his character and deeds have been unique. Winston Churchill, a citizen of the British Empire by birth and loyalties, is now a citizen of America by congressional action, as indeed he is a citizen of the world by his life and deeds.

The following editorial in the Washington Post well expresses the affection we feel for Sir Winston Churchill:

CITIZEN CHURCHILL

By its unanimous vote, the U.S. Senate has fittingly and appropriately concluded congressional action upon the resolution which directs the President to declare Winston Churchill an honorary citizen.

There is no action that this Government could take that would be more in harmony with the sentiments and feelings of the American people, who will welcome with joy into the fellowship of this new and formal association one who long has been united to America and Americans by bonds that no political body could either devise or dissolve.

This unanimous act of the Senate will gladden the hearts of all Americans. A great legislative body has as its primary duty the affirmation in the statutes of those resolves already confirmed in the minds of a free people; but it has an equal duty to affirm by solemn enactment the sentiments that stir the hearts of citizens. This is such an enactment.

It is to be hoped that it will also gladden the heart of Winston Churchill. There is reason to think it will. Like Henry V, he could always say: "I am not covetous for gold * * * but if it be a sin to covet honor, I am the most offending soul alive." Such men may have a surfeit of everything else upon this fair earth, but of honor they can never have enough. And so, there is reason to hope that his honor, heaped high although it is upon a life already filled with honor, will find the taste for more not staled by all that has befallen him, the appetite for honor undiminished. And may the savor of this honor stay sweet upon his tongue in all his days to come, comforting him in the hours of his old age and nurturing to brighter recollection the memory of his great deeds.

To construe this act as a mark of that special relation which exists between this country and England would be to underestimate the honor and overestimate that historic bond, for the special relationship out of which this action springs is that between these greatly led and those who greatly lead them. Freemen everywhere shared for a while in the greatness of this man, revealed in his glorious phrases, roused to his brave sentiments, rejoiced in his bold challenges. This is the special tie that binds us all to him and him to us. It is good to have it unanimously affirmed by the U.S. Senate.

BY THE PRESIDENT OF THE UNITED STATES OF AMERICA

A PROCLAMATION

WHEREAS Sir Winston Churchill, a son of America though a subject of Britain, has been throughout his life a firm and steadfast friend of the American people and the American nation; and

WHEREAS he has freely offered his hand and his faith in days of adversity as well as triumph; and

WHEREAS his bravery, charity and valor, both in war and in peace, have been a flame of inspiration in freedom's darkest hour; and

WHEREAS his life has shown that no adversary can overcome, and no fear can deter, free men in the defense of their freedom; and

WHEREAS he has expressed with unsurpassed power and splendor the aspirations of peoples everywhere for dignity and freedom; and

WHEREAS he has by his art as an historian and his judgment as a statesman made the past the servant of the future;

NOW, THEREFORE, I, JOHN F. KENNEDY, President of the United States of America, under the authority contained in an Act of the 88th Congress, do hereby declare Sir Winston Churchill an honorary citizen of the United States of America.

2

IN WITNESS WHEREOF, I have hereunto set my hand and caused the Seal of the United States of America to be affixed.

DONE at the City of Washington this ninth day of April, in the year of our Lord nineteen hundred and sixty-three, and of the Independence of the United States of America the one hundred and eighty-seventh.

By the President:

Acting Secretary of State

White House Ceremony

Remarks by President John F. Kennedy at proclamation ceremony conferring honorary citizenship on Sir Winston Churchill, the White House, Washington, D.C., April 9, 1963

We meet to honor a man whose honor requires no meeting—for he is the most honored and honorable man to walk the stage of human history in the time in which we live.

Whenever and wherever tyranny threatened, he has always championed liberty.

Facing firmly toward the future, he has never forgotten the past.

Serving six monarchs of his native Great Britain, he has served all men's freedom and dignity.

In the dark days and darker nights when Britain stood alone—and most men save Englishmen despaired of England's life—he mobilized the English language and sent it into battle. The incandescent quality of his words illuminated the courage of his countrymen.

Given unlimited powers by his citizens, he was ever vigilant to protect their rights.

Indifferent himself to danger, he wept over the sorrows of others.

A child of the House of Commons, he became in time its father.

Accustomed to the hardships of battle, he has no distaste for pleasure.

Now his stately Ship of Life, having weathered the severest storms of a troubled century, is anchored in tranquil waters, proof that courage and faith and the zest for freedom are truly indestructible. The record of his triumphant passage will inspire free hearts for all time.

By adding his name to our rolls, we mean to honor him—but his acceptance honors us far more. For no statement or proclamation can enrich his name—the name Sir Winston Churchill is already legend.

SIR WINSTON CHURCHILL

KNIGHTSBRIDGE 7972.

28, HYDE PARK GATE.
LONDON. S.W.7.

6 April, 1963

Mr. President,

I have been informed by Mr. David Bruce that it is your intention to sign a Bill conferring upon me Honorary Citizenship of the United States.

I have received many kindnesses from the United States of America, but the honour which you now accord me is without parallel. I accept it with deep gratitude and affection.

I am also most sensible of the warm-hearted action of the individual States who accorded me the great compliment of their own honorary citizenships as a prelude to this Act of Congress.

2.

It is a remarkable comment on our affairs that the former Prime Minister of a great sovereign state should thus be received as an honorary citizen of another. I say "great sovereign state" with design and emphasis, for I reject the view that Britain and the Commonwealth should now be relegated to a tame and minor role in the world. Our past is the key to our future, which I firmly trust and believe will be no less fertile and glorious. Let no man underrate our energies, our potentialities and our abiding power for good.

I am, as you know, half American by blood, and the story of my association with that mighty and benevolent nation goes back nearly ninety years to the day of my Father's marriage. In this century of storm and tragedy I contemplate with high satisfaction the constant factor of the interwoven and upward progress of our peoples. Our comradeship and our brotherhood in war were unexampled. We stood together, and because of that fact the free world now stands.

Nor has our partnership any exclusive nature: the Atlantic community is a dream that can well be fulfilled to the detriment of none and to the enduring benefit and honour of the great democracies.

Mr. President, your action illuminates the theme of unity of the English-speaking peoples, to which I have devoted a large part of my life. I would ask you to accept yourself, and to convey to both Houses of Congress, and through them to the American people, my solemn and heartfelt thanks for this unique distinction, which will always be proudly remembered by my descendants.

Winston S. Churchill

Sir Winston Churchill, April 11, 1963, at Hyde Park Gate just after American Ambassador David K. E. Bruce had presented to him the Proclamation and Passport declaring him an Honorary American Citizen

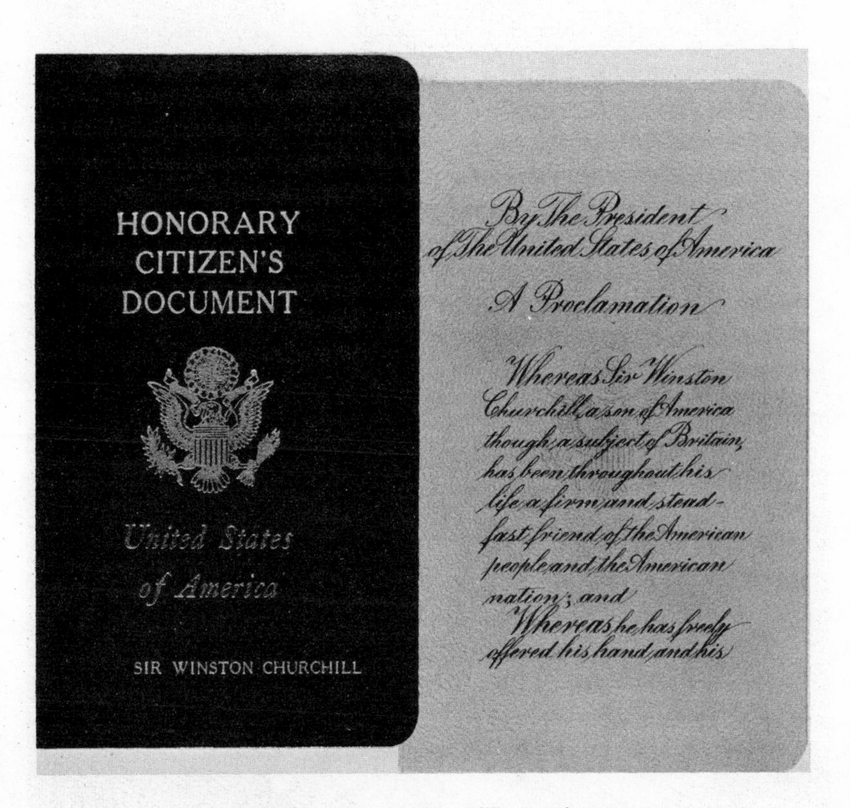

Photograph of Sir Winston Churchill's American passport

Memorial Addresses

In Eulogy of

Sir Winston Churchill

In The

House of Representatives

Of the United States

January 25, 1965

Memorial Addresses

In the

UNITED STATES HOUSE OF REPRESENTATIVES

January 25, 1965

Prayer by the Chaplain

Rev. Bernard Braskamp, D.D., used this verse which Sir Winston Churchill quoted when he addressed a point session of the Congress: Psalm 112: 7: *He shall not be afraid of evil tidings, his heart is fixed, trusting in the Lord.*

O Thou who are the companion of our hearts and the counselor of our minds, may we feel that Thy eternal truth is our guiding light and Thy love the bond of unity among men and nations.

Fill us with generous impulses and sympathetic attitudes toward all mankind and may each day bear witness to new adventures and advances in faith and in friendship.

Hear us as we daily pray for our beloved President, beseeching Thee to share Thy healing ministry with the doctors and nurses at the Naval Hospital, enabling them to know just what to do for his complete and speedy recovery.

We mourn the passing of our greatly esteemed and beloved Sir Winston Churchill but we rejoice that Thou hast opened for him the gateway to the larger life and received him into Thy nearer presence, leaving us to dream and imagine how wondrous fair that life must be since he is there.

In Christ's name we pray. Amen.

ADDRESS BY

HON. JOHN W. McCORMACK

OF MASSACHUSETTS

Mr. Speaker, it is one of the great truths of this hour that the only individual in more than a hundred years, who is not an American, and yet could evoke the profound sense of bereavement Americans feel so emotionally today, is Sir Winston Spencer Churchill. What he did in our time established for him and for the people of Great Britain an immortality on the noblest levels of human achievement. The depth of our pride, as Americans, in this man, is the more astonishing for its intensity because this hero of our century was so distinctively and so absolutely an embodiment of the greatest qualities of his people. His voice, even, as we heard it on the floor of this very Chamber, his stance, his language, made him the incarnate hero of the hour during one of the world's most agonizing periods of travail. Yet this Englishman, born of an American mother, became more than ever one of our own, by the principles he espoused and the cause he fought for.

It is to the enormous credit of this greatest European statesman of the last several hundred years that at no time during the grand alliance or after, did the slightest stigma arise between the two greatest English-speaking nations on basic questions of mutual integrity, mutual good will, mutual respect. The great man on this side of the Atlantic, Franklin Delano Roosevelt, and the great man of 10 Downing Street—Winston Churchill—represented within themselves the lofty idealism and the decency of character of their respective peoples. It is not so much that the oratory of this brilliant Englishman was touched with flame and the quality of endurance so long as English will be spoken, but that he used this mighty tool on behalf of freedom. It was a weapon that in its time will be equated by historians with the majesty of moving armies and the power of the most intrepid battalions in the chronicle of warfare.

It is not enough to say that we so intensely admired Winston Churchill because, of course, he intensely admired the American people, and the American tradition of liberty. We have been, as two nations in two World Wars, ideologically on the same track, fighting against what became in world history an affliction of afflictions when the unspeakable Nazis took over in Germany. What Winston Churchill did not only for his people, but for all the free world, was to sharpen the confrontation so that no one could fail to understand the monumental meaning of the cause of freedom against the ferocity and the ruthlessness of this barbaric threat. By the same token he has since—and mostly in a speech on American soil—revealed with identical sharpness to the whole of mankind, the meaning of the newly expanded threat he defined under the term "Iron Curtain."

Most of all to the average man Winston Churchill presented the human personality in its finest manifestation of courage, conviction, and solidity. In this, we like to think, he was most like us, and essentially one of our own. Indeed, in our own way and with the highest regard for the English people, we sought to claim him as one of our own when we here in the Congress voted him an honorary citizen of our country. He was the very personification of valor when he led his people and the free world to victory under the guns and the overwhelming might of the German onslaught, finally with the fullest support and cooperation of President Roosevelt and the American people, fighting shoulder to shoulder. We join with the British people and the free people everywhere in the expression of the grief we feel and the pride we take in having lived in the same period of world history with this great man, this American citizen, this outstanding hero in the crisis of crises that finally brought an ugly despotism of our time to book.

ADDRESS BY

HON. CARL ALBERT

OF OKLAHOMA

Mr. Speaker, the whole world shares the sorrow of the family and friends of Sir Winston Churchill, a world citizen of extraordinary dimensions, who on yesterday departed this life in the city of London.

Of all men who have lived in the 20th century, Sir Winston may well have lived the fullest life. For more than 90 years he walked among us as one of God's noblest and most remarkable creatures.

Sir Winston, the articulate spokesman for the cause of freemen in World War II, was unquestionably the one man behind whom all the forces of freedom rallied in the fight against Nazi and Fascist tyranny.

He was the first outstanding public figure in the world to warn against the threat that Hitler posed.

He was the first to raise the warning flag, as disciples of appeasement began to raise their heads among the free nations of Western Europe. There are many, he said, who would feed the crocodile only to be devoured by him in the end.

Among all public men whose lives and careers were identified with World War II, Churchill's name stands preeminent.

But, Mr. Speaker, Winston Churchill's leadership in this era is not his only claim to historic recognition. Had he passed on even before Hitler's armies began to march, he would have had a prominent place in the annals of his country. He was acclaimed as the best debater in Parliament and was the unchallenged prince of British orators for more than half a century. He was a fighting man of great courage and talent—an author of rare distinction. Of all those who spoke the English language in this century, Winston Churchill spoke it best. In his speeches and in his writings, he demonstrated again the strength and the beauty of Shakespeare's language. Rugged, determined, articulate, witty, courageous, he was every inch a man. Historian, philosopher, and statesman, he as much as any other human being understood and raised his voice against the dangers of tyranny from both the right and the left.

This generation and the world in which it lives—future generations and the world of tomorrow—all who will ever cherish freedom will owe a lasting debt of gratitude to Sir Winston Churchill.

Today in sorrow, respect, and affection, we salute this great man. This man whose life was wholly affirmative. This man who in battle would accept only victory. This man whose courage never faltered. This champion of liberty who was unbending in his determination to preserve Christian civilization against the onslaughts of evil despots.

Mr. Speaker, we in America proudly and rightfully share in the glory of Churchill's fame and rejoice in the scope of his accomplishments. The son of an American mother, the first and only honorary American citizen in the history of this country, an ally and friend in every major battle, we can say that Winston Churchill was in a very real sense one of our own.

Now, Mr. Speaker, as the flags fly at half-mast—as prince and pauper offer their last farewells—all good men rejoice that Winston Churchill passed our way in our day and generation. He hung his star high. Among history's most distinguished statesmen, he has set new patterns of human achievement which aspiring youth may seek to emulate for years and centuries to come.

As his countrymen mourn him and lay his remains to rest, decent men and women everywhere will surely proclaim: Well done, thou good and faithful servant, in whom we are well pleased.

ADDRESS BY

HON. FRANK CHELF

OF KENTUCKY

Mr. Speaker, England, the United States of America, and all of the world have lost a vigorous, effective, and most successful champion of freedom, democracy, and decency, the Right Honorable Sir Winston Spencer Churchill.

During World Wars I and II, Sir Winston was the cannon, the ammunition, the ramrod, the warhead, and the marksman which literally blew Britain's enemies and those of world peace out of the water with a direct hit. Of course, our great Nation came to Britain's aid—but Sir Winston had called the war shots with the phenomenal accuracy endowed with a clairvoyant mind.

His famous "blood, toil, sweat, and tears" speech in the House of Commons on May 13, 1940, mobilized the talents, the ingenuity, and the challenge, stirred the hearts, and provided the inspiration that turned the tide against Hitler. It came at a time when Britain stood all alone.

My colleagues on March 12, 1963, I made a speech here in the House urging the passage of legislation that would confer honorary citizenship upon this truly great statesman of the world. This legislation had been introduced by all of us who were members of the Immigration and Nationality Subcommittee of the Judiciary Committee of the House of Representatives.

Mr. Speaker, no matter how hard I try here today, I sincerely do not believe that I could pay Sir Winston a better tribute than was contained in my March 1963 Churchill speech. So, my colleagues, if you will please be so kind as to forgive me and bear with me, I will quote a few excerpts from my previous remarks about this resolute, valiant, unconquerable Englishman. I quote:

To find words adequate to describe properly this distinguished man is comparable to gilding the lily, bringing cotton to Alabama, the derby to England, and good bourbon to my native Kentucky.

His bravery, his fortitude, his tenacity of purpose, and his unyielding desire to win shall never be forgotten.

In my opinion, his achievements shall stand out forever like the Washington Monument, Big Ben, the Eiffel Tower, and the pyramids. By his unselfish service to mankind, he has emblazoned his name with honor and everlasting distinction in huge letters of gold on the silver pages of world history. Why? Because during war, travail, "blood and tears and sweat," fear, want, privation, devastation, chaos, and despair—at a time when it seemed all was lost—this incomparable leader was the epitome of hope, the very embodiment of courage, the preserver of time, the protector of faith, the guardian of destiny, the inspiration for victory, and the successful negotiator of peace.

Quoting further:

To paraphrase one of his own famous statements: "Never in the field of human conflict was so much owed by so many to one man."

May he have a full fruition of his dreams and a happy realization of all of his endeavors. May his leaf never wither and whatsoever he doest, may it prosper. May God in His infinite wisdom spare and protect our beloved friend, Sir Winston, for many years to come and may He who reigns as the King of Kings, the Master of all lodges, nations, and men, smile graciously, abundantlly, beautifully, and everlastingly from His wide blue canopy of heaven upon this, our worthy candidate for the position of the world's most honored peacemaker since that lowly Man walked the shores of Galilee many centuries ago. * * *

Thank the Lord, he did not place his light under a bushel, but on a candlestick and it giveth light unto all in the house.

I trust that Sir Winston will forgive my inadequate words of praise—and I say this from a humble heart—because, unfortunately, not in America nor in England nor any place else on the face of the globe, is there another Churchill with the command of the King's English which he alone possesses.

My colleagues, this great but humble man when he had heard that I had made this speech, wrote me the following letter which I prize so dearly and so highly that the original is now framed along with a picture of President Kennedy signing the legislation into law, and one of the pens with which he signed it:

> My Dear Chelf: I am indeed obliged to you for the very agreeable things you say about me and for the graceful way you expressed them. Pray accept my good wishes.
>
> Yours very sincerely,
>
> Winston Churchill.

May the Good Lord bless Lady Churchill and all of their wonderful family in this great void which has come to them.

The Good Lord, in his infinite wisdom, as I see it, literally lent us Sir Winston and allowed us the benefits and fruits of his labors for lo these past 90 years. Obviously, He could not allow us to retain forever this magnificent leader of men and so the Master has called Sir Winston back to that mansion of rest on high. The free world thanks you dear Lord for the loan of Sir Winston.

Again, I repeat from my 1963 speech: "Hail, noble Englishman. Hail, great American."

Mr. Speaker, I want to take this opportunity to personally thank our outstanding majority leader for his not only reserving this time today but being so generous and so magnificent in giving those of us who really idolize this great man, Sir Winston Churchill, an opportunity to say a word about him.

ADDRESS BY

HON. JOHN J. FLYNT, JR.

OF GEORGIA

Mr. Speaker, with countless others I mourn the death of Sir Winston Leonard Spencer Churchill, but even more—much more—I am grateful for his life and the contributions which he made during that life of four score years and ten.

Unquestionably he was the outstanding Briton of this century. It is possible that he was the outstanding leader of the English-speaking people. More than that of any single person, his courage, his faith, and his indomitable will provided the leadership which led the United States, Great Britain, and our allies to victory in World War II.

His prescience was a marvel of both warfare and international politics. He foresaw events before they occurred; and when they did occur, he already had the answers to questions and the solutions to problems. Fortunately for us those answers and solutions were accurate ones—this was fortunate not only for his country, but for ours as well.

We shall gratefully remember him as long as there lives an American or Englishman who remembers 1939–45. We who have heard or seen or met him will never forget him. History will honor him and accord him a high place on any list of great men of all time.

As head of the Government of Great Britain and as British leader in war and peace, he is without a peer.

As both a speaker and a writer he was a master of the English language. On June 4, 1940, I vividly remember listening to a radio rebroadcast of his speech on Dunkirk to the House of Commons; and I especially remember these words:

> We shall not flag or fail. We shall fight in France, we shall fight on the seas and oceans, we shall fight with growing confidence and growing strength in the air, we shall defend our island, whatever the cost may be, we shall fight on the beaches, we shall fight on the landing grounds, we shall fight in the fields and in the streets, we shall fight in the hills; we shall never surrender.

Winston Churchill did not surrender and he never had any intention of doing so.

A fortnight later, on June 18, 1940, he said:

> Let us therefore brace ourselves to our duties, and so bear ourselves that, if the British Empire and its commonwealth last for a thousand years, men will still say: "This was their finest hour."

And men will also say with accuracy that in "their finest hour," that Winston Churchill was their finest man.

In a radio broadcast on July 14, 1940, he said:

> We shall defend every village, every town, and every city. The vast mass of London itself, fought street by street, could easily devour an entire hostile army; and we would rather see London laid in ruins and ashes than that it should be tamely and abjectly enslaved.

Winston Churchill loved his country, his people, and his island. Even more, he loved freedom and he meant to maintain freedom for his people and his island. This he did.

He has earned an enviable place in English literature. He was a prolific writer and with his pen he mastered our language as he did with his speech.

As President Kennedy said when he proclaimed Sir Winston an honorary citizen of the United States:

He mobilized the English language and sent it into battle.

The contributions of few writers can compare with his three-volume biography of the Duke of Marlborough; his multivolume history of World War I, "The World Crisis"; the six volumes comprising his "The Second World War": "The Gathering Storm," "Their Finest Hour," "The Grand Alliance," "The Hinge of Fate," "Closing the Ring," "Triumph and Tragedy." Following that, he published "The History of the English-Speaking People" and "Island Race."

In war he demonstrated resolution. In victory he was magnanimous. In peace he provided good will. Now in death, he leaves behind a grateful people in England, in this United States, and throughout the world.

In the minds and hearts of freemen he will be their patron saint—the patron saint of freedom.

ADDRESS BY

HON. CLEMENT J. ZABLOCKI

OF WISCONSIN

Mr. Speaker, we are all much the poorer today for the passing of one of the truly outstanding men of our century, Sir Winston Churchill.

His wisdom, his courage, his wit, his proficiency as a writer and speaker, his artistic ability, his foresight, and his indomitable will have all been remarked upon time and again in the days which have elapsed since his death last Sunday.

As one priviliged to be a Member of this body, however, I like to recall Sir Winston as a man of politics. It was in this very

Chamber, Mr. Speaker, that this towering figure of our times said, "I am a child of the House of Commons."

He meant that, I believe, as a compliment to those of use who serve in this House of Representatives. He knew the rigors of practical politics, of legislative compromise, of parliamentary strategy. He knew as well that service as a representative of the people is an opportunity for measureless good and accomplishment.

The course of his political career was far from smooth. He never feared to speak his mind in the face of countervailing public opinion and it often cost him dearly. Today we know that what he spoke was very often the truth.

It was he who first saw the dangers inherent in the rise of Hitlerism and tried to warn his complacent people against the coming tyranny. It was he who first crystallized for us the postwar threat in the advance of the Soviet Union across Europe.

As Winston Churchill is taken from us, let our prayer be that the Almighty, seeing the needs of humanity, will favor the world with other leaders of his kind to show the way should the sky again darken and the hour once again seem late.

ADDRESS BY

HON. GERALD R. FORD

OF MICHIGAN

Mr. Speaker, from time to time in the history of nations there emerges a man, as human as the rest of us, but one able to capture for himself and his country the respect and imagination of all of us. By native intelligence, force of personality, diligent effort, determined leadership, and a sense of the historical, Sir Winston Churchill became that kind of man.

He belongs, first of all, to Great Britain; but every nation in the free world is richer because he lived. The entire world has felt the impact of his work and the fullness of his spirit.

England has lost a leading public figure. Mankind is bereft of a symbol which has stood for the finest qualities in our humanity: courage, tenacity, ability, dedication—all used in the eternal struggle for freedom and justice.

We in the United States join our fellow men everywhere in mourning the passing of one of the great men of our time. He is gone, but his work remains as an inspiration to us and all who follow.

ADDRESS BY

HON. SAMUEL S. STRATTON

OF NEW YORK

Mr. Speaker, I want to join with the distinguished majority leader in paying my own small tribute to a great statesman, a great man and a great Englishman, Sir Winston Churchill. We are all in his debt, as the majority leader has already indicated, whether we be Americans or citizens of some other country.

The quality that has always stood out above all others, in my judgment, in the career of Sir Winston Churchill, is courage. He displayed physical courage as a war correspondent and when he was a young subaltern on the fields of India and of Africa. He displayed great courage and indomitability as the leader of the free world and of his own country in the dark days of World War II.

But, Mr. Speaker, I think there is another aspect of courage that perhaps has been overlooked in the career of Sir Winston Churchill, and that is the courage he displayed, the moral courage, in his unwillingness to alter or compromise or ignore his own beliefs and convictions simply because they were not at the time very popular. We know Sir Winston as the great leader of his country. But let us not forget that only a few months before he was called, on May 10, 1940, to take over the war leadership of his country, he had been at age 65 already tabbed as a has-been, a back-bencher, a dissenter who was unable to agree with members of his own party and sometimes members of other parties, too, simply because he had refused to back down from his deep conviction which he held throughout the 1930's of the urgency of rearming England to deal with the growing menace of Hitler's Nazi tyranny.

The fact that Sir Winston was right after all was brought out only because of his courage and determination in sticking by those views even though they were for too long a time unpopular with the majority of Englishmen.

Mr. Speaker, last November 30, on the occasion of the 90th birthday of Sir Winston Churchill, I happened to be in London as a member of the Naval Reserve on training duty. Although I realized that it would be difficult if not impossible to see Sir Winston at that time, and though I had never seen him personally at all, I could not resist the temptation to walk around to Hyde Park Gate, and to walk down that little cul-de-sac and stand there for a few minutes in front of his home at No. 28.

As we pause here today in this Chamber, Mr. Speaker, to pay tribute to Sir Winston Churchill, I cannot help feeling grateful that I had this opportunity last month to stand there for a minute or two to pay a small and silent tribute to one who has done so much for the free world; who so brilliantly demonstrated that the institutions of democratic, parliamentary government can indeed deal effectively and efficiently with the forces of totalitarianism in time of crisis; and who has been and will surely always continue to be an inspiration to every one fortunate enough to serve in elected public office.

ADDRESS BY

HON. WILLIAM S. MOORHEAD

OF PENNSYLVANIA

Mr. Speaker, never have so many people of so many nations owed so much to the courage of just one man.

A friend described the courage of Sir Winston Churchill as "a fixed resolve to see the thing through to its end."

The glory of the courage or Sir Winston Churchill was that he had courage in sufficient quantity to share it with and bestow it upon 50 million people of the British Isles.

When the Battle of Britain was on, when invasion of England seemed imminent ,Winston Churchill, as the late President Kennedy said, "Mobilized the English language and sent it into battle." He marshaled words the way generals marshal their troops.

Who knows what caused Hitler to postpone and later to cancel his invasion plans, but when he did so, he must have had ringing in his ears those Churchillian words:

We shall fight on the landing grounds, we shall fight in the fields and in the streets, we shall fight in the hills; we shall never surrender.

On a later occasion, Sir Winston said:

It was the British that had the lion's heart: I had the luck to be called upon to give the roar.

The roar of that brave man will echo throughout eternity.

ADDRESS BY

HON. ROMAN C. PUCINSKI

OF ILLINOIS

Mr. Speaker, I should like to congratulate our distinguished majority leader, the gentleman from Oklahoma [Mr. Albert], for taking this time today. I would like to join in the stirring remarks delivered here today in tribute to one of the great giants in history, Sir Winston Churchill.

Mr. Speaker, it would be my hope that the epitaph on Winston Churchill's tomb would read, "He dared to be different."

Throughout his entire life of public service, the world saw this man time and time again rise above the clamor of popular opinion. Time and time again he spoke out in defense of positions he felt to be just. He was not concerned with popularity, but with principle. His soaring individuality kept him from marching in a single cadence with men too blinded by tradition and prejudice to see the stars above them. He was able to capture and lead the spirit of the world in its darkest moments and its moments of ultimate victory. He was "Winnie"—and unconquerable.

It would seem to me that a study of Sir Winston's illustrious career in public service, and his great contribution to literature and to the arts, should be an inspiration to all of us. "Each of us," in the lines of an old poem, "passes this way but once." Winston Churchill trod that path with three generations of men. Yet, in his record of achievements in that single lifetime we can fine solace, confidence, and courage. He did, indeed, dare to be different and the results will illuminate the history of the world. May he rest in peace.

ADDRESS BY

HON. HOWARD H. CALLAWAY

OF GEORGIA

Mr. Speaker, the world will remember Sir Winston Churchill in many different ways—the politician, the statesman, the world leader. But the people of the Third District of Georgia will particularly remember those dark years during which our boys left their training bases at Fort Benning and Warner Robins to fight beside Sir Winston's gallant British forces.

Winston Churchill's memory will long live in the hearts of Georgians—and freedom-loving men everywhere. Perhaps, at this moment in our history, it is fitting to consider the words of this great man:

> If you will not fight for the right when you can easily win without bloodshed; if you will not fight when your victory will be sure and not too costly; you may come to the moment when you will have to fight when all the odds are against you with only a precarious chance of survival. There may even be a worse case. You may have to fight when there is no hope of victory, because it is better to perish than to live as slaves.

May America, Mr. Speaker, be ever mindful of his words, as we carry on his work in search of freedom for all men.

ADDRESS BY

HON. WILLIAM J. RANDALL

OF MISSOURI

Mr. Speaker, as a member of the Missouri delegation I should like to recall one of the great contributions made to the world by Sir Winston Churchill in an appearance at Fulton, Mo., the home of Westminster College.

It was back in March of 1946, as the personal guest of my fellow townsman President Truman, that Sir Winston Churchill first coined the expression "the Iron Curtain," which now has become a symbol of the barriers separating the free from the enslaved world. In prophetic words he warned us that unless the free world banded together in common defense against Stalin, Europe would undergo the same order of tragedy she had experienced under Hitler.

> I do not believe that Soviet Russia desires war—

He said—

> What they desire is the fruits of war and the indefinite expansion of their power and doctrines.

Then the indomitable Englishmen defined the Communist character in a way that was to be echoed over the next few years by President Truman, by our Secretaries of State, and by the other leaders of the free world:

> From what I have seen of our Russian friends and allies during the war—

He said—

> I am convinced that there is nothing they admire so much as strength, and there is nothing for which they have less respect than for weakness, especially military weakness.

These remarks, Mr. Speaker, set the tone for the alliance policy of the next decade and a half.

The man who uttered these words is no longer with us. But his spirit and his forceful ideas will continue to live on, both in the written history of the post-war epoch and in the policies of the Western Alliance.

We owe an incalculable debt to him. We have already recognized that indebtedness once by bestowing honorary American citizenship upon him, the same honor given once before to French General Lafayette after the Revolutionary War. We must now acknowledge that indebtedness in another more lasting manner. Our greatest tribute to him would be to remember his message and his example.

Mr. Speaker, I know that I speak for the all of Missouri and particularly for the city of Fulton and for Westminster College, when I say that today we are all filled with grief and are all mindful of the lasting contributions of this heroic public figure. We all share the grief of his loved ones. May his good soul rest in peace.

ADDRESS BY

HON. RICHARD H. FULTON

OF TENNESSEE

Mr. Speaker, I would like to take a few moments to join with those millions of persons around the world in paying tribute to Sir Winston Churchill.

He is gone. Yet his words, deeds, and spirit will live as long as freemen walk this earth. History will record few men who answered the call and met the challenge of public service with the wisdom, intelligence, statesmanship, and determination of Sir Winston. His achievements were remarkable in view of the formidable tasks which he faced.

Americans have admired, respected, and held Sir Winston in warm personal regard for decades.

The people of Tennessee were among the first in the Nation to show their esteem for this great leader. In 1963, the Tennessee General Assembly adopted a resolution making Sir Winston an honorary Tennessean.

Two years ago, as a Member of this body, I was honored to join in sponsorship of the resolution granting him honorary U.S. citizenship.

A great man has passed our way and the world is a better place for his service to the cause of freedom and liberty.

ADDRESS BY

HON. DONALD RUMSFELD

OF ILLINOIS

Mr. Speaker, the world mourns the passing of Sir Winston Churchill, whose words and deeds, whose courage and dedication to the cause of freedom and peace will be long remembered. But particularly must his own people feel a deep sense of loss, for in their darkest and most perilous hours they called upon him to lead them against their most bitter and destructive enemy. He gave all of his talent, all of his strength, and all of his wisdom to this struggle, and called forth from his people the determination and valor which brought victory.

And we in this country feel a close kinship with this man of our age, whose friendship and warmth for our people have given us a sense of pride that we were privileged to know him. He has gone from the scene, but the substance of his greatness will live in the pages of history and be a source of inspiration to future generations.

ADDRESS BY

HON. WILLIAM E. BROCK 3D

OF TENNESSEE

Mr. Speaker, this day we stand in tribute to the great statesman of our time, Sir Winston Churchill. In such a moment the deep sense of loss felt by all can only be second to our continuing gratitude that the world was given his example to follow, an example of integrity, courage, and faith.

His mark has been dramatically recorded not only on the character of his beloved England, but on the other nations for which he fought so gallantly.

Sir Winston was time and again tested; without fail the challenges were met. He was an honorable winner who knew the responsibilities of victory. He was a noble loser, gracious yet proud in defeat. This tremendous fighter for good, this statesman and soldier, has always been close to the heart of America.

As Churchill made history he also recorded it, leaving a wealth of documentation on our times and guideposts for the future. Though the man is gone, his spirit lives on. His strength of character and record of service to humanity will continue to inspire men to ever nobler achievements in generations yet unborn.

ADDRESS BY

HON. JOE L. EVINS

OF TENNESSEE

Mr. Speaker, I desire to join with my colleagues in an expression of deepest sorrow at the passing of Sir Winston Churchill, and in paying a brief but sincere tribute to the memory of this distinguished world statesman.

In common with American citizens throughout our country, and with freemen everywhere, the people of the district I have the honor to represent regarded Winston Churchill as one of the greatest men of our century.

He was indomitable in time of war and a great champion of freedom and liberty in days of peace and always.

We mourn his passing as we would the loss of a cherished member of our own family circle.

He spoke our deepest thoughts in times of stress and great difficulty.

He taught us anew the meaning of courage.

He asserted the greatness of the human spirit in words and deeds that gave inspiration to multitudes of freemen everywhere.

As he was fond of recalling, Winston Churchill was half American and he made us feel that we were bound together by something even greater than ties of blood, shared traditions, and our common language.

Many of us recall when he came to America as Prime Minister and spoke to a joint session of the Congress. He commented on his relationship to our country and the fact that his mother was born in America. He told the Congress that if his father had been an American and his mother British instead of the other way around, that he "might have made it here," on his own.

The fact is that he did "make it here" on his own.

His permanent constituency does include all of America.

In voting last year to confer honorary American citizenship on him, the Congress acted to formalize the universal recognition of Citizen Winston Spencer Churchill as one of our own.

In America, we have no titles of nobility. The designation of "citizen" is the highest honor than can be bestowed on an individual in our land.

We loved this gallant Englishman as a warmhearted friend and ally at the same time, that we acclaimed him as a peerless leader. We can never forget Citizen Winston Churchill. We can never forget his command to fight, to preserve, and never to surrender, in the struggle for liberty, justice, freedom, and peace.

ADDRESS BY

HON. BARRATT O'HARA

OF ILLINOIS

Mr. Speaker, my constituents in the Second District of Illinois would wish me to express their grief at the passing of Sir Winston Churchill and to join in this tribute to his memory.

In a very large sense he was one of us. Perhaps no man more completely blended the spirit of the peoples of two great nations, that of the United States of his mother's birth and the England of his father and his father's family.

He was truly beloved by the people of the United States as he was beloved by the people of his native land. He gave a new depth of meaning, of eloquence, and of force to our common language.

It was not long ago that the Congress voted to confer honorary American citizenship upon Sir Winston Churchill, and now that he is gone I am sure we all feel more than ever a quiet sense of satisfaction that during the lifetime of this good and remarkable man this recognition was given.

Mr. Speaker, while the youth and the prime of Winston Churchill were active and colorful, it was not until he had reached the age of 65 that the mantle of greatness began to envelop him. If there had been a rule or a law in England such as obtains in some businesses, and some of little vision would fasten upon all public as well as private employment, that anyone on reaching 65 must be eliminated by compulsory retirement, Sir Winston Churchill in the dazzling brilliance of his genius would have been lost to the world.

ADDRESS BY

HON. J. EDWARD ROUSH

OF INDIANA

Mr. Speaker, when one feels compelled to speak out on the passing of a great man the limitation of one's own vocabulary becomes sharply defined. When the great man is Winston Churchill this deficiency of expression becomes even more acute.

It has been said that for Englishmen, of all the races on earth, any task undertaken in an adventurous spirit acquires the merit of romance.

Winston Churchill personified the spirit of adventure. For him life was one long romance. It was a relationship in which the past was only a prelude to be thoroughly understood so that he could better appreciate today in preparing for the challenges he anticipated tomorrow.

For Winston Churchill, history was a subject to be studied, a record to be set down, events to be directed. All of these he did in what has become known as the Churchillian manner.

He himself commented that it is foolish to waste lamentations upon the closing phases of life.

We shall follow his counsel. These few words are not voiced to lament his passing but to express our appreciation he was here.

ADDRESS BY

HON. EMILIO Q. DADDARIO

OF CONNECTICUT

Mr. Speaker, I rise to join in the tribute we pay today to an honorary citizen of this country, the son of an American beauty, who accomplished so much in his lifetime to maintain the freedom of the West.

His deeds are many and they are worth study and emulation. He was a giant among men. Though he once said that it was the British people who had the lion's heart and he only had the luck to give the roar, it was his voice of defiance, his spirit of determination, which was more than a frail reed, more than an uncertain trumpet in the West's hour of need.

Because he took positive stands in so many trying moments, there are those who find it difficult to forgive. Yet the world has benefited from his pugnacious and resolute being, from his imaginative and fighting spirit, and from his leadership.

This leadership transcends all petty worries and leads us to sorrow with the British at the passing of such a great figure. We saw him, in the world's moment of crisis, working closely with our own great leader, Franklin D. Roosevelt, in bringing victory to the West. We have seen him, in his waning years, giving counsel to the West, contributing history of first water in quality to the traditions of our youth.

Let me add my condolences today to those which are being expressed by the House to his family, to his nation, and to the world.

ADDRESS BY

HON. ROBERT McCLORY

OF ILLINOIS

Mr. Speaker, it is entirely fitting that the American flag should be flown at half staff in memory of Sir Winston Churchill.

It is appropriate, also, that we pause today in this House of Representatives to pay tribute to a great Member of the British House of Commons.

Winston Churchill's great talents developed and flourished in the British House. His skill in debate, his wise and ominous warnings to the British nation and to the world, and his long, difficult experiences in behalf of unpopular causes prepared him for the hours of greatness which came to him. This greatness, associated as it was with courage and fortitude, enabled Great Britain to survive amidst the most devastating attacks upon the British Isles.

The strength and courage of this man provided hope and inspiration to Britain's Western allies, as the long, hard road to victory began—and Winston Churchill challenged one and all with fingers raised in a symbolic "V" for victory.

It was a personal privilege to be part of the 88th Congress and to support H.R. 4374 which made Winston Churchill the first and only honorary citizen of the United States.

The people of the 12th District of Illinois, as well as citizens of the entire world, join in tribute to Winston Churchill's life of service and leadership.

It was a glorious hour when Winston Churchill rose to encourage faith and strength in his British countrymen and the free world. Today, it is a dark hour as the world mourns his passing.

ADDRESS BY

HON. DON FUQUA

OF FLORIDA

Mr. Speaker, today the world mourns a great statesman.

In the passing of Sir Winston Churchill, all mankind has lost a friend and leader. Today, as we mourn his passing, we are consoled with the realization that we have been privileged to have had such a man among us.

A lifetime of training, of bitter disappointment, was suddenly shunted aside at a time when many men have retired from life's labor, as he was called to lead his nation, and even the world, in one of its most trying hours.

The freedom of dignity of every man was at stake as the Fascist hordes enslaved vast areas of the earth's surface. And it was Winston Churchill's lot to fall heir to the most trying position that a man has ever tried to fill.

With his cheery countenance, his bulldog determination, his unflinching patriotism and devotion to the cause of freedom for every man everywhere, he became the man of the hour. Never in history has so much been demanded of a man.

And in response, he gave.

We cannot know the agonizing suffering which must have been his. We cannot know the full impact that these responsibilities must have had, as he realized that what he did might well determine the course of freedom. And it did.

His flashing "V" for victory sign gave hope to a beleaguered people. Where there was no hope, he gave hope; where there was misery he gave comfort; where it was darkest, he gave light. Truly it was one of the finest hours for all men everywhere.

Today we are blessed because he gave. As his mortal remains are deposited with all the honor that his beloved land can give him, he has the love and appreciation of all freemen everywhere.

History has just begun to judge his contributions. They are legend. To paraphrase his own immortal words, "Never have so many owed so much to just one."

The world is richer because of his life. From him we should draw inspiration. Never can a statesman study the past for the key to the future without drawing on the life and works of Winston Churchill.

He is gone from us, and we mourn his passing.

But we are richer for his having been with us. Nations and men from this day forth will humbly thank the Creator for having allowed such a leader to emerge when one was so needed.

From his determined spirit, we willingly accept the torch and the responsibilities which he passes to us. A new generation now must lead, and they will lead better because of his example, his courage, wit, and determination.

The pages of history will record his deeds. As has been so aptly stated, surely this was the man of our century. From his passing, let us resolve that we will have learned from his life, that we may strive for a world where hunger, disease, ignorance, and enslavement may be abolished. His dream was our dream. And it shall come to pass if we have faith, and we give of ourselves as unselfishly as did this man we honor today.

He is gone, but he can never be forgotten.

ADDRESS BY

HON. ROBERT B. DUNCAN

OF OREGON

Mr. Speaker, a titan has left our midst. Those legendary and historical inhabitants of Mount Olympus and Valhalla have willingly moved over to make room on the front bench for one of our age who need acknowledge no peer.

No human throughout our history has faced more herculean challenges successfully than he. No one has been vested both with the prescience and the courage, ability, and opportunity to both combat evil and advance the cause, not just of his own people, but of humanity everywhere.

His life spanned generations; his talents knew no bounds. Greatness never marred his humility; reverses never dampened his integrity or his resolve.

Those of us who shared, even briefly, Sir Winston Churchill's time on earth know that the age of heroes is not over.

ADDRESS BY

HON. FRANK HORTON

OF NEW YORK

Mr. Speaker, with profound sorrow I join my colleagues and countrymen in expressing grief over the loss our world suffered yesterday with the passing of Sir Winston Churchill.

We have lost a stalwart statesman whose four score and 10 years of vigor and vitality occupy a prominent part of the history of our times.

Let it not be forgotten that the United States has lost not only a fond friend and able ally but also an honorary citizen. I shall always remember the honor which I felt as a freshman Congressman in voting for the legislation which became Public Law 88–6 bestowing honorary U.S. citizenship on Sir Winston. I said at that time and I repeat now: It was a great privilege in behalf of a great man.

ADDRESS BY

HON. FRANCES P. BOLTON

OF OHIO

Mr. Speaker, last evening with millions of other people here in this great country of ours, I listened to the CBS hour "Sir Winston Churchill—Man of the Century." Today I take this opportunity to thank the network for giving us these reminders of this great man's contribution's to Britain, to the free world, and to his other country.

What a life was his. What a channel he was for the forces of good. How privileged we have been to have lived during the long years when he challenged all free people to match his courage to meet the full measure of his faith in his country.

"We will win." How often those words rang out loud and clear in those terrible years—in the voice that carried them across the world.

Undaunted, he never accepted defeat. Unfaltering, he led his people to victory.

In deepest gratitude for the "Churchill Hour," I would say to you who share with me the privileges and responsibilities of this U.S. Congress that there never was a time in our history when we so needed that same courage and vision and determination.

I challenge each one of you to renew your faith in these United States—to say to yourselves, to our country, and to the world "We can and we will win this battle for decency and honor which is being waged within our borders and in all corners of the globe."

Is there no one who will come forth and give us a clarion call to the battle we must wage against the false gods of discouragement and despair? Is there no one who will challenge us to fill our Government positions with men whose blood is the blood of heroes that we may hear on all sides the call that Sir Winston gave the free world in its darkest days: "We will win."

ADDRESS BY

HON. DURWARD G. HALL

OF MISSOURI

Mr. Speaker, I think the gentlewoman from Ohio, the Honorable Frances P. Bolton, has made an inspiring statement and I commend her, and would like to associate myself with her thoughts.

With the death of Sir Winston Churchill, England has lost, a great leader, statesman, and soldier, maker and recorder of history. And the free world has lost the greatest fighter for freedom of this century. When England stood alone against the onslaught of Nazi tyranny, it was Churchill who summoned the English language to battle and in so doing prepared his people for the dark days that followed. Surely hindsight must tell us that his leadership, his perseverance, and his courage not only changed the course of history, but may indeed have saved it from entering a new dark age in the midst of the 20th century.

As an author, Churchill has left us with a valuable insight for our own future course of action. In his book, "The Gathering Storm," he perceived:

> If you will not fight for the right when you can easily win without bloodshed; if you will not fight when your victory will be sure and not too costly; you may come to the moment when you will have to fight when all the odds are against you and only a precarious chance of survival. There may even be a worse case. You may have to fight when there is no hope of victory, because it is better to perish than to live as slaves.

In evaluating Sir Winston's place in history, his own comments during the Battle of Britain could well be paraphrased: never have so many owed so much to one man.

ADDRESS BY

HON. SEYMOUR HALPERN

OF NEW YORK

Mr. Speaker, the world has lost a great champion of liberty, a man who in character and deed embodied the grandeur of an upsetting time.

We mourn the quiet passing of Sir Winston Churchill; may our remembrance of him stir within us the will and faith which distinguished his life.

To his family and the British people, we extend profound sympathy on their loss, which is also ours.

There is no end to the honor and respect owing to this giant among men. In an age of growing specialization and polarization, he epitomized skill and wisdom in all fields. Statesman, politician, warrior, author, painter, and bricklayer, the life of Winston Churchill is of heroic dimension.

We can never forget that Winston Churchill more than any other person, rallied the forces of civilization against Hitlerite tyranny. At that hour when Europe quivered, helpless, before the onslaught of evil incarnate, the island kingdom found a man who would not surrender. He stirred the conscience of his nation, of the free world, returning to the democracies that vital respectability which had been lost in weakness, pettiness, and defeat.

Sir Winston Churchill, his character and his achievements, will endure as long as freemen have the strength to protect the liberties which he cherished.

ADDRESS BY

HON. EDWARD J. DERWINSKI

OF ILLINOIS

Mr. Speaker, I join Members of the House in paying tribute to a great world statesman, the late Sir Winston Churchill. Americans certainly appreciate and recognize his unique role in history. The Nation mourns his passing as a true friend of freedom whose memory will always be held in special reverence by all Americans.

Winston Churchill's greatness was in large part seen in his personal courage and the inspiration he gave to his countrymen and people throughout the free world. His heroic leadership of the British people during World War II, coupled with his statesmanlike qualities in recognizing the postwar designs of international communism, were outstanding high points of his career.

The free world has lost a great leader, but he has left a rich and inspiring history that will continue to be a source of strength and inspiration to us.

ADDRESS BY

HON. EARLE CABELL

OF TEXAS

Mr. Speaker, my good constituents from the Fifth District of Texas will think me remiss in my duty if I do not express in their behalf that we of Dallas County join with those in this august body and those of the world who have expressed their deepest sorrow at the passing of one of the century's ablest leaders and statesmen, Sir Winston Churchill. Particularly, representing Dallas do I feel motivated to speak out in praise of this man's life and in sorrow at this man's death, for we in Dallas owe him a debt. Three years ago, while I was the mayor of the fine city of Dallas, Sir Winston was made an honorary citizen of Dallas. In responding to this city's tribute to him, Sir Winston paid Dallas one of its most revered compliments. We will never fortget this great man or his warm remarks about our city.

ADDRESS BY

HON. OTIS G. PIKE

OF NEW YORK

Mr. Speaker, most of us, in this body of Members truly representative of our Nation, are of that generation which President Kennedy in his inaugural address referred to as "tempered by war." We had, from the tragic years from 1938 to the triumphant year of 1945, our own great leader in the person of Franklin D. Roosevelt, but we and all people who fought tyranny during that dark convulsion which shook the earth had another leader in the person of Sir Winston Churchill.

England has the honor to call him her own, but we have the honor to call him ours, too, by adoption and by affection. From the beginning of that conflict there was tragedy, and there was fear, and a new language was imposed upon the minds and hearts of the American people. As the German armies overran Poland, the first nation proud enough to fight rather than surrender, the word "blitzkrieg," "panzer," "Stuka," and "Gestapo" became household words, and brought a foreboding of a terrible and irresistible force which could menace us even across the Atlantic, and as those armies overran France this fear increased.

And then that doughty, cocky, magnificent voice was raised, and a more familiar language went to work, and phrase after eloquent phrase rolled across England, and across America, and put heart in her people and our own.

"Give us the tools," he said, and America produced the tools.

"Look west, the land is also bright," he quoted, and the conscience and honor of America were awakened.

"We shall fight on the landing grounds, we shall fight in the fields and in the streets, we shall fight in the hills; we shall never surrender," he said, and courage and resolve flowed from this one man into all who enlisted in the cause of freedom.

For that generation which was tempered by war, he provided both the fire and the steel; he articulated courage and honor; he brought out the best in all of us, and made that generation greater than it had been.

For all those, in all lands, who have ever engaged in public service, he did something more. He demonstrated the value of standing hard by one's beliefs. Sir Winston Churchill did not always leap mightily from triumph to triumph. He had his political defeats, his public repudiations, and must at times have despaired for the future of all those principles in which he most deeply believed, but he held to those principles and in the fullness of time they were recognized, needed, and used to save his nation and our own.

Not many men live to be recognized as great in their own time. None will be recognized as greater in our own. Warrior, statesman, author, artist—this was a man. This was the titan of our time. From his life each of us has gained greatly; with his death we join gratefully to do him honor.

ADDRESS BY

HON. JAMES C. CORMAN

OF CALIFORNIA

Mr. Speaker, freedom-loving people the world over today mourn the death of Sir Winston Churchill. The great warrior is stilled. The final battle is over.

But the tears in our eyes and the grief in our hearts are not so much for Sir Winston, himself, who lived a rich, full life and tasted the fruits of honor and glory and the respect and admiration of his fellow man.

No, I think we mourn for ourselves, for we have lost a valiant and farsighted man. We have lost a statesman and a patriot who rallied an entire country to the cause of liberty, giving it the fortitude and courage to withstand the forces of oppression and tyranny which besieged it. We have witnessed the passing of a leader who helped inspire an alliance of nations to turn back the enemy so that freedom might prevail. We have lost a great orator and writer who gave the English language new eloquence. Indeed, we mourn for ourselves because we have lost one of the great men of our time.

Yet, we cannot really mourn for our children who will never know him as we did. We cannot grieve for them because they are the richer because Sir Winston lived. They are the heirs of the liberty into which he breathed new life and the heirs of the freedom he fought so steadfastly to perpetuate.

ADDRESS BY

HON. THOMAS N. DOWNING

OF VIRGINIA

Mr. Speaker, all too often it seems that the true worth of a man is recognized only after his death. This was not true of our beloved Winston Churchill.

This man became a legend in his own time. He became the symbol of a proud people and a proud nation and an enduring, prideful relationship between our great Nation and his own. The extent of his personal contribution to the world is simply awe inspiring—virtually impossible to measure in any mortal terms. His passing takes Winston Churchill into the realm of the immortal, but to so many of us he has seemed immortal while he was among us.

Winston Churchill has always seemed to me to be a man who defies description in any reasonably human terms. His contributions have been so extensive, so valuable, so fulfilling that he demands description in language that is too poetic because despite the immortal character of the man, he was a warm, sincere, and genuine human. He enjoyed his life and he obviously enjoyed life's pleasures, even though he had dedicated his life to service to his fellow man. And, there is no man in public life in any time who has so richly deserved the deference he received during his lifetime and now. His greatness found its origins in his own character and he was one of the few men on this earth who has been able, by the great force of his magnetic ability, to influence people and nations and the world.

He has seemed, in recent years, to gain in stature and in the admiration of his colleagues, friends, and admirers and in human warmth. It has become evident to every citizen of every nation that Winston Churchill had given his every thought, his every action, and his life to the best interests of Britain and the world. The affection that has been showered on him in recent years seemed to please him and I am very deeply grateful that this man who gave so much was able to know—as one of our great leaders was never able to know—that the people loved him.

It has become commonplace in recent times for men in public life to talk about their place in history. Winston Churchill who himself has gained a hallmark reputation as a historian will be recorded in history as the man who perhaps best represents the Western World's image of leadership in modern times. The symbol of leadership that he is leaving behind may never again be matched on this earth. His mastery of men and events and issues was not only uncommon—it was gigantic. His own people have recognized him as a superb author, orator, patriot. Here in the United States we have known him for all these things and as a friend.

I am personally very deeply sorry that he is no longer with us, and yet I know that he will live forever in the hearts of his own people, on the pages of history, and in our hearts.

ADDRESS BY

HON. BURT L. TALCOTT

OF CALIFORNIA

Mr. Speaker, we have received the tragic though not unexpected news of the passing of the truly remarkable Sir Winston. His great works will live forever in the history of our planet as shining guide-posts for those who follow.

Mere words fail as we seek to eulogize Winston Spencer Churchill. The greatest of the great falls far short of the mark in describing the impact of this man upon our century. It is clear to all that he was the greatest of our era—and one of only a few of the truly outstanding mortals in all of recorded history.

Mr. Speaker, we are aware that Sir Winston was a man of many rare qualities. He leaves a rich personal heritage which we may study to our very great benefit.

His statesmanship is legendary. By the force of his own personality and will, Prime Minister Churchill crystallized the determination of his own nation and of the entire free world during times of extreme danger to repel and overcome the most serious threat to civilized society in the history of the world to that point. It seems probable that this "uncommon commoner" affected the course of human affairs more profoundly than has any other single individual since Jesus of Nazareth.

Mr. Churchill was an early and implacable foe of communism, recognizing it as a most dangerous form of tyranny.

As a member of the House of Commons for 62 of his 90 years, Mr. Churchill was a parliamentarian without equal—a politician in the most honorable sense of the word.

Mr. Churchill was perhaps the foremost craftsman of the English language of all time—written and oral, formal and extemporaneous—a towering figure in the area of human expression.

Mr. Churchill was a renowned painter throughout most of his life—one of the outstanding artists of his time. His place in history would have been secure with his contributions in this field alone.

As the son of an American mother, and an honorary citizen of the United States—a distinction of which he was enormously proud—we cherish Mr. Churchill as one of our own.

It would seem, Mr. Speaker, that we might honor the great Sir Winston best—and simultaneously benefit all of mankind—by studying his life, emulating his works as best we can, heeding his admonitions, pursuing his dreams, and keeping alive his ideas.

May God grant us a small portion of his indomitable courage, his profound foresight, his selfless, sustained dedication to the preservation of freedom for all men.

ADDRESS BY

HON. CHARLES E. BENNETT

OF FLORIDA

Mr. Speaker, belief in evil equals fear. Belief in good equals courage. Sir Winston Churchill's death reminds us of these truths. He was, in fact, the world's greatest living person; and his passing over to the realm of spirit makes us look again at his predominant tool for leadership and victory, namely, courage. Even the most humble are important in the eyes of God; and we Christians believe that all become great with the acquisition and practice of courage for right things. Churchill's life will always be a symbol of the value of courage for proper objectives. I am glad I lived in his age, met him, and have his memory to strengthen me. As to his life, we all respond: "Well done."

ADDRESS BY

HON. PAUL H. TODD, JR.

OF MICHIGAN

Mr. Speaker, Sir Winston Churchill is dead. And it is right and proper for all who love freedom and admire man to do him honor.

But it must be done in the correct way. It is not enough merely to recite lists of deeds done, or name battles won, or chant a string of adjectives with his name. Nor should it be maudlin or idolatrous.

He would not have liked it.

More important, it would have missed the point. For Churchill was a man, and a very human one. He made mistakes, sometimes enormous. He was hard to get along with, and sometimes pettish. He was always stubborn, and he could be tyrannical.

But it was precisely that humanity—set in a grand scale and raised to a high power—that made him what he was: One of the giants of our times. Churchill the man was bigger than lifesize, and it was partly through this that he led men as he did. But he led men from a position in their midst, rather than trying to lead from above. He went out into the streets during the agony of London, to be with his people. As a man, then, we must see him and do praise to his measure.

Merely to have lived in the same century with Sir Winston was an honor and an inspiration and, unquestionably, fun. For Churchill had that lashing sense of humor and quick flash of wit which importantly complemented his iron will and fierce resolve. He was big enough and strong enough to direct it against himself, as well as others.

His wit, coupled with his impatience, helped him lead. "Pray submit to me, by 4 p.m. today, on one-half sheet of paper, the preparations undertaken by His Majesty's Navy to pursue the coming war," he supposedly wrote the First Sea Lord after becoming the First Lord of the Admiralty.

He led with words, written sometimes but more effectively spoken. To an extraordinary degree, his language had always expressed his unusual character. It came, in time, to express not only what Great Britain must be, but what the Western World must do. It was good, tough language and it had a majesty that made the important things seem vitaly alive and immediate. He could never say, as had his predecessor, Neville Chamberlain, that England would not fight "for a small, faraway country, between people of whom we know nothing."

Instead, Churchill rallied his people and the world to the struggle at hand and to the problems to come. He did so by combining, to a degree unmatched since President Lincoln, the qualities of a great man and a towering writer in a setting of dark peril. The result was the true criterion of leadership; he made people feel directly, personally, and passionately involved in the great events of their time. Not only people in Great Britain, but also in France, America, and around the world.

Winston Churchill did this himself, through the force of his personality and the power of his words. The setting did not make the man, though it called him forth. Once emerged, he changed it entirely. His life was one of the rarest of all historical events; in living, he did not make a difference. He made the difference.

His death was right and proper. It was expected and dignified, quiet and fitting, after such a life. His going leaves us all the poorer, as his living left us all the richer.

Winston Churchill will always be with us, for in large measure he molded our world. He will particularly be in our hearts during moments of crisis and fear, his words and his example giving fiery thrust to our hopes:

In war, resolution.
In defeat, definance.
In victory, magnanimity.
In peace, good will.

ADDRESS BY

HON. W. J. BRYAN DORN

OF SOUTH CAROLINA

Mr. Speaker, one of the highlights of my service in the Congress was a visit with Sir Winston Churchill at 10 Downing Street in London in the fall of 1951. Mr. Churchill was again Prime Minister following Prime Minister Atlee and his Labor government. I was with a group of my colleagues headed by the distinguished gentleman from North Carolina [Mr. Bonner].

As our congressional group was leaving Mr. Churchill's office, the Prime Minister called me back to inquire of his good friend, Jimmy Byrnes. The Prime Minister was very familiar with the history of our country and he knew of my States rights philosophy and devotion to the private enterprise system. Mr. Churchill with tears in his eyes said that England could no longer lead the free world and this responsibility now belonged to the United States. He said that England could become a second-rate power due largely to one party in England being wholly conservative and the other extremely liberal. Mr. Churchill said that after 6 years of the Labor government under Mr. Attlee, he could do nothing to undo socialistic measures which had been instituted by the Labor government. Churchill said it was impossible to induce businessmen to return and take over certain utilities that had been nationalized by the Government because these businessmen knew that someday the liberal government would come back to power and that business would be again nationalized.

Mr. Churchill, in referring to socialized medicine, said that it would be impossible for him to take a pair of pliers and pull the teeth from the mouths of the people given to them by the Government. He said they would howl to high heaven. He used this as an example to illustrate that there is no turning back from socialism and the erosion of initiative, private enterprise, and individual effort.

Mr. Churchill suggested that if the United States were to remain the heart and core of the free world, our two great political parties must continue to embody in each conservatives, liberals, and moderates. He warned that the United States would deteriorate and lose its prestige and position as a world power if one of our great political parties became completely conservative and the other totally liberal. Sooner or later, Mr. Churchill warned, the liberal party would come to power and the United States and its great institutions would be treated to socialistic schemes from which there is no return. Mr. Churchill said in order for the United States to continue its world leadership it would be necessary to keep a balance in both political parties so that the Nation could move forward in the middle of the road. I was amazed at Mr. Churchill's keen insight into American political philosophy and was amazed with his foresight. I will always believe that Mr. Churchill called me aside for this word of warning because at that time I was a young man in my early thirties, and he knew that I was associated with the philosophy of States right and devoted to the private enterprise system and was a member of the Democratic Party which has traditionally encompassed all elements and classes of our American society.

Mr. Speaker, I have wished many times that the world had listened to Winston Churchill, a man of unsurpassed wisdom, culture, education, training, and experience in world leadership in the most critical time in our modern history. No one was more aware than Winston Chruchill that the Polish corridor created after World War I was the immediate cause of World War II. Churchill was well aware that a Berlin corridor would set the stage for world war III. It will always remain a mystery to me how the incredible tragedy of the Berlin corridor was foisted on the world. War lords and agitators in their wildest imagination could have never dreamed up a more perfect way to insure another war. Winston Churchill knew, which many of us seem to forget, that Communist Russia was equally as guilty as Adolf Hitler in launching World War II. He kept constantly in mind that Communist Russia violated the integrity of Poland and invaded that nation and in its deal with Hitler received the largest slice of Polish territory.

Churchill was one of the greatest men in the history of the world but he did not have to be great to see the folly and stark tragedy of turning central Europe over to Communist Russia. Churchill knew in the end that we won no victory in Europe. We only made it possible for Communist Russia to win the ultimate victory. It was with such sadness that Churchill saw Poland, the very nation that the free nations went to war to preserve, gobbled up by the ruthless Communist aggressor, thus depriving the Western World of a victory over the forces of oppression, dictatorship, and aggression.

Mr. Speaker, Winston Churchill typified all that was great, all that was grand, gallant, and magnificent about the British Empire. Winston Churchill is an example of British statesmanship at its best. Churchill was incomparable as a patriot, soldier, historian, and statesman. We are all indebted to him today for standing like a stone wall guarding the ramparts of freedom when the chips were down.

ADDRESS BY

HON. JOHN O. MARSH, JR.

OF VIRGINIA

Mr. Speaker, the life and character of Sir Winston Churchill has been the subject of countless sincere and eloquent encomiums in recent days, and I would not presume to undertake an inclusive eulogy. I cannot let his passing, and the impressive funeral ceremonies, retreat into history, however, without a brief and heartfelt comment.

Sir Winston Churchill was the best of everything British. He was a man who could bring to the modern world the finest traditions of the past. Yet for all his achievements that would make him a legend in his lifetime, we saw in him, particularly, the greatness of human spirit. In many ways, he captured the spirit of Kipling's "If," and shining through a brilliant career we cannot help but see the greatness of an individual that would be translated into magnificent accomplishments in the realm of public service.

Sir Winston Churchill was the embodiment of the British spirit. He represented the greatness of the British past and British traditions. Yet for all of his achievements in the field of politics, in military affairs, in art and letters, he shall be marked by the indomitable spirit in a man whose pole star for greatness was courage. This was a personal courage that would be translated into the courage of a nation, an empire, and a cause. It was physical, and it was moral.

One cannot look at him without a sure conviction that here was a man who, without hesitation or fear, would undertake any task, perform any duty, make any sacrifice which he might demand of others.

His stature will grow in history, and the posterity which owes him so much will study again and again the character of this man who not only inspired the free world by the leadership of his country in Britain's darkest hour but who had the vision, the courage, and the foresight after the end of World War II to direct the world's attention to the tyranny of communism and the aggressive aims of the Soviet Union. It could well be that the greatest debt the free world shall owe to this man who towered above others in our tumultuous 20th century shall be found centered in his leadership in the postwar years to prevent the enslavement of mankind by the Sino-Soviet bloc.

ADDRESS BY

HON. JOHN B. ANDERSON

OF ILLINOIS

Mr. Speaker, one of the acts of the 88th Congress was to confer honorary citizenship on Sir Winston S. Churchill. We did so in recognition of the vast and heroic part that he played in the prosecution of the allied war effort which gave us victory over our common foes, the Axis Powers. We did it also because he exemplified more than any other living mortal of foreign nationality those essential traits of devotion to liberty on which the whole American experiment was initially founded. The fact that this experiment, begun 189 years ago, has not only endured but flourished and prospered beyond measure is due in large part to the fact that these ideals of liberty, respect for truth, and love of justice have been fought for by courageous men of purpose and vision.

Sir Winston Churchill will surely live forever in the annals of history. We mourn today his passing; yet, we rejoice in the imperishable heritage which he has not only helped to preserve but which his shining deeds and magnificent words of courageous counsel in times of adversity have helped to strengthen. For in the course of human events there will surely come other times of decision; yes, even times when once again our whole democratic system will come under the siege guns of those who would overcome us. Yet, we can remain confident that in times like these the inspiration of Sir Winston Churchill's life and writings will continue to strengthen other men in the purpose and resolve to resist tyranny and remain free. The world has truly lost a great man, but as freedom's champion he lives on in the immortal garb of historic greatness. He will forever remain joined in the effections of the American people with the great patriots of our Republic.

ADDRESS BY

HON. ALBERT H. QUIE

OF MINNESOTA

Mr. Speaker, we pause to pay tribute to one who in perilous times fought for the freedom of the entire world. This was the late Sir Winston Churchill, a man among very few who saw his name chronicled in history during the course of his own lifetime.

Mr. Churchill was a giant among great men and grand events, his hallmark being supreme tenacity in the face of adversity. Over and above this, he had a facility for bringing forth the best in men during times when it was most needed.

During World War II, he proved a great light in long hours of darkness; and because he remembered the high purpose of freemen in their hour of trial, mankind will never forget Winston Churchill.

ADDRESS BY

HON. JAMES C. CLEVELAND

OF NEW HAMPSHIRE

Mr. Speaker, Sir Winston Churchill's name is forever associated with the cause of freedom and its finest hours. A politician in the highest sense of the word, he set standards of courage, vision, and leadership on which public servants and all freedom-loving men of every nation may model themselves without reservation.

Born an aristocrat, Churchill touched the hearts and stirred the finest feelings in men of every walk of life. Throughout his long, extraordinary career, he did nothing cheap or mean and no breath of scandal touched him.

He was also born half-American and died in the enjoyment of full citizenship bestowed on him by Congress in the name of a grateful people allied with him in the common cause of freedom.

Every American laments his passing.

Freemen everywhere will long walk in the titanic shadow of this great and good man.

ADDRESS BY

HON. WILLIAM G. BRAY

OF INDIANA

Mr. Speaker, we all mourn the passing of Sir Winston Churchill, probably the greatest man of this century.

He possessed so many great attributes and so many attributes of greatness that we hardly know which are the most important to remember.

He had indomitable courage and perseverance, proven both in his personal life and his leadership of Great Britain and the free world.

He had a capacity for being absolutely honest, even when his candid assessments of things as they actually were, were not appreciated and were not popular.

We should remember especially that he was always skeptical about Russian intentions. At Teheran, it was Churchill who tried in vain to safeguard the interests of the Western democracies, rightly guessing that after World War II we would find our peace and security endangered by international communism.

The Russians, even during his final illness, have castigated Churchill as the man who started the cold war. Of course, that is preposterous. It is one thing to start something; it is something else to be able to see clearly what is happening in the world.

Churchill early perceived the course of international communism and the treachery of the Russians. Had we in the United States heeded his advice sooner, many of communism's advances would never have been achieved.

The greatest need of the world today is for more men of the caliber of Winston Churchill.

ADDRESS BY

HON. OGDEN R. REID

OF NEW YORK

Mr. Speaker, Great Britain and the United States have lost a son without peer. Sir Winston Churchill bestrode the free world like a mighty colossus. He was—as President de Gaulle has said of his role in the great drama of World War II—"the greatest."

Our century may not see his like again. His courage was indomitable. His sense of the course of history was clear and ofttimes prophetic. His eloquence was unmatched. His flashing wit could uplift a nation or devastate a mean thrust. His leadership in the House of Commons, in power and out, was formidable and farseeing.

Few men in high public life have written of history—and of history they made—with such authority and with such sweep.

For the future, Churchill will in some measure be part of all of us. His voice and his words will always beat the call to courage and to principle—whenever freedom and human dignity stand in danger; wherever tyranny raises up its head and whenever the time comes for freemen to stand together undaunted and unafraid.

I am sure all in this House deeply mourn his passing and extend all sympathy to his family, to his Queen and to Great Britain and the Commonwealth.

Resolution of Respect By

Hon. Carl Albert, of Oklahoma

Mr. Speaker, I offer a resolution and ask for its immediate consideration.

The Clerk read as follows:

H. Res. 136

Resolved, That the House of Representatives has learned with profound sorrow of the death of Sir Winston Churchill, former Prime Minister of the United Kingdom, honorary citizen of the United States, beloved elder statesman of the world.

Resolved, That the House of Representatives tenders its deep sympathy to the members of the family of the late Sir Winston Churchill, and to his countrymen, and expresses the hope that the burden of their personal loss will be diminished by the knowledge that it is shared by his fellow citizens on this side of the Atlantic who were sustained by his eloquent words and courageous deeds when lesser men despaired and by all those throughout the world who are the beneficiaries of his dauntless defense of freemen.

Resolved, That the Secretary of State be requested to communicate these expressions of sentiment to the family of the deceased and to the Parliament of the United Kingdom of Great Britain and Northern Ireland.

Resolved, That as a further mark of respect to the memory of the late Sir Winston Churchill the House do now adjourn.

The resolution was unanimously agreed to.

Accordingly (at 2 o'clock and 15 minutes p.m.) the House adjourned until tomorrow, Tuesday, January 26, 1965, at 12 o'clock noon.

Memorial Addresses

In Eulogy of

Sir Winston Churchill

In The

Senate of the United States

January 26, 1965

Memorial Addresses

In the United States Senate

January 26, 1965

Prayer by the Chaplain

Rev. Frederick Brown Harris, D.D., offered the following prayer:

Our Father, God, in the noise and confusion of these baffling days, when world peace with justice and righteousness still hang in the balance, we would this day lift our Te Deum for one who in the darkest night, with indomitable courage, was the embodiment of freedom and human dignity in its finest hour—Thy servant, Winston Churchill, to whom, as he lies now in peace, all the world is indebted.

We are grateful that to him came the summons of the words to the prophet of long ago: "I sought a man among them who should build up the wall and stand in the breech before me for the land, that it should not be destroyed."

To that ringing challenge, he cried, "Here am I; send me." And Thou didst send:

> The greatest captain of our times—
> Great insaving commonsense,
> And as the greatest only are
> In his simplicity sublime.

Thanks be to Thee that such have been, though they are here no more.

We bring our prayer in the name of the master of all good workmen. Amen.

ADDRESS BY

HON. MIKE MANSFIELD

OF MONTANA

Mr. President, the world has received a shock in the passing of one of the great statesmen of our time. I refer, of course, to Sir Winston Churchill, funeral services for whom will be held on Saturday next.

While his death had been anticipated, nevertheless the news aroused a feeling of shock on the part of all people because of the many contributions which this man made to the welfare of Great Britain, Western Europe, this country, and to the world as a whole.

No man was able to do so much with so little for so many people in an hour of great emergency. His monument will be his words and his deeds. His passing will, in effect, mark the end of an era.

We shall miss this eminent statesman, this honorary citizen of the United States, the only one, I believe, besides the Marquis de Lafayette.

Mr. President, on behalf of the distinguished minority leader [Mr. Dirksen] and myself, I submit a resolution and ask that it be read.

The Vice President. The resolution will be stated.

The legislative clerk read as follows:

Resolved, That the Senate of the United States has learned with profound sorrow of the death of Sir Winston Leonard Spencer Churchill, former Prime Minister of Great Britain, a great and revered friend and honorary citizen of the United States of America.

Resolved, That the Senate expresses its deepest sympathy to the family and the people of Great Britain in their great loss.

Resolved, That the President of the United States be requested to communicate this expression of sentiment to the widow and members of his family assuring them of the condolence of the people of our Nation in their irreparable bereavement; and be it further

Resolved, That when the Senate adjourns today, it does so as a further mark of respect for the former Prime Minister.

The Vice President. Is there objection to the present consideration of the resolution?

There being no objection, the resolution was considered and unanimously agreed to.

ADDRESS BY

HON. EVERETT McKINLEY DIRKSEN

OF ILLINOIS

Mr. President, I can recall no individual, certainly in the past 100 years, who has been so honored by the entire world as Winston Churchill—and rightly so. In a dark hour, his words went into every corner of the world and restored confidence, restored strength in the cause of freedom, and somehow brought the entire world together in that hour, as the struggle for freedom was pursued to victory.

He was indeed a distinguished statesman in every sense of the word. I am sure that in all the corners of the world this week, and particularly on Saturday, there will be mourning in places high and humble to mark the passing of a truly great man.

ADDRESS BY

HON. LEVERETT SALTONSTALL

OF MASSACHUSETTS

Mr. President, those of us who love freedom and have an understanding of what war means have lost our hero and idol. No one individual ever represented more completely the qualities of leadership in times of great crises than did Sir Winston Churchill—courage, resourcefulness, energy, and the ability to stimulate an entire nation and others throughout the free world.

I shall always remember the day I spent with him at Harvard University, when that institution honored itself by offering him an honorary degree. He spoke to the many boys in training, he lunched with the officials of the college, and he stimulated the alumni in the afternoon. Then he returned to Washington.

But he left us all wiser about our duties and enthusiastic about our past in winning a war that would keep our country and his nation secure for the advancement of freedom and opportunity.

We owe him a debt of gratitude which we can never repay.

ADDRESS BY

HON. THOMAS H. KUCHEL

OF CALIFORNIA

Mr. President, the life and labor of the late Winston Churchill are completely unparalleled in all recorded history. This good, noble, and complex man demonstrated, in a long lifetime of service in the legislative branch of his government, an unmatched leadership, a bulldog devotion to the independence of the United Kingdom, and in the cause of man's freedom, as well as a capacity for constructive labor in many fields. He rallied his people in their very dark day—in their night of peril when another "Dark Age" hovered over them. Finally, when Pearl Harbor came, the New World stood by his side in vanquishing oppression and dictatorship bent on enslavement of the human race.

I have no doubt that every Senator has read and reread, as I have, that superb history of the Second World War which was one of the gifts of his pen to the ages.

I recall many times these days the last volume of that history, which is entitled "Triumph and Tragedy." I recall vividly the theme of that volume which he set down:

> How the great democracies finally emerged triumphant and so were able to resume the follies which had so nearly cost them their life.

Once again, does it not appear that the follies of the great democracies which have been, and are being resumed, undermine the Grand Alliance which ought steadfastly to continue as a deterent to new aggression?

The prescient wisdom this great human being demonstrated in all his long, productive life represents a remarkable gift to the strength of freedom-loving peoples on both sides of the Atlantic and in every sphere, in which human kind strives today for freedom against the new kind of tyranny.

Surely the lesson is clear for the people of the United States. We have a duty of leadership in the world today to continue those cherished goals which Churchill represented with his voice and his deeds as the indomitable figure of human dignity and leadership.

I rise as an American citizen to express the profound sense of loss to all mankind at the passing of this giant. I join my senior colleagues in expressing condolences to his family and to stand in solemn salute to the majestic, illustrious life he led. Americans recognize in their hearts that it was Churchill who rallied freedom against tyranny at a time when our mother country stood alone. That kind of dark day must never occur again. If America respects the Churchill legacy, the darkness will not return.

ADDRESS BY

HON. A. WILLIS ROBERTSON

OF VIRGINIA

Mr. President, I share the sorrow of the millions of friends and admirers throughout the world of Sir Winston Churchill, whose death occurred last Sunday. He was the greatest man that I have ever known. He was the greatest statesman of the 20th century. I believe history will record him as one of the truly great statesmen of all recorded time.

It was my happy privilege to know Sir Winston Churchill over a long period of time, and I regard him as having been the greatest statesman of our century.

I believe history will rate him with the great statesmen of all time.

I not only had the privilege of meeting Sir Winston on all of his official visits to Washington, but on two occasions away from the Capital, which stand out in my memory.

The first time was in 1929, when Sir Winston, then 54, visited Richmond, Va., to study the surrounding battlefields with Dr. Douglas Southall Freeman. The distinguished British visitor was entertained at the Governor's mansion by the then Governor, now Senator Harry F. Byrd. I was a member of the Governor's staff, having served in World War I and retired as a major. Senator Byrd invited me to come to Richmond and assist him in entertaining the visitor.

Seventeen years later, after World War II, I met Sir Winston again and had my longest personal conversation with him, at Palm Beach, Fla. I was there with Raymond Guest, visiting his mother, Mrs.

Frederick Guest, whose late husband was a cousin of Sir Winston. Sir Winston and Mrs. Churchill had come over from Miami Beach to spend the day at the Guest home.

This occurred early in 1946, while I was still a Member of the House. Realizing that the House would soon be debating the bill to make a postwar loan of about $3.7 billion to Great Britain, and being fearful that the Labor government would pour that money down the rathole of socialistic schemes, I discussed the matter for about an hour with Sir Winston and followed his advice to support the loan.

Although I was on the Ways and Means Committee at the time, and the British loan bill had been reported from the Banking and Currency Committee, I took a leading part in the debate in support of the bill, because of the information I had received from Mr. Churchill, and my great respect for his opinions. The great wartime British leader felt that the money was absolutely necessary for Great Britain's survival.

None of us will ever forget the courage he displayed following the fall of France in World War II. I am glad that Congress acted a few years ago to confer honorary U.S. citizenship on this champion of democracy. I shall always cherish the memory of my contacts with him.

ADDRESS BY

HON. RALPH W. YARBOROUGH

OF TEXAS

Mr. President, the passing of Sir Winston Churchill has stilled the most eloquent orator the English-speaking peoples have ever produced.

He was the modern Prince Valiant of mankind, rising like the answer to prayer from the rubble of wartorn England to lift up a torch of hope for freedom that spread its glow to the outer limits of the free world.

He exemplified the courage and steadfastness and the will to win that saved England and all Europe from a tyranny worse than the Dark Ages. No man has done more for freedom.

His genius for inspired leadership, his understanding of the human ideals combined to produce a legend that will live as long as men work and hope for a finer civilization.

It was my privilege to cosponsor the resolution conferring honorary American citizenship on Sir Winston Churchill.

On Monday morning, January 25, I recommended to Postmaster General John A. Gronouski that a stamp in tribute to Sir Winston be issued as soon as possible by the U.S. Post Office Department, and am pleased to learn that this is being done. It is my hope also that other memorials will be forthcoming, suitable to commemorate the memory of this great man, whose record now belongs to the ages.

It will be particularly beneficial to young Americans to know as much as possible of the magnificent record of the man who became a symbol of courage in the most trying hours for his country and ours, and of freedom itself.

ADDRESS BY

HON. FRANK J. LAUSCHE

OF OHIO

Mr. President, I rise to express my sorrow at the passing of Sir Winston Churchill.

During the war, I was mayor of Cleveland for part of the time and Governor of Ohio for the remainder. Those hours were critical. The citizenry of our Nation and its public officials were looking for signs of hope that might give them courage to withstand the agony and the portents of disaster which appeared on the European battlefield.

It was in 1940, the darkest hours of the war, when the retreat from Dunkirk was made. Nothing but darkness seemed to hover over the nations struggling to repel the assaults of the tyrants. Each day their hopes grew fainter.

Then there came a voice from England calling upon the citizens devoted to freedom to stand up, not to surrender hope, but to fight to the end.

As mayor of Cleveland, I knew the state of thought among the citizens of that community. Although we might have been divided prior to that time, we were consolidated in action at the time when the portents grew darkest.

In my judgment, one man stood out in rallying the forces of freedom, and that was this distinguished, brave, intrepid statesman of England—Winston Churchill.

When I learned of his passing, though it was anticipated because of the illness which beset him, I felt as though I had lost my closest friend.

The world has suffered a great loss in his passing. Winston Churchill will go down in history as the greatest man of the 20th century.

ADDRESS BY

HON. STEPHEN M. YOUNG

OF OHIO

Mr. President, free men and women everywhere and people who yearn for freedom the world over are saddened by the death of Winston Churchill. Very few individuals in history have made as many notable contributions to their time as Winston Churchill has to the 20th century. The entire world is indebted to him for his leadership in the struggle of freemen against nazism, fascism, and communism.

He is one of the honored few whose names themselves speak for their achievements. As a writer, historian, and orator—indeed, one of the great masters of all time in the art of the English language—he has earned himself a place among the literary giants of the English-speaking world.

Throughout the years he has been one of our Nation's stanchest friends. All Americans are grateful to him for his contributions to freedom and democracy. A thousand years from now people in faraway places will give thanks that in a dark and grave period in history this man grasped leadership of freemen and freewomen and threw back in bitter defeat the powerful forces of tyranny.

His enthusiasm, power, and leadership helped crush the terror of nazism, and men and women the world over were restored to their simple dignity as creatures of God.

Mr. President, on August 9, 1962, I introduced in the Senate the first resolution introduced in the Congress authorizing the President of the United States to declare Winston Churchill an honorary citizen of the United States. Two weeks later Representative Frances Bolton introduced the same joint resolution in the other body and other Representatives in that body later introduced the same joint resolution. Early in 1963 this joint resolution was passed by both Houses of Congress and a short time thereafter the late, great President John F. Kennedy declared him an honorary citizen at a ceremony at the White House at which Miss Kay Halle and I were guests along with many others, including Randolph Churchill and young Winston Churchill, grandson of this great leader of the world.

The person most responsible for this was Miss Kay Halle, radio and television commentator, journalist, author, world traveler of note, and one of our country's outstanding women. During World War II, Miss Halle served in an executive capacity in the Office of Strategic Services and most recently has been a member of the President's Advisory Committee on the Arts.

She first met Winston Churchill in 1931 when she was writing a column from London for the Cleveland News. During her stay in England, she spent many weekends at Chartwell with the Churchill family.

For many years Miss Halle has been urging that this great man be honored with American citizenship as a token of the esteem in which all Americans hold him. It was an article written by Miss Halle entitled "Hero of Two Nations" that appeared in the Plain Dealer, a great newspaper in Ohio and in our Nation, on July 23, 1962, that prompted me to introduce the joint resolution which would confer honorary citizenship on Winston Churchill. I spoke on this subject in the Senate and inserted her column in the Congressional Record. The Nation is indebted to Miss Kay Halle for her tireless efforts in urging the Congress to take this action.

Mr. President, I join with my colleagues and with free men and women everywhere in expressing deep sorrow at the passing of Great Britain's great war leader, one of the great men of all time.

ADDRESS BY

HON. THOMAS J. DODD

OF CONNECTICUT

Mr. President, nowhere will it be possible to fully record for historians the total sense of loss felt by peoples the world over at the death of Sir Winston Churchill. His death has cast a shadow on the hearts of people everywhere. From his youth, and for almost a century, his motto was: "Trust the people." He did, and was repaid in kind. There is no finer tribute.

He died as he lived, a symbol of what man can do in the face of adversity. And to the end, without flinching, he fought the certainty of death with the same audacity he confronted the trials of life. He was the epitome of the civilized man, revered by those whom he led to victory and respected by the vanquished.

I feel a personal loss at his death. As was said of Abraham Lincoln, "He truly belongs to the ages."

ADDRESS BY

HON. JACK MILLER

OF IOWA

Mr. President, all people throughout the world who love and cherish freedom have been saddened by the loss of Winston Churchill.

If one were to name the greatest man of the 20th century, it would have to be the one whose loss we mourn this week.

His life history reads like a historical novel. His accomplishments and experiences are so many and so far reaching as to stagger the imagination.

For all that he will be remembered, however, it is likely that he will be most remembered for his strength of character and the magnificence of his leadership in transferring that strength not only to the people whom he officially led, but also to the people in other lands whom he inspired.

We may pray that this inspiration will continue, even though he is gone, because it is through such inspiration that freedom for all people will come.

ADDRESS BY

HON. WAYNE MORSE

OF OREGON

Mr. President, I wish to pay my respects to the memory of the great British statesman, Mr. Winston Churchill, in the following one-sentence eulogy:

Freedom continues to live in the world because Winston Churchill lived and defended it.

ADDRESS BY

HON. WINSTON L. PROUTY

OF VERMONT

Mr. President, few persons in this century, indeed, in this age have left their mark on mankind as has the late Sir Winston Churchill. Few persons, indeed, have contributed so much and, at the same time, have so endeared themselves to men of all walks of life.

The passing of Sir Winston to yet another glory, is not a fact that we should mourn. For, he shall certainly receive in full measure as he gave.

Our hearts should, rather, swell with a sense of pride to have lived as contemporaries of this great man.

We are enabled to attain greater ends for mankind, though we may have to endure hardship, because his example has shown us how to do both.

Sir Winston Churchill will most probably not be memorialized in great marble monuments to his memory in this country. He will be among the greatest American citizens for whom this will not be done.

He did, however, give his consent to become one of us. In doing so, he honored us as highly as he possibly could. In doing so, also, he permitted us to honor him.

ADDRESS BY

HON. CLAIBORNE PELL

OF RHODE ISLAND

Mr. President, all who respect courage, faith, truth, and wisdom today deeply mourn the death of Sir Winston Churchill. He was a giant of our times in all these attributes. We will always remember the resonance of his voice, its inspiration, and the way he marshaled our thoughts and energies in the cause of justice. In the dark and tragic days of World War II he offered to all who fought oppression that unforgettable challenge of blood and tears. Now the world responds with tears at the loss of this great man.

His remarkable career spanned some of the most difficult times mankind ever faced. He met these difficulties with that soaring quality of spirit which transcended national boundaries and instilled itself into our own hearts and minds. He was the young cavalier, the superlative leader of his people in periods of crisis, the elder statesman who imparted both wisdom and strength. Among those who especially admired him, I feel privileged to have shared in the same century in which we lived.

Mankind stands in respect. Freemen everywhere mourn his passing.

ADDRESS BY

HON. JOHN G. TOWER

OF TEXAS

Mr. President, our hearts are full and no mean words that we might muster could appropriately eulogize the most heroic figure of the century whose death the free world mourns.

As a chronicler of our English speaking civilization, he articulated an appreciation for the inherent greatness of our race of which he was a living manifestation. He was, too, a manifestation of the notion he so lucidly advanced that the sweep and course of history has been influenced by a succession of great men. He was possessed of an infinite and unequaled capacity for leadership. He distinguished himself in so many ways that it staggers the imagination. His deeds and achievements are so vast and so well known to us all that it would be superfluous to recite them here. His eloquence not only inspired us but brought to our ears the soaring majesty of the English language.

If from some eternal domicile the immortals of the past—Richard the Lionhearted, Edward III, Elizabeth I, Wellington, Nelson, Disraeli—could look upon the earthly procession of this era, they would concede that this leader of epic proportion was the greatest Englishman of them all.

His passing marks an epoch in human history. Those of us who have Anglo-Saxon blood coursing through our veins can think better of ourselves because we belong to a race that produced Winston Churchill.

ADDRESS BY

HON. SAM J. ERVIN, JR.

OF NORTH CAROLINA

Mr. President, the people of the free world were saddened to learn on Sunday that their champion and longtime leader had left them.

As I stand here today, I am reminded that North Carolina's great educator and Governor, Charles B. Aycock, said on one occasion, if a man requires a eulogy, he does not deserve one, and if he deserves one, he does not require it. Certainly, no one in this century has been more deserving of a eulogy and, certainly, no one requires one less, for Winston Spencer Churchill was known well and loved well by freemen everywhere. Surely, history will honor him well, and when the finest hours of the free world are recorded, those during his leadership will be at the pinnacle.

Each of us is saddened by the death of this great man, and we recall the gallant leadership that he gave to us during our most desperate hours and the direction that he gave in preserving the peace. It would be virtually impossible for one to enumerate the accomplishments of our honorary American citizen, and I shall not attempt to do so. His accomplishments and eloquence were such they could not be embellished by anything that I might say. Even so, I should like to reflect a few minutes upon what he has meant to me through the years.

I have long been an admirer of Sir Winston Churchill. To me, he has been a source of inspiration because he always had tenacity of purpose, however great was the opposition at the time. He persevered against tremendous odds, and even in the face of inevitable defeat, he never hesitated to say and do what he felt was right.

I go back to his childhood and the difficulty that this genius had in adjusting to a set curriculum, and although he may have been one who never mastered the classical languages, he certainly mastered the English language. Our language is the richer for that. As First Lord of the Admiralty, the Gallipolian fiasco would have shattered a lesser man, but not Winston Churchill. As Chancellor of the Exchequer, he faced the great depression and worked for fiscal stability against tremendous odds that would have discouraged most men; and finally, at 65 years of age, having lived longer than most men of his generation, and, certainly well beyond the age when men think of their greatest and most effective productivity, he took the mantle of leadership for the entire free world, and his steadfastness and determination played a major part in saving it. Of course, his service to mankind did not end there.

Seemingly rejected by the electorate at the war's end, he continued to speak out for principles he held dear. And again he emerged to lead his people. He served long and well, ever true to those democratic concepts that made England great and which form the bulwark of our political system.

Winston Churchill's example in fighting to preserve freedom and justice for all, in providing a body politic under law rather than men, is exemplary for those who would govern.

I recall that I was presiding as a superior court judge in Lincolnton, N.C., at the time of the Dunkirk evacuation. I went to my hotel room after the court had adjourned and heard a broadcast by Adolf Hitler, translated by an interpreter, in which he told the British people that the might of the Third Reich was against them and that the only sensible thing for them to do was to surrender. I remember Churchill's defiant reply, which not only aroused the pride of the peoples of the free world but strengthened the determination of the British people to fight on, to the death, if necessary, in the preservation of liberty.

He may no longer be among us, but Winston Churchill lives on in the hearts of freemen everywhere, and his great spirit will forever permeate the history of our times.

ADDRESS BY

HON. ROMAN L. HRUSKA

OF NEBRASKA

Mr. President, the peoples of the world today are mourning the loss of a great leader and an eloquent spokesman for freedom. It remains for each of us to be a little less because of the loss of Winston Churchill.

Sir Winston said on his 88th birthday, "I feel on both sides of the Atlantic." Today we feel this tragic loss on this side of the Atlantic for he was one of our own. But we cannot claim exclusive possession because in fact, everyone on every side of every ocean feels this loss to the cause of mankind. Out of our ranks has departed a noble warrior and prince of peace with a passion for humanity.

It was nearly 2 years ago that we in the United States out of respect and thankfulness fittingly conferred, by an act of Congress, citizenship upon this elder statesman. Prior to this the State of Nebraska had conferred its citizenship upon Sir Winston because of "his courage, tenacity, wisdom, and leadership both in war and in peace." One of our own has gone out from among us.

The loss is limited not to the nations of the world alone. The impact of this tragic loss has been keenly felt in the town of Clearwater, Nebr. A kinship had grown and was strengthened between this eminent world leader and the citizens of the town. They had early made Sir Winston an honorary citizen of their little town—the highest honor they could grant and the finest expression of his inspiration for them.

In a letter to Sir Winston they pointed out that the "climate ranges from unspeakably hot to unbearably cold, but our land and people are productive." Productive—here was an element in the kinship between this great man of history and the citizens of Clearwater. In addition, the letter went on:

> We offer you as your residence in the United States of America a fine little home here in Clearwater, which will be maintained for you.

Where else can one find such an expression of kinship between a rural community and this cosmopolitan world figure?

Each of the 420 citizens of Clearwater, just as the peoples of all Nebraska and in the far reaches of the earth, poignantly feels the loss of this great actor from the stage of life. Indeed, his life was a "triumph of life itself."

ADDRESS BY

HON. E. L. BARTLETT

OF ALASKA

Mr. President—

> For Heaven's sake, let us sit upon the ground,
> And tell sad stories of the death of Kings.

Saturday, they bury Sir Winston Churchill with no less the pomp and honor with which were buried Wellington and Marlborough; and this is fitting, for Churchill was no less than they.

His was a life of heroism anl leadership, lived in the full glory of historical perspective. Churchill and the triumph of the Battle of Britain stand proud and sure with Nelson at Trafalgar and Marlborough at Blenheim. Churchill's greatness and his victory, and Britain's greatness and Britain's victory—for they were one and the same—will last for a thousand years, and the name of this splendid man will never be forgotten.

The beginning of all things, says the Bible, is with the word. All that Churchill was and all that he did were wrought with words. His supreme power was in his language. It is his words that cause a man to rise up or that cast him down. It is language that inspires, that leads and directs. No man writing in the English language—at least, in this century—has better understood or made better use of the power of our language.

It is a mawkish thing for us who live after to attempt to pay full and lasting tribute to Sir Winston. We cannot do it. He has done it for us. What he meant and what he was are seen in his words during those agonizing months in 1940. Those words have already taken their place with the greatest speeches ever addressed by leader to nation.

Three times, in modern times, the enemy stood at English gates, and England was outnumbered and ill prepared. Three times, great men have come forth, and, using English as their weapon, have triumphed.

In 1415, young King Henry addressed his troops on the eve of Agincourt:

> This day is call'd the Feast of Crispian:
> He that outlives this day, and comes safe home,
> Will stand a tiptoe when his day is named,
> And rowse him at the Name of Crispian.
> He that shall see this day, and live old age,
> Will yeerely on the Vigil feast his neighhours,
> And say, to morrow is Saint Crispian.
> Then will he strip his sleeve, and shew his skarres:
> Old men forget; yet all shall be forgot:
> But hee'le remember, with advantages,
> What feats he did that day. Then shall our Names,
> Familiar in his mouth as household words,
> Harry the King, Bedford and Exeter,
> Warwick and Talbot, Salisbury and Gloucester,
> Be in their flowing Cups freshly remembered.
> This story shall the good man teach his sonne:
> And Crispine Crispian shall ne're goe by,
> From this day to the ending of the World,
> But we in it shall be remembered;
> We few, we happy few, we band of brothers:
> For he to day that sheds his blood with me,
> Shall be my brother: be he ne're so vile,
> This day shall gentle his Condition.
> And Gentlemen in England, now a bed,
> Shall thinke themselves accurst they were not here;
> And hold their Manhoods cheap, whiles any speakes,
> That fought with us upon Saint Crispines day.

In 1588 Elizabeth, the Virgin Queen, addressed her troops as the greatest armada in the history of nations bore down upon the island people:

> My loving people, we have been persuaded by some that are careful of our safety, to take heed how we commit ourselves to armed multitudes, for fear of treachery; but I assure you, I do not desire to live in distrust of my faithful and loving people. Let tyrants fear. I have always so behaved myself that, under God, I have placed my chiefest strength and goodwill in the loyal hearts and goodwill of my subjects; and therefore I am come amongst you, as you see, at this time, not for my recreation and disport, but being resolved, in the midst and heat of the battle to live or die amongst you all; to lay down for God, for my kingdom, and for my people, my honour and my blood, even in the dust. I know I have but the body of a weak and feeble woman; but I have the heart and stomach of a king, and a king of England, too, and think it foul scorn that Parma or Spain or any prince of Europe, should dare to invade the borders of my realm; to which, rather than any dishonour should grow by me, I myself will take up arms, I myself will be general, judge, and rewarder of every one of your virtues in the field.

And in 1940, after Dunkirk, the King's First Minister, Winston Churchill, stood before the Parliament, and said:

> What General Weygand called the Battle of France is over. I expect that the Battle of Britain is about to begin. Upon this battle depends the survival of Christian civilization. Upon it depend our own British life and the long continuity of our institutions and our empire. The whole fury and might of the enemy must very soon be turned on us. Hitler knows that he will have to break us in this island or lose the war. If we can stand up to him, all Europe may be free and the life of the world may move forward into broad, sunlit uplands. But if we fail, then the whole world, including the United States, including all that we have known and cared for, will sink into the abyss of a new Dark Age, made more sinister, and perhaps more protracted, by the lights of perverted science. Let us therefore brace ourselves to our duties, and so bear ourselves that, if the British Empire and its Commonwealth last for a thousand years, men will say, "This was their finest hour."

Churchill's speeches—like that Shakespeare gives Henry before Agincourt, like Elizabeth's before the coming of the armada, or Nelson's before Trafalgar—have the force of a thousand atom bombs; but they do not destroy—they create. They give formulation to the nameles—and, until then, wordless—yearning of the national soul for the greatness of which it is capable and the courage of which it is shaped. By giving form to this force, they make it real; and, made real, it becomes invincible.

Churchill in 1940 made freedom invincible.

Adjournment By

Hon. Russell Long, of Louisiana

Mr. President, I ask unanimous consent that when the Senate adjourns, it do so in accordance with the resolution previously adopted, as a further mark of respect to the deceased Sir Winston Churchill and his bereaved family.

I now move that the Senate adjourn until 12 o'clock noon tomorrow.

The motion was unanimously agreed to; and (at 3 o'clock and 45 minutes p.m.) the Senate adjourned, under the order previously entered, until tomorrow, Wednesday, January 27, 1965, at 12 o'clock meridian.

Memorial Tributes

To

Sir Winston Churchill

In The

Congress of the United States

TRIBUTES BY

SENATOR SAM J. ERVIN, JR.

OF NORTH CAROLINA

Mr. President, I ask that the following editorials on Sir Winston Churchill be included in this tribute:

[From the Winston-Salem (N.C.) Journal, Jan. 25, 1965]

SIR WINSTON CHURCHILL

When history beckoned, Winston Churchill was ready.

For most of his 65 years he had stood in the shadows of mistrust. His countrymen found him brilliant—yes, attractive. But he was too impulsive, too erratic, people said. England would never trust him with what he wanted most, the supreme power; he was a dangerous man.

Yet when the field-gray hordes of Hitler rolled like an opaque fog over Flanders, when the freedom of the sceptered isle lay in the balance, England turned to Winston Churchill.

And from that moment in 1940 greatness enveloped him.

It was a token of that greatness that he never looked back in anger. He never reproached the Tories who had mocked him in the House of Commons when he warned them time and again of the coming peril. He never reminded the Laborites that they had made him their whipping boy during those bitter years wtih taunts of "warmonger" and "imperialist." Instead, he gathered them round him and made them see the glory of their place in history. He called on them to make this—the moment of England's greatest danger—their finest hour. And they made it their finest hour.

And always, together with the courage, the eloquence, there was the blessed humor.

"We shall fight on the beaches, we shall fight on the landing grounds, we shall fight in the streets * * * we shall never surrender," he said when the German blow seemed ready to fall. And then, according to the legend in the pubs, he put his hand over the microphone and added. "We shall hit them with beer bottles, because God knows that's all we've got."

To Americans he was such an ally as we may never see again. Tenacious in argument, stubborn in advocacy, he still was always loyal. His faults, our leaders found, were of the kind that make us love a man; his qualities were those that enrich and inspire the human spirit. There is no record that, even in the most trying days of the alliance, he ever uttered an ignoble word against us.

When Churchill returned to Britain to enter politics, he did what Franklin Roosevelt emulated later—he deserted his "class." He infuriated the Tories by becoming a Liberal. After a tumultuous career in the World War I government, which ended in the Dardanelles fiasco, he joined Lloyd George's government. At its downfall, Churchill was a broken man—politically despised by his former Tory associates and discredited among the Liberals.

At that dark moment Winston Churchill returned to the party of his fathers—the Tories. When he heard the "distant hoofbeat" in the late thirties, he was ready to catch the horseman's coattails.

During all of his years in the political wilderness, Winston Churchill wrote strong splendid nouns and verbs in 27 books, including a biography of his famous ancestor, the first Duke of Marlborough, and a beautiful history of the English people. But the events of World War II gave him the material for his finest literary work, which led to the Nobel Prize. Once, addressing the House of Commons, Sir Winston warned it to "leave the past to history, particularly since I intend to write the history myself."

And he did.

It was the doing, however—the imposition of his imagination and his will upon his countrymen during their dire crisis—that made Winston Churchill most memorable. Isaiah Berlin, in an analysis of "a great man at a great moment," notes that "Churchill was successful precisely because he appeared to them (his people) larger and nobler than life and lifted them to an abnormal height in a moment of crisis."

This has happened many times in history with dangerous results; dictators and demagogs have transformed "peaceful populations into marching armies." It was Winston Churchill's unforgettable achievement, Mr. Berlin reminds us, "that he created this necessary illusion within the framework of a free system without destroying or even twisting it; that he called forth spirits which did not stay to oppress and enslave the population after the hour of need had passed; that he saved the future by interpreting the present in terms of a vision of the past which did not distort or inhibit the historical development of the British people. * * *"

Here was a man, then, who reminds us of Pitt, Marlborough, Nelson, Wellington, Leonardo da Vinci, Washington, Julius Caesar, and even Lincoln. Here was a man who possessed great and versatile talents and used them effectively in the service of a besieged civilization. Sir Winston was soldier, scholar, historian, "naval person," correspondent, statesman, orator, artist, and wit. This splendid renaissance man made history and then wrote about it in words of magnificence.

Two quotations from his own pen may befit this hour of his passing—one which he delivered on the occasion of the death of his old adversary, Sir Neville Chamberlain:

"The only guide to a man is his conscience; the only shield to his memory is the rectitude and sincerity of his action. It is very imprudent to walk through life without this shield, because we are so often mocked by the failure of our hopes; but with this shield, however the fates may play, we march always in the ranks of honor."

And finally his own words at Harrow in 1941:

"Never give in. Never give in. Never, never, never, never—in nothing great or small, large or petty—never give in except to convictions of honor and good sense."

[From the Charlotte (N.C.) Observer, Jan. 25, 1965]

Churchill and History Met To Create Our Finest Hour

The times of Sir Winston Leonard Spencer Churchill were the best of times and the worst of times for all who lived through them with him. He has been bone of our bone and flesh of our flesh.

Americans have more cause than any other people in the world save the British to say of Sir Winston, "Ah, there was a man." For there was a man of such splendid proportions that we would search in vain for his peer among us.

Churchill was the essence of the history we have had a part in making. When Hitlerism threatened the freedom of the English-speaking peoples in World War II and our nations formed the grand alliance, Churchill was its omnipresent symbol.

He rallied his nation and the cause of freedom with the literary brilliance of his words. He exuded a self-assurance that without his boyish charm would have bordered on arrogance. He was brave, he was stubborn, he smoked and he drank, he made political and military mistakes that detracted but little from the brilliance of his life.

We were drawn to him because to be remote from him was to turn our backs on the meaning of our lives and the significance of our years.

HISTORY

The week was simultaneously mournful, majestic, and momentous.

Sir Winston Churchill died at the age of 90, one of the greatest and best loved statesmen in the history of statesmanship. He had served Britain under three kings and two queens, beginning with Queen Elizabeth II's great great-grandmother Victoria.

Britain's Parliament was 700 years old last week. Historians generally consider 1295 to be the beginning of Parliament as it is known today, but in 1265 Simon de Montfort summoned Britain's first known national legislative gathering of peers and commoners together, establishing the precedent on which today's Parliament is based.

Lyndon Johnson's inauguration as President last week was the 44th since George Washington took the oath on April 30, 1789.

Surely it does neither Sir Winston nor President Johnson a disfavor to point out that without Parliament (and possibly all 700 years of its life) and the nation that produced it, the death of a man named Churchill might have gnoe unnoticed by all but a handful of relatives, and the inauguration of the 36th U.S. President might never have occurred at all.

The Old World and the New met and blended in Sir Winston. His 90 years were practically a span between the muzzle loader and the hydrogen bomb, with two World Wars in between. He was in the thick of all of it.

Soldier and journalist par excellence, chronicler of military engagements in all parts of the world, successful politician, social reformer, historian and prophet, world leader—all these and more.

We loved Winnie for many things. We revered his words for what they did to keep the world from being plunged into a new dark age.

There was that moment in May 1940 when in his first appearance as Prime Minister before the House of Commons, with Hitler's panzer divisions sweeping through the Low Countries, he said:

"I have nothing to offer but blood, toil, tears, and sweat."

At that moment it became clear what the lifelong preparation of Sir Winston Churchill had been about. A point in history came to be matched with a point in the life of a man, as if they had been proceeding toward each other by radar for more than half a century.

And the debacle at Dunkirk, that dark hour for Great Britain when Churchillian prose broke through the gloom:

"We shall fight on the beaches, we shall fight on the landing grounds, we shall fight in the fields; we shall never surrender, and even if, which I do not for a moment believe, this island or a large part of it were subjugated and starving, then our Empire beyond the seas, armed and guarded by the British fleet, would carry on the struggle, until, in God's good time the New World, with all its power and might, steps forth to the rescue and the liberation of the Old."

A voice to bring the power of justice and truth surging through the veins of men. A conscious purpose of demanding that man be true to the majestic purposes for which he was created. And, later:

"Let us therefore brace ourselves to our duties, and so bear ourselves that, if the British Empire and its Commonwealth last for a thousand years, men will say, 'This was their finest hour.' "

And so we bury Winnie, that utterly individualistic, rotund figure of a man who nevertheless managed to be the personification of his people and the power supply of the free world.

His death is swallowed up in victory.

[From the Twin City (N.C.) Sentinel, Jan. 25, 1965]

Winston Churchill: Our Tallest Giant

Until yesterday, Winston Churchill belonged to us. Now he belongs to the ages.

He was an aristocrat in the truest sense—a master among men who knew and honored his responsibilities and had the power to inspire others to rise to superhuman effort in hours of peril and crisis.

In the darkest hours of World War II, when England was under a cloud of terror from the skies, the appearance of Winston Churchill the "former naval person" as he often called himself, on a bomb-threatened London street, in an obscure English town, or at a military installation, instantly evoked wild enthusiasm and cheers. A man among men, he caused all freemen to lift their heads a little higher and grow a few inches taller.

When Winston Churchill spoke, men listened and their hearts beat faster. For this man spoke with a tongue of fire, and his words had a curious power over the heart and mind. No matter how desperate seemed the free world cause, no matter how invincible appeared the hordes of Hitlerian tyranny, when Churchill spoke, all men who believed in human freedom and dignity breathed new hope and went forward with the feeling that theirs was the ultimate victory.

He had human faults and weaknesses, of course. But there was something about Winston Churchill that always spoke of greatness. Greatness of courage. Greatness of will, of resolution, of loyalty to the great traditions of an Anglo-Saxon civilization. So to millions he became a father image, a constant inspiration, an assurance that helped men still find sense in an upended, confused, and broken world.

So, in his own lifetime he became a legend, a symbol of all that is finest in the traditions of the West. Yesterday he belonged to us all, our tallest towering giant of the 20th century. Today indeed, he belongs to the ages.

[From the Smithfield (N.C.) Herald, Jan. 27, 1965]

Sir Winston Churchill and the West's Darkest Hour

Sir Winston Churchill deserves the title "savior of Western civilization."

In the summer of 1940, following the fall of France, there was no military might capable of preventing a Nazi conquest of Britain. There was only a man with an indomitable will to preserve Western traditions. And that man, Sir Winston, making the most of his opportunity as leader of Britain, rallied the human spirit in his own land and in all lands where love of democratic freedom prevailed. The courageous leadership of Prime Minister Churchill discouraged Hitler from carrying out his threat to invade England.

The words Mr. Churchill spoke in the House of Commons on June 18, 1940, not only gave heart to the people of Britain and the Americans who sympathized with them; those words rang clearly in the ears of Hitler, giving him reason to pause lest he commit a foolish act in his determination to extend the Nazi system to the great island citadel of freedom. This is what Mr. Churchill said on that fateful day, just 4 days after the Germans had occupied Paris:

"Hitler knows that he will have to break us or lose the war. If we stand up to him all Europe may be free, and the life of the world may move forward into the broad sunlit uplands; but if we fail, then the whole world, including the United States, and all that we have known and cared for will sink into the abyss of a new dark age, made more sinister, and perhaps more prolonged by the lights of a perverted science. Let us therefore address ourselves to our duty and so bear ourselves that if the British Commonwealth of Nations and Empire last for a thousand years, men will still say: 'This was their finest hour.' "

Britain responded nobly to Mr. Churchill's appeal. It, indeed, "stood up" to Hitler, not only with a will to resist, but also with all the military strength it could muster through skillful use of its limited number of Spitfire planes. The Battle of Britain raged as the summer of 1940 wore on.

It was a trying time for civilians as well as for military personnel. In the words of one British writer (H. E. Bates), for the first time in British history "a housewife carrying her shopping bag could pause, look up into the sky and watch armed men engage in the bloody business of exterminating each other; a farm laborer at harvest could for the first time also look and see the victims of battle dropping into his barley." The German bombs fell on the aged, the young, the weak, the strong.

It is difficult for us in the United States, who have been spared the horrors of modern warfare on our own soil, to imagine the ordeal which the British survived in the months before Britain and her allies could mobilize full strength for the counterattack that ultimately crushed the Nazi menace. It was an ordeal that no people could have experienced successfully without a strong leader. Sir Winston was the "man of Britain's finest hour." And all that he did for Britain, he did for the United States and all the world that stood in danger of conquest by the Nazi maniacs.

With the British, we mourn Sir Winston's passing. With the British, we share the pride that rises in the human breast as Sir Winston's uncommon achievements for the benefit of mankind are contemplated.

[From the Asheville (N.C.) Citizen, Jan. 26, 1965]

SMALLER MEN COWERED, SO FATE SENT A GIANT

It took Winston Churchill a long time to become a legend, but he worked hard at it and he wore the aura comfortably, even a little smugly, as one who had earned it.

His claim was undoubtedly valid.

Here was a brave man, with a special genius for inspiring bravery in others.

Regarded as the symbol of British courage during the dark days of World War II, he was more the catalyst of a spirit that carried the English people through the rubble of certain defeat and staved off an invasion by Hitler's triumphant armies.

You know this classic warning to the Nazi Fuhrer ("We shall fight on the beaches, we shall fight on the landing grounds, we shall fight in the fields and in the streets, we shall never surrender"). A few years later, after American and Russian entry promised an Allied victory, Churchill called his speech a bluff. "We had not, at that time, 50 tanks," he said. "We had a couple of hundred field guns, some of them brought out of museums."

Bluff or not, it worked—and Winston Chuchill, a master of the written and spoken word, became the hero-father figure for millions of Britons as he scrambled though the bomb-scarred sections of London, chewing his cigar, raising his fingers aloft in his "V" for victory" sign.

Since that time, and despite temporary setbacks, the Churchill legend has grown and mellowed, nourished by the affection of Britons, Americans, and the free world masses.

Winston Churchill was not, as Anthony Eden once said in a public address, "the greatest man that ever lived." He had many faults, including a stubborn resistance to social-political change and a longing for return to the age of empire when "the sun never set on British soil." He was not a military superman and he may have been, indeed, a military romanticist. But he learned, through words, to light a glow in men's hearts and he walked with majestic poise through the shambles of a time that needed his confidence. That was his test of greatness and he met it heroically.

Winston Churchill is dead at 90, but the legend still lives and will continue to grow as long as men gather to honor their memories. And somebody, somewhere, will always turn down a glass.

DEATH OF A GREAT STATESMAN

The world shares England's saddest hour in mourning the death of Sir Winston Churchill. The man who rallied England in her darkest hour in World War II, and thus set the stage for the forces of freedom to prevail against tyranny and oppression, has left monumental works for all mankind.

Death at 90 from the onset of illness, injury, and advancing years, was not unexpected. Yet, even during the last, lingering days, when the world stood a hopeless vigil, Sir Winston's fight for survival demonstrated his indomitable spirit and resoluteness which characterized his 90 years of living.

It was his destiny, not only to make history, but also to shape the course of human events for generations to come. This was done through the combination of firm and steadfast leadership combined with compassion and feeling for his fellow man. No figure in modern history is perhaps so indelibly etched into the minds and hearts of men everywhere as the Churchillian posture of courage and bravery.

Those who remember the war years of the forties will never forget the giant of a man who emerged as the British Prime Minister and rallied his people and his allies in one of freedom's darkest periods of history.

But his great works will be remembered even beyond his gigantic contribution to victory. As a statesman, a soldier, an author, a painter, a man of dignity and humbleness, he has left a legacy worthy of his place in history.

And today's children will know of his greatness, for their lives, too, have been influenced by this man who strode magnificently across the world's stage and became the symbol for brave men everywhere.

There is no more fitting monument to this world statesman than that he will be remembered by the ages.

So now he leaves us—head forward, jaw thrust out, shoulders hunched—for that lofty shrine where the English-speaking peoples guard the memory of their noblest heroes.

And in all truth we Americans have reason to cherish him. For he was generous to our mother tongue, and we may pray that schoolboys for centuries to come will recite his words. He was prodigal with his foresight and his wisdom, and we may hope that our leaders in these uncertain years will profit by the legacy he leaves us.

And as a guide to national conduct we can find nothing better than the moral he drew from the great crisis that he helped to master:

In war: Resolution.
In defeat: Defiance.
In victory: Magnanimity.
In peace: Good will.

[From the Greensboro (N.C.) Daily News, Jan. 25, 1965]

THE SPLENDOR OF SIR WINSTON CHURCHILL

The Lion of Chartwell is dead.

Sir Winston Leonard Spencer Churchill, among the handful of great men of the 20th century, has quietly passed away in London after the final valiant fight of his illustrious career.

It was Bismarck who said that political genius consists of the ability to hear the distant hoofbeat of the horse of history—and then by superhuman effort to leap and catch the horseman by the coattails.

Sir Winston did that in 1940. Later he wrote of that time: "It is impossible to quell the inward excitement which comes from a prolonged balancing of terrible things." When Churchill came to the fore in the crumbling dreamworld of Baldwin and Chamberlain, he again inspired the the island race—his name for the British people—to magnificence.

Sir Winston was born at Blenheim Palace during a dance attended by his American-born mother. Visitors marvel that the event took place in a small anteroom when there were many vast apartments upstairs. His good friend Virginia Cowles noted: "Winston Churchill was 2 months ahead of his time. In subsequent years he continued on that schedule."

The Lion of Chartwell began life as a misfit. In school as a "fat and loutish boy" he refused to learn Greek or Latin. This assured him of the lowest place in his class at Harrow. But while his fellows concentrated on Greek and Latin, Winston concentrated on English; it repaid him handsomely. Once he reminisced about his early days: "I am surprised in my later life I should have become so experienced in taking degrees when as a schoolboy I was so bad at passing examinations. In fact, one might almost say that no one ever passed so few examinations and received so many degrees."

Ineptness in school led directly to his military career. Lord Randolph Churchill sent his wayward son to Sandhurst where, after two failures, he managed to pass the entrance examination. His military career led him to India seeking a post of danger. Then he resigned from the army to become a newspaper correspondent; he achieved world fame at the age of 25 when he was captured by the Boers in South Africa and managed to escape.

TRIBUTE BY

SENATOR JACK MILLER

OF IOWA

The lead editorial in the Washington Evening Star of January 26 is but one of many which are appearing to eulogize this great statesman and humanitarian. But the writer of this editorial has uniquely expressed Winston Churchill's imprint on history, and he appropriately ends with the prayer, in which all of us join—"May angels attend him." The editorial is as follows:

WINSTON CHURCHILL

Churchill is dead, gone from the world he saved. And the world he saved, distracted still by the flow and eddy of the aftermath, has not yet reckoned its debt to him.

Perhaps that sum cannot be reckoned up, so great it is. Our very troubles of this time derive from that more nearly mortal evil that Churchill fought and ended.

Are the emerging nations irritated and frustrated at what they take to be survivals of the British Raj? Had it not been for Churchill, they would have been spared their hurt feelings, for they would never have emerged at all.

Does Charles de Gaulle grow restive at the failure of the nations to see his glory? The question would not have arisen without Churchill to fight for a France that had been captured.

Are we ourselves troubled with the problems of the alliance? We'd have been spared our troubles had not Churchill stood when all else fell. Is it hard and endless to achieve the unity of Europe? There was a European unity of slavery and depravity designed to last a thousand years. Because of Churchill it is no more.

The Russians themselves may count their debt to that great man. Had England made its peace with evil, the Soviet state would have dropped into the dark of history or have become, in the extension of the Stalin-Hitler pact, the complete political expression of the worst shadows in Stalin's mind.

But Churchill did not fail. He lived and spoke and fought, and so all of us live as we do.

In an age of progressive thought, he seemed an odd man to become a hero. He liked cigars and brandy and high cuisine. He believed deeply in the virtue of royalty. He believed in the British Empire, in gallantry, in chivalry.

He believed in language and in the golden deeds of the English past. In an age that wrote history in terms of social movements and philosophical evolution. Churchill read history as a glorious record of brave men and the things they did for their country.

He was old fashioned and out of date. But when the hour struck it was his alone. For the evil that rose in Germany was a timeless evil. To meet it required a cast of mind that Churchill had, a dedicated innocence, a belief in battles and in courage. The monstrous German war gods came up from under mountains and brandished again their hammers and axes. Their shadow of death spread through the heart of Europe, north to the polar ice, south to the Sahara, over all of France and paused for a moment at the little strip of water before England.

In that moment Churchill spoke and his voice was like Roland's horn at Roncesvalles. He broke the spell of the evil magician and roused the world to fight for its freedom. Against the Wehrmacht's mechanical might, he had, for a while, only the gallantry, the courage, the spirit, of his people. These old-fashioned virtues held the battle.

He saved the world and his world at home replied by turning him out of office, for a new time had come. He said that he would not preside over the dissolution of the British Empire, but it is dissolved and it had to be dissolved. Yet whatever hope of freedom and dignity all men have today, they owe in part to the last glorious fight of that Empire and to the ability of the Empire to bring forth, as its last gift, the man, Winston Churchill.

May angels attend him.

TRIBUTE BY

SENATOR FRANK CHURCH

OF IDAHO

Mr. President, among the many who will try, few will succeed in writing eulogies that do justice to the greatness of Winston Churchill. One such tribute, written with brilliance and singular perception, appeared in the January 26 edition of the Washington Post. Captioned, "He Was Us as We Would Like the World To See Us," Patrick O'Donovan has contributed an article worthy of the extraordinary man we mourn.

He Was Us as We Would Like the World To See Us

(By Patrick O'Donovan)

London.—His death had been long expected. And when it came, it was gentle and discrete. He was prodigiously old. We had not seen or heard him in many months. He had lived a great roaring life and somehow shared it with the nation.

He had written great books and had relished adventures that others knew only in fantasy. He had wielded unimaginable power. He was a man who could weep at a school song or bow before his sovereign with the awe of a courtier or walk in procession to the Garter Chapel muffled in a great cloak, buried under a preposterous Tudor hat, looking like a giant blue mushroom.

He could express his displeasure at a modern portrait presented by Parliament and be applauded for unbending prejudice. He could be tyrannical or petulant, he could be patently wrong, he could be monstrously unfair to an opponent, he could sail through life with more sails out than any ship was made to carry, and we relished it all.

He will not be mourned in the usual way. He was no father figure. He was us as we would like the world to see us. We enjoyed him vastly. We are glad to have lived to see him. We shall not forget him.

Those who are middle aged or more will remember him, almost as if they knew him. That is the strange thing about him. The innumerable barroom bores putting on their imitations of his voice to tell some apochryphal story are only adding their incoherent praise to one of those rare legends that are also fact.

Above all, he will be remembered as he was in war, and when the war is recalled with him at its center it is somehow less horrible and more of an adventure. This is essential, because in the war he did something remarkable to Britain and, for once, Britain has recognized and remembered the achievement.

UNREALITY OF WAR

He was not really a great national figure before the war. He was already an elder statesman. He had an aura of failure, of incomplete fulfillment, about him—though it must be said that he did not recognize this himself. He was a little suspect, because he was forever issuing terrible warnings that seemed unnecessary and wrongheaded. He was admittedly brilliant and amusing. But we left our government to more solid men, to Baldwins and Chamberlains. They were the responsible 20th century figures.

And when war did come, the solid men were at a loss. The madness and the vulgarity of Hitler seemed unreal rather than menacing. There were expeditions and defeats and men died or became prisoners, but Britain did not really feel like a nation at war.

We were amateurs at a distasteful game. We were dutiful rather than wholehearted. And then the real though undeclared prospect of defeat toppled the solid men and we had this old and slightly suspect adventurer to lead us. And we were reassured and confident from the start.

The new Premier came at the worst possible moment and he made no bones about what lay ahead. He seemed positively to relish the prospect. He, and we, perked up at the possibility of disaster.

He brought a relish for old wars to new. He made what we were doing seem natural and inevitable. He convinced us that we could do it and do it greatly. He called up the old Adam in us and gave us back the power to be aggressive.

AN ACTOR'S TIMING

It was partly his eloquence, though he was not truly an eloquent man but an unsurpassed reader of speeches. You could see the joke or the epigram coming; he would rootle and fumble for it, and suddenly brandish it aloft as if he had dug it out of a deep packing of cotton wool. And he did it with an actor's timing.

The language he used was inflated and Augustan, and it served to dignify the messy things we were doing. He snarled and ranted, and the whole country crowded in to listen to what he said, because this was how we were beginning to feel—exasperated, defiant, and prickly proud.

He boasted for us, but not outrageously. He talked like a great captain whose only trade was war and found it a good one. He would "strangle the U-boats" and "wage great battles." And somehow he brought the past in as an ally. It could be said that somehow he brought out the best in war.

Or he would come down to look at his troops, and stump, scowling, along the ranks. He would wear a preposterous billycock hat and hold a cigar and brandish a stick and suddenly relax and grin wickedly and make a gesture toward victory with his fingers that meant something else to a soldier. The whole act was so confident and natural and superb that the troops grinned back from the ranks and cheered and forgot for a little to complain. They went back to their tents or billets with the vague feeling that they came of great stock.

Or, after a bad night of bombing in London, he would pick his way down a ruined street, crunching the glass underfoot, looking now angry, now almost indecently cheerful. And exhausted men and women, picking over the ruins of their homes, would straighten up with a broken toy or a soiled curtain in their filthy hands and shout out, not a demand for protection or aid, but a reassurement to him.

SCHOOLBOY HEROICS

Or he would sneak oft to watch the war, with an air of conscious delinquency, and be seen with his exasperated generals by the side of the road munching a sandwich with a flask in his hand. Or he would order a gun to be fired toward the enemy or insist on seeing the Rhine. It was all very reprehensible and it is not a fashionable attitude today. But, at the time, it served marvelously to increase the sum of national courage.

He made war seem more noble and less squalid.

He was not, of course, a one-man band and he did not win the war singlehanded. Others did the dying and the crawling with fear. He was surrounded by men who had to work impossibly hard and none of them who survived were sycophants. And yet he utterly commanded the stage. For a few years he summed up Britain and gave life to Britain and gave her confidence and was himself the more than life-sized image of Britain. That was his achievement.

THE CLOSING YEARS

The retirement and old age of the great and the powerful can be a pathetic spectacle. Lloyd George frittered away his long years in bitterness and crankiness. But this man, as he came closer to the inevitable end, still seemed to enjoy the last drops at the bottom of the glass that others have found so bitter. He possessed a curious quality of inner freedom about him.

In large part, this was due to his origins. He was born, quite simply, into a highly privileged aristocracy. Such people are accorded a special liberty. So are those at the bottom of the pyramid. For both classes pretense is not necessary. They are the truly liberated. And between this aristocrat and the least privileged of the British there was an instinctive understanding, even when they chose not to vote for him.

UNCONVENTIONAL TO END

He relished the solid, rather vulgar luxury of unfashionable watering places in the sun. He never courted the press. He kept a few racehorses for a time and did well with them. He maintained an ironclad privacy. He was sentimental. He loved great occasions. He expected to dominate conversation. He was unconventional. He was untouched by scandal.

TRIBUTE BY

SENATOR THRUSTON B. MORTON

OF KENTUCKY

Mr. President, most of us, I am sure, were impressed by the inspiring remarks of General Eisenhower in tribute to Winston Churchill, made over the facilities of the British Broadcasting Co. during the dramatic ceremonies the past weekend. I ask that his historic statement be printed as follows:

THE TEXT OF EISENHOWER'S TRIBUTE ON TV

Upon the mighty Thames, a great avenue of history, move at this moment to their final resting place the mortal remains of Sir Winston Churchill. He was a great maker of history, but his work done, the record closed, we can almost hear him, with the poet (Tennyson) say:

"Sunset and evening star,
And one clear call for me,

* * * * *

Twilight and evening bell,
And after that the dark.
And may there be no sadness of farewell
When I embark."

As I, like all other freemen, pause to pay a personal tribute to the giant who now passes from among us, I have no charter to speak for my countrymen—only for myself. But, if in memory, we journey back two decades to the time when America and Britain stood shoulder to shoulder in global conflict against tyranny, then I can presume—with propriety, I think—to act as spokesman for the millions of Americans who served with me and with their British comrades during those 3 years of war on this sector of the earth.

HE WAS BRITAIN

To those men Winston Churchill was Britain—he was the embodiment of British defiance to threat, her courage in adversity, her calmness in danger, her moderation in success. Among the allies his name was spoken with respect, admiration, and affection. Although they loved to chuckle at his foibles, they knew he was a stanch friend. They felt his inspirational leadership. They counted him a fighter in their ranks.

The loyalty that the fighting forces of many nations here serving gave to him during the war was no less strong, nor less freely given, than he had, in such full measure, from his own countrymen.

An American, I was one of those allies. During those dramatic months I was privileged to meet, to talk, to plan, and to work with him for common goals.

Out of that association an abiding—and to me precious—friendship was forged; it withstood the trials and friction inescapable among men of strong convictions, living in the atmosphere of war.

FRIENDSHIP GREW

The war ended, our friendship flowered in the later and more subtle tests imposed by international politics. Then, each of us, holding high official posts in his own nation, strove together so to concert the strength of our two peoples that liberty might be preserved among men and the security of the free world wholly sustained.

Through a career during which personal victories alternated with defeats, glittering praise with bitter criticism, intense public activity with periods of semiretirement, Winston Churchill lived out his 4 score and 10 years.

With no thought of the length of the time he might be permitted on earth, he was concerned only with the quality of the service he could render to his nation and to humanity. Though he had no fear of death, he coveted always the opportunity to continue that service.

At this moment, as our hearts stand at attenion, we say our affectionate, though sad, goodby to the leader to whom the entire body of freemen owes so much.

CHAMPION OF FREEDOM

In the coming years, many in countless words will strive to interpret the motives, describe the accomplishments, and extol the virtues of Winston Churchill—soldier, statesman, and citizen that two great countries were proud to claim as their own. Among all the things so written or spoken, there will ring out through all the centuries one incontestable refrain: He was a champion of freedom.

May God grant that we—and the generations who will remember him—heed the lessons he taught us; in his deeds; in his words; in his life.

May we carry on his work until no nation lies in captivity; no man is denied opportunity for fulfillment.

And now to you, Sir Winston—my old friend—farewell.

TRIBUTES BY

REPRESENTATIVE OGDEN R. REID

OF NEW YORK

Mr. Speaker, I submit the following editorials from New York newspapers which reflect the esteem in which Sir Winston Churchill was held by the people of my State:

[From the New York Times, Jan. 25, 1965]

SIR WINSTON CHURCHILL

The power and the glory are gone, the soaring oratory, the eloquent pen, the cherubic face, the impish twinkle in his eyes, the jaunty cigar, the vitality that sparked a world.

One measure of Churchill's greatness is that no one today, now that the blaze of his genius has subsided into dust and ashes, need explain or describe or grope for words. He is one of those rare figures in history who stand like skyscrapers above the merely great. Usually history waits to recognize its supreme leaders, but there is no need to wait in Churchill's case.

He was Britain's glory in a special way, for he somehow managed to personify what is magnifient in the English race, and what is most appealing—John Bull with imperfections and eccentricities, but with the courage, the doggedness, the loyalty, the strength. Many who sought to isolate the essential quality of his greatness fastened upon his astonishing vitality. Never was there a man so durable, so indefatigable, so indomitable. It is almost incredible that there was a man among us yesterday who rode in the charge of the 21st Lancers at Omdurman and was a Member of Parliament under Queen Victoria, but who served as his nation's Prime Minister as late as 1955.

Yet durability and vitality are not in themselves a guarantee of greatness. They only assured him life and dominance at a moment of history when all his gifts and those of his people could combine to produce the miracle of Britain in the Second World War.

There was some quality of anticlimax about the rest. When the Great War was won, Winston Churchill was rejected as his nation's leader. A few of his military commanders were critical in their memoirs of some of his wartime decisions—as an earlier generation had been critical of his Gallipoli campaign in 1915–16.

A decade ago his work was done, in the sense that he no longer had the strength to carry on in his beloved House of Commons, although he remained an M.P. almost to the end. In some ways the whole of his life was devoted to the House of Commons. He did go on writing and, in fact, the fourth and last volume of his monumental "History of the English-Speaking Peoples" was only published in 1958. Writing for him was always an avocation although for years he had to make a living out of it and he wrote superbly.

He was, too, an orator whose speeches were never dull and sometimes reached the most inspiring heights of which our language is capable. Like Shakespeare, he will be full of quotations so long as the English language lives. But no one in later generations will ever recapture the thrill that came to us, listening over the radio in moments of glory and agony, as we heard Winston Churchill speak of blood, toil, tears and sweat, of their finest hour, of fighting on the beaches, in the fields, in the streets, of so much being owed by so many to so few.

In the sweet, sad process of looking back we have the consolation of these memories. A man like Winston Churchill makes everyone a part of his life, as if a little of that greatness were shared by each of us. That he should have been half American as well as all English was a special source of pleasure to Americans. Nowhere beyond his native land will he be more sincerely mourned than throughout the length and breadth of these United States.

Winston Churchill was the glory of a tremendous era in history encompassed by the two World Wars. He leaves one feeling that an age has gone into history with him. Years ago he wrote that he gave sincere thanks to the high gods for the gift of existence. We, too, have reason to be thankful for that gift.

One would like to think of his passing in terms jotted down in a notebook by another supremely great human being, Leonardo da Vinci: "Just as a day well spent brings happy sleep, so a life well spent brings happy death."

[From the New York Herald Tribune, Jan. 25, 1965]

John Crosby in London: The Greatest Man

London.—I love the story about the little boy whose mother took him to Chartwell and promised to introduce him to the greatest man in the world. Unfortunately, Winston Churchill was ill that day and the visit was called off. But the little boy slipped off down a corridor and followed a waiter into the sickroom. There he marched up and asked: "Are you the greatest man in the world?"

"Yes, I am," snarled Sir Winston. "Now push off."

He was, too, but I've always felt his greatest moments were, not during the war, but before it. England stood alone in 1940 and the great speeches—"Blood, toil, tears, and sweat," "We shall fight in the fields and in the streets, we shall fight in the hills, we shall never surrender," "This was their finest hour" and the rest—thundered throughout the free world.

This was England's great ordeal but Winston Churchill's great ordeal came earlier, when with his monumental vision, he thundered unheard, unheeded, virtually unread, and unprinted his great warnings about the growing military power and intentions of Germany. Then, Churchill stood alone, against virtually all of England, to say nothing of its allies.

In 1936, when Hitler reoccupied the Rhineland, the shock waves rocked the chancelleries of the world but it was Churchill alone who specifically spelled out in precise terms, in a speech before the House of Commons, the military significance of this action.

"The creation of a line of forts opposite to the French front will enable German troops to be economized on that line and will enable the main forces to swing through Belgium and Holland," he said. This was in 1936, mind you, 2½ years before World War II started. Four years later, the German forces did exactly that.

"The whole aspect," Churchill said in his speech, "of the Baltic States, Poland, and Czechoslovakia, with which must be associated Yugoslavia, Rumania, Austria, and some other countries are all affected very decisively the moment this great work of reconstruction is completed." All these prophecies were appallingly accurate.

It was not a popular speech. England was in a mood of business as usual. Stanley Baldwin was Prime Minister and a very popular one. Some of Churchill's greatest speeches were blasts of withering scorn against the flaccidities of Baldwin's government:

"The Government cannot make up their minds, or they cannot get the Prime Minister to make up his mind. So they go on in strange paradox, decided only to be undecided, resolved to be irresolute, adamant for drift, solid for fluidity, all powerful to be impotent. So we go on preparing more months and years—precious, perhaps vital, for the greatness of Britain—for the locusts to eat."

Six months later Baldwin resigned and Churchill later wrote: "[Baldwin] laid down his wide authority he had carefully gathered and maintained but used as little as possible. He departed in a public glow of gratitude and esteem." Churchill was in anything but a public glow of gratitude or esteem.

In July 1936, 4 years before England was to be saved by a handful of Spitfire pilots, Churchill told a select committee of great public figures in the Prime Minister's room at the House of Commons: "We are facing the greatest danger and emergency in our history. At all costs, we must draw the flower of our youth into piloting airplanes. We must accelerate and simplify our aircraft production and push it to the largest scale. We are in danger as we have never been in danger before—no, not even at the height of the submarine campaign (of 1917)."

This prophetic utterance was totally discounted. The Government told Churchill his views were too gloomy, that nothing in the international situation justified upsetting the industrial life of the country or alarming the populace.

These were Churchill's finest hours when he was making prophecies of such stunning accuracy they could be put unchanged into the history books.

Churchill's darkest hours came well before World War II. One was Neville Chamberlain's rebuff of President Roosevelt's offer to mediate which Churchill considered "the last frail chance to save the world from tyranny otherwise than by war." The darkest hour was when Anthony Eden resigned as Foreign Secretary in protest against Chamberlain's appeasement policies on February 20, 1938.

"In a long life," he wrote, "I have had many ups and down. During all the war soon to come and in its darkest times, I never had any trouble sleeping. In the crisis of 1940, when so much responsibility lay upon me, and also at many other very anxious, awkward moments in the following 5 years, I could always flop into bed and go to sleep after the day's work was done. I slept sound and awoke refreshed and had no feelings except appetite to grapple with whatever the morning's boxes might bring. But on this night of February 20, 1938, and on this occasion alone, sleep deserted me. From midnight till dawn I lay on my bed consumed by emotions of sorrow and fear. I watched the daylight slowly creep in through the windows and saw before me in mental gaze the vision of death."

That was Churchill's darkest hour. England's came 2 years later in the Battle of Britain—September 15, 1940—when Churchill asked a subordinate: "How many Spitfires have we in reserve?"

"None, sir," was the reply.

"Then we must press forward the attack," said Churchill lightheartedly. That was the night the German air armadas finally desisted and the Battle of Britain was over just when Germany might have won it.

By then, Churchill was the beloved, indomitable hero of the whole free world. But I like him best when he was unloved—and still indomitable. That's the true best.

TRIBUTES BY

REPRESENTATIVE FRANK J. HORTON

OF NEW YORK

Mr. Speaker, Sir Winston's passing was the subject of an editorial eulogy published January 25 by the Democrat and Chronicle of Rochester, N.Y. I take pleasure in sharing this eloquent expression with my colleagues:

A Giant Passes

So the old gentleman died, and the very fact of his death, even as the achievements of his life, had the quality of perfect timing.

For Sir Winston Churchill's death reminds us—at a time when the free world needs reminding—that nations can rise above bickering and name calling and apathy; that there is a nobility and a willingness to sacrifice in mankind, when the right figure steps forth to lead.

His death reminds us of the days and months and years that his shattered stubborn little island stood against the might of organized barbarism—we called it the Axis then—and held it at bay until the rest of the free world could mobilize to join the fight. So we are reminded that while one oasis of freedom remains, there is always hope for man.

His death reminds us that the price of always is too great, for victor as well as vanquished. This practical thought should cause the free world to look up from its mourning and renew its dedication to peace. For in ultimate victory, the British nation overspent its strength in the cause of honor and freedom in that last great war. After the war it entered upon the twilight of greatness, but it did this without a whimper, knowing it had done what had to be done.

His death reminds us always to seek for giants, of whom we have so pitifully few today. We need giants who can see—as did Sir Winston—danger massing against the free world when others cannot see it; who can describe the danger with icy or fiery words; and who can thus arouse freemen to action.

We need to think of all those things now, we who live in this bickering, threatening world. And the death of the old gentleman reminds us to think hard, even while we mourn.

Mr. Speaker, in this same edition, the editors of the Democrat and Chronicle carried an article by Reporter George Murphy which traced the little-known ancestry aspects of Sir Winston that so directly relate to Rochester, N.Y. All who are interested in this history, I am sure will find Mr. Murphy's article a fascinating story:

Coowner of Democrat and Chronicle Progenitor—Churchill's Grandfather Was Rochesterian

(By George Murphy)

Winston Leonard Spencer Churchill, who typified England and the English people, had Yankee blood in his veins.

His maternal grandfather, Leonard Jerome, once lived only a stone's throw from where this story is written—74 Fitzhugh Street South, now the site of the Civic Center Garage.

As a matter of fact, the connection between Britain's great leader and this newspaper is more than geographic, for Leonard Jerome and his brother Lawrence owned the Rochester Daily American from 1846 to 1850, and that newspaper eventually was combined with the Democrat and in 1870 became an integral part of the Democrat and Chronicle.

It was prophetic that Churchill's grandfather once dealt with the printed word, for it was Winston who rallied Britain when she stood alone in World War II with these historic words:

"We shall fight on the beaches, we shall fight in the fields and in the streets; we shall fight in the hills; we shall never surrender."

One wonders also if Winston Churchill did not inherit his audacity, his gusto, and his gift for the stirring phrase from ancestors who were pioneers in upstate New York.

His grandfather was born on a farm at Pompey, south of Syracuse. Young Leonard was sent as a lad in his teens to live with his uncle, Hiram K. Jerome, a lawyer in Palmyra. There he prepared for college, leaving for Princeton in 1836, but a desire to economize prompted him to transfer 2 years later to Union College in Schenectady, where he was graduated in 1839.

Returning to Palmyra, he studied law in the office of his uncle, recently named judge of Wayne County. And when Judge Jerome decided in 1842 to move to Rochester, Leonard and his younger brother, Lawrence, likewise moved to the Flour City.

The Jeromes located in the fashionable third ward where the judge rented a house at No. 72 (later renumbered 83) Fitzhugh Street South, while his two nephews boarded across the street at No. 63 (later 74). Neither Leonard nor his brother developed a strong attachment to law, and in 1845, after Lawrence married Catherine Hall, a wealthy heiress of Palmyra, the brothers bought an interest in the Daily American.

Shortly after their marriage in August 1844, Lawrence and his wife rented the Pond House at No. 65 South Sophia (No. 219 Plymouth) Street, taking Leonard in as boarder, but they moved back to 63 South Fitzhugh the next year, renting the entire house.

Leonard settled there with his wife, too, when in April 1849 he married Clarissa Hall, younger sister of Lawrence's Catherine. It must have been a lively household, but the spacious house afforded ample room for the two Jerome-Hall couples.

The first two sons of Lawrence and Catherine Jerome, Roswell W. and Lovell Hall, were born in the house at 63 Fitzhugh Street South but Jennie Jerome (Churchill's mother), one of Leonard and Clarissa's four daughters, was not.

But local myths have waxed with the Churchill fame until finally some Rochesterians were insisting that this city was the birthplace of the statesman's mother.

Lady Churchill, who should know, wrote in her autobiography, "I was born in Brooklyn." But her son, ever the politician, at times seemed to concur in the Rochester claim while not denying Brooklyn's.

In 1941 when Winston received—via radio—an honorary degree from the University of Rochester, he replied to the honor in these diplomatic words:

"As you tell me, my mother was born in Rochester."

In 1952 City Historian Blake McKelvey's passion for historical accuracy swept away the cobwebs spun by local wishful thinking. His careful research showed that Jennie Jerome was born in Brooklyn 4 years after her parents moved away from Rochester and the Fitzhugh Street house.

A bronze tablet which once stood on that house told the true story in its inscription:

"Leonard Jerome, publisher and grandfather of Britain's Winston Churchill resided on this site, 1844–50. He married Clarissa Hall of Palmyra, April 5, 1849."

Winston Churchill visited Rochester on two occasions. He came the first time as a young Boer War correspondent to address a sparse audience in the Lyceum Theater on January 28, 1901. Winston Churchill was not a celebrated name then.

He was better known on his second visit, February 10, 1932, when he spoke on "The World Economic Crisis" at the Eastman Theater. But the Labor Party was in power in Britain and Winston was on the sidelines, picking up a few dollars on a lecture tour.

On neither visit is there any record he visited the houses where his forebears had dwelt.

Mr. Speaker, I also want to share with the Members of the House a historical account of the Churchill ancestry which was printed a few days ago in the Palmyra Courier-Journal which serves a large part of my Wayne County constituency. Editor Carol Clark and her staff have provided us with details of the special relationship which the community of Palmyra had in the life of Leonard Jerome, Sir Winston's maternal grandfather:

WINSTON CHURCHILL—WE CLAIM ONE "FINEST HOUR"

Winston Churchill, citizen of the world, the United States only honorary citizen, of early Palmyra stock—Palmyra can claim him as a son, a part of our vital heritage.

Churchill never formally recognized Palmyra's claim to his birthright through his maternal grandparents here. We are among the many who entered his bloodline—Marion, Rochester, New York City, Philadelphia, New England.

A blood right Churchill did claim. Of his address to our Congress in December 1941 he wrote, "To me, who could trace unbroken male descent on my mother's side through five generations from a lieutenant who served in George Washington's army, it was possible to feel a blood right to speak to the representatives of the Great Republic in our common cause."

That Christmas Eve Churchill had told the American people, "I cannot truthfully say that I feel far from home. Whether it be the ties of blood on my mother's side, or the friendships I have developed here over the many years of active life, or the commanding sentiment of comradeship in the common cause of great peoples, I have a right to sit at your fireside."

Palmyra was 2 years in the making when in 1791 Rhode Islander David Wilcox joined the settlement. A daughter, Clarissa, in the early 1820's wed Ambrose Hall, newly come from Massachusetts, and raised a family of six daughters in their home where the village park bandstand now stands.

Their daughter, also Clarissa, married Leonard Jerome, a prosperous Marion farmer formerly of Pompey in Onondaga County.

The Jeromes moved to Rochester, then to New York, where Leonard became a publisher, arts' patron, racetrack owner, diplomat, world traveler, a man of wealth.

A daughter, one of four, Jenny Jerome, married Englishman Lord Randolph Churchill.

Ninety years ago a son was born to the granddaughter of Ambrose Hall and the son of the Duke of Marlborough.

He was named Winston Leonard Spencer Churchill.

The Jerome farm still stands on the Boss Road in Marion, now the home of the Leo Allen family.

Still standing on West Canal Street is the home of newlywed Leonard and Clarissa Hall Jerome.

And, still remembered is the Market Street site of the law office where Leonard Jerome studied law with an uncle, Judge Hiram Jerome.

Whatever strain of pioneer spirit that typified the industry of the early Palmyra coursed through the generations to Winston Churchill, however small the part a Palmyra ancestry played in his formation, of the preponderance of greatness that has marked Churchill's 90 years, Palmyra can rightly claim at least one of his finest hours.

TRIBUTES BY

REPRESENTATIVE EDWARD J. DERWINSKI

OF ILLINOIS

Mr. Speaker, typical of the press commentary across the country on Churchill's career were the editorials which appeared in Chicago's American and the Chicago Daily News on January 25:

[From Chicago's American, Jan. 25, 1965]

CHURCHILL

(*The life we are today honoring is unique. The oldest amongst us can recall nothing to compare with it. The younger ones among you, however long you live, will never see the like again.*—HAROLD MACMILLAN, before House of Commons, July 1964.)

With Sir Winston Churchill, an age of heroes has passed. There are living reminders of it still; there are even still heroes, but they have survived their time. The world does not stir to their voices as it stirred to Churchill's.

We should not really grieve for Churchill. His death was not a tragedy. His life had to end and it ended, in peace and honor, after one last, gallant fight; and we could have wished no better for the old warrior.

What a life it was. Churchill was famous, a leader and shaper of events, in an age so different that it is hard for most of us to imagine. He saw and fought in battles that rang as far off and strange as the wars of the Old Testament. Malakand and Tirah, the world's last great cavalry charge at Omdurman against the dervishes, the siege of Ladysmith in the Boer War.

And not once but twice, before the two Great Wars, he fought the most crucial and heartbreaking battle of all with his own countrymen; he had to plead and argue and flog them into arming themselves against deadly danger.

More than any one man, Churchill could claim a proud title: He was the enemy of Adolf Hitler. He stood against the monstrous indecency of Nazi Germany, rumbling anger and defiance and indomitable will. And his stern, splendid language led the Western World like a banner.

We feel grief at Churchill's passing, of course; we cannot help it. But there is no real cause for grief, unless it is for this world that has grown smaller now.

[From the Chicago Daily News, Jan. 25, 1965]

SIR WINSTON CHURCHILL

Death finally bested the indomitable little man whose mark lies more boldly than any other on our time. But Sir Winston Churchill had given so much of himself to history that the victory, when it came at last, had lost much of its meaning. The imprint had already hardened when Churchill, battered by two successive strokes, gave over the reins of government to Anthony Eden in 1955. It was, and will remain, a mighty imprint.

A man who rises by his own force to tower above his peers may often be a single-minded man, but he will never fall into an easily defined mold.

In the complex interworkings between the man and his times, certain salient characteristics will show through—the resiliency, the humor, the daring, the eloquence, and with Churchill above all, the stubborness so deeply ingrained that it shaped the very contour of his jaw. But the whole somehow emerges greater than the sum of the parts.

It could not be said in this case that history largely made the man, because history did its persistent worst to destroy him. The great military academy of Sandhurst rebuffed young Churchill twice, and on the third desperate try he crashed the academic gate. The Boers captured him, and when he escaped put a price on his head, but he hid out for days in an old mine and finally made his way to freedom.

His own people rejected him time and again—the Gallipoli disaster was laid to his mishandling as First Lord of the Admiralty, and he was banished to a niche so obscure that he took to painting as a relief from the boredom.

It was such first-rate painting that one of his works was later hung in the Royal Gallery.

His incessant oratory against the rising menace of nazism was scorned ("We have sustained a total and unmitigated defeat," he roared after Munich) until Hitler sent his panzers into Poland in September of 1939. Then he won his old Admiralty post back, and, when the war was nearing its lowest ebb and there was no one else to turn to, the King summoned him to be Prime Minister on May 10, 1940.

No one could have known how apt was the choice, until 3 days later Parliament heard words that shaped history in their very saying:

"I have nothing to offer but blood, toil, sweat, and tears. You ask what is our policy? I will say it is to wage war—by sea, land, and air—with all our might and with all the strength that God can give us; to wage war against a monstrous tyranny never surpassed in the dark, lamentable catalog of human crimes. That is our policy."

Stubbornness, a zestful almost insolent daring—and humor; these, more than any genius, were what Britain needed, and what Churchill provided. When Dunkirk fell he delivered his solemn, stirring address: "We shall go on to the end; we shall fight in France, we shall fight on the beaches, we shall fight in the fields, in the streets, in the hills." And at the end put his hand over the microphone and muttered: "And we shall hit them over the heads with beer bottles, which is all we really have got."

His memorable tribute to the Royal Air Force after the Battle of Britain was well deserved—but seldom, too, had so many owed so much to a single man.

Cast aside once again when the war was won, the old campaigner returned with undiminished zeal to his writing, to emerge, for his final triumph, to public life in 1951 when, at 76, he regained the premiership in his own right. When he stepped down 4 years later, it was by his own wish.

Churchill lived, wrote, and guided history—but so have many great men. What is unique with Churchill, Lincoln, and their kind is that in gaining a world's respect they also won its love. As long as there is a Britain, that love will endure for the square-jawed little man with the bowler hat, the cigar, and the twinkling eye who lifted a great people to their finest hour.

TRIBUTE BY

REPRESENTATIVE ABRAHAM J. MULTER

OF NEW YORK

Mr. Speaker, Winston Churchill—the embodiment of Western civilization's struggle toward peace in the 20th century—has departed from us. The uniqueness of the man is best summed up in the following editorial which appeared in the New York Journal-American of January 25, 1965:

CHURCHILL

The great man is dead. With him has died a part of the 20th century.

Sir Winston Churchill was a towering figure of our age, a unique man who grasped and molded history as few before him.

Those fortunate enough to have lived during his day can treasure this knowledge: they are contemporaries of one who ranks with such titans of history as Caesar, Napoleon, George Washington, and Lincoln.

Who of us will forget how he rumbled defiance when Britain stood alone during World War II? Who of us has not thrilled to the rolling resonance of his words?

His brandy, his cigars, and famed V-sign became his unmistakable hallmarks, and he relished them as one who loved life and his fellow man.

We are proud that his mother was an American and that he accepted honorary American citizenship, the sole individual so honored in this century.

Soldier, journalist, statesman, and historian—he was all of these in a manner seldom equaled. Yet he was more than any of them.

He was the embodiment of a stubborn determination to preserve honor, decency, and dignity in the affairs of men. For him, civilization and all it implied, built up over the centuries, was sacred.

A giant is gone from our midst.

TRIBUTE BY

REPRESENTATIVE WILLIAM F. RYAN

OF NEW YORK

Mr. Speaker, the famous 369th Veterans' Association, Inc., had its installation of national officers at the 369th Regiment Armory on Sunday, January 31, 1965. At this very impressive ceremony William K. De Fossett, who has served the association with unusual dedication, was again installed as the national president. I extend my congratulations to him and the other officers of this splendid organization. It was a special privilege for me to speak at the ceremonies, and I am honored to belong to the 369th Veterans' Association.

Rabbi William F. Rosenblum, of Temple Israel, chaplain, 369th Veterans' Association, delivered a commemorative prayer for Sir Winston Churchill. Dr. Rosenblum's prayer is so beautifully written and so fitting that I wish to share it with my colleagues.

Dr. Rosenblum's inspiring tribute to Sir Winston Churchill follows:

COMMEMORATIVE PRAYER FOR SIR WINSTON CHURCHILL DELIVERED AT THE INSTALLATION OF OFFICERS CEREMONY OF THE 369TH VETERANS' ASSOCIATION, INC., SUNDAY, JANUARY 31, 1965

(By Rev. Dr. William F. Rosenblum, chaplain, 369th Veterans' Association, rabbi, Temple Israel of the city of New York)

Our God and Father of us all, into Thy presence a saddened yet grateful Nation, indeed a sorrowful but grateful world but yesterday committed one of their noblest sons: Sir Winston Churchill.

Unyielding in war, he was equally steadfast in peace in the defense of freedom and justice. He served not alone his native land, but all to whom liberty is dear.

O Lord, may we, who understand how precious and imperative are justice and freedom, resolve that the remembrance of this great man of our century, whose pen was ever as mighty as his sword, will inspire us to walk in his path; to make his design for living our guide for the future—never seeking only what is convenient, never hesitating to become involved and to sacrifice, never surrendering to the wrong.

Thus will we be able to establish here among men that brotherhood which will reflect Thy fatherhood and bear witness to Thy majesty, Thy glory, and Thy unity. Amen and amen.

TRIBUTE BY

REPRESENTATIVE RALPH HARVEY

OF INDIANA

Mr. Speaker, I insert a letter to the editor by Albert Ferris, of Milton, Ind. It was carried in the Eastern Indiana Farmer edition of February 16, 1965, and is a fine tribute to Winston Churchill.

The article follows:

Churchill Was Frank

Much has recently been written in tribute to the late Winston Churchill. Perhaps one of the greatest tributes came during his life as we made him an honorary American citizen. Some have even suggested that he would have made a great leader for our country. However our thoughts may have wandered in this direction, it is quite evident he would actually not have fit too well into the pattern of our prevailing social and political philosophy.

Churchill was ever frank with the English people. If things were going badly, he never concealed the truth from them. "I bring you bad news," he told Parliament on one of the darkest days, "and fear there may be even worse." As he never watered down defeat, so he never exaggerated triumph. Win or lose, he gave the people the unvarnished facts. No, Churchill would not have fit into the pattern of our Great Society adventure. He could not have consented to the limiting of the people's right to know. He would not have glossed over our obvious blunders in Vietnam or in our dealings with the Communist world. As an ardent foe of socialism, he would never have fit into our welfare state. He would never have stood mute before the covert operations of Billie Sol Estes and Bobby Baker. He most certainly would not have represented as an accomplishment in economy a budget under $100 million, the while his projected expenditures were actually billions higher. No, "Winnie" would not have fit into our present political philosophy at all. And yet, as Morrie Ryskind predicted, "Centuries hence, when the Great Society has tumbled into the oblivion that awaits all schemes built on its quick-stand of bread and circuses without toil, the little country churchyard at Bladon will still be the shrine to which the world will make its grateful pilgrimage."

TRIBUTES BY

SENATOR MILWARD L. SIMPSON

OF WYOMING

Mr. President, there was hardly a community in the Nation in which the people and the press did not mourn the passing last month of Sir Winston Churchill, a man who, had the respective nationalities of his mother and father "been the other way around," might well have won election to this legislative body. It is fitting that members of the free press with whose British counterpart Sir Winston was associated in his memorable days as a war correspondent would carry mention of this man in their editorial columns.

The leading daily of Wyoming's capital city, the Cheyenne, Wyoming, State Tribune, of Cheyenne, has carried two such editorials. The first, under date of February 1, paid tribute to Sir Winston as well as questioning the composition of the delegation which represented official Washington at the funeral. A later editorial, February 3, concerned a summary of Sir Winston Churchill's capacities as a leader written by Denis Brogan, a professor of political science at Cambridge University.

The Thermopolis Independent Record, in a February 11 editorial, affirmed that Churchill's "place in history is a towering one and will always remain so"—an observation with which few could disagree.

Mr. President, I feel these three editorials should be made a part of this body's permanent record on the illustrious living legend whose biography is virtually the history of man's last century.

[From the Wyoming State Tribune, Feb. 1, 1965]

REPRESENTATIVE OF THE AMERICAN PEOPLE

It seems deeply unfortunate that the United States of America which had made Sir Winston Churchill one of its own and to whom it had accorded so many honors as well as the love and admiration of its millions of people, was not appropriately officially represented at the final tribute paid him in London Saturday.

It is excusable that the President of the United States, who had evinced a sincere desire to do so, could not personally attend. But in his stead it would appear to us there could have been no more proper officially designated representative of the people of this country than Gen. Dwight D. Eisenhower.

It is not enough to say that General Eisenhower has twice served this country as its President; more fitting to the occasion is the fact that he, too, is an old warrior and one of our very great living heroes of the holocaust that molded Churchill forever in the hearts not only of Britain and the English-speaking world but the champion of freedom everywhere.

The people of America deserved to have General Eisenhower as a comrade-in-arms and one of the few survivors of the topmost echelons of command of World War II, named to represent them in the absence of this country's Chief of State.

But unofficially, Generall Eisenhower did go, at the personal invitation of Lady Churchill; and in their hearts we are sure that he really represented the people of this country.

His moving discourse on his old friend and associate delivered over the British Broadcasting Co.'s television network Saturday as Sir Winston's cortege moved along the Thames, stirred the emotions of people everywhere.

Said the general: "Upon the mighty Thames, great avenue of history, move at this moment to their final resting place the mortal remains of Sir Winston Churchill.

"He was a great maker of history, but his work is done and the record closed."

General Eisenhower then recited Tennyson's "Crossing the Bar," and thereafter proceeded to speak at length on the great figure being mourned.

"I would, like all other freemen, to pay a personal tribute to the giant who now passes from among us," said General Eisenhower. "I have no charter to speak for my countrymen, only for myself. But if in memory we journey back to the time when Britain and America stood shoulder to shoulder in global conflict against tyranny, then I act as spokesman for the millions of Americans who served with me and their British comrades, in 3 years of war in this sector.

"To those men Winston Churchill was Britain. He was the embodiment of British defiance to threat, courage in adversity, calmness in her danger, moderation in her success."

General Eisenhower reviewed the war years and he spoke briefly and modestly of his own association with the Prime Minister and their precious friendship.

Then he concluded:

"At this moment, as our hearts stand to attention, we say an affectionate though sad goodby to the leader to whom the entire body of freemen owes so much.

"In the coming years, countless words will strive to interpret the motives and describe exactly the virtue of Sir Winston Churchill—leader, statesman, citizen, that two great countries were proud to claim as their own.

"Of the many things so written and spoken there will ring out through all centuries one incontestable refrain: 'Here was a champion of freedom.'

"May God grant that we and the generations who will remember him heed the lessons he taught us in his deeds, in his words, in his life.

"May we carry on his work until no nation lies in captivity, no man is denied opportunity for fulfillment.

"And now to you Sir Winston, my old friend, farewell."

A most moving and eloquent final testimonial; and although General Eisenhower had no formal charter, as he called it, from his Government to represent us at Sir Winston's funeral, the people of America can feel grateful and proud that their sentiments were so well and capably conveyed—and by one who himself is enshrined in their hearts.

[From the Wyoming State Tribune, Feb. 3, 1965]

LESSON IN LEADERSHIP

Denis Brogan, a professor of political science at Cambridge University, has written a brief summary of Sir Winston Churchill's capabilities as a leader. It is deserving of some study not only in connection with Churchill's life but with the leadership role throughout government and private industry.

Standing in direct contrast to the "Naw-zi" he hated so thoroughly as well as Mussolini (that "guttah-snipe" as Sir Winston called him), Churchill accepted leadership with the limitations peculiar to free institutions.

"Never for a moment," writes Mr. Brogan, "did he forget that he had his mandate from the House of Commons—and so from the people to whom he was responsible not only for the achievement of victory, but for the preservation of the old liberties of the land."

First, he was a loyal, devoted, and obedient member of the House of Commons; and thus, writes Mr. Brogan, it was the leadership of a man who also was proud to be a servant; and to submit to often ignorant criticism and to the answering of silly questions.

This was in stark contrast to the dictators—this controlled, almost humble leadership, if one may call Sir Winston humble.

Another characteristic was candor; no reluctance to have people see things as they really were. And with this, he also called on courage in such a fashion, says Mr. Brogan, that "even quite timid persons found their hearts filled with new energy as they listened to that indomitable voice."

Again, he points out, this was no command from above but a summoning of common courage and common resolve.

"In inspiring this courage, this common confidence, Sir Winston called on all his great resources as an orator," writes Mr. Brogan. "Never has a democratic leader spoken with equal force to so many millions, including the many millions of the subdued nations of Europe, and the many millions across the

Atlantic who found in these brilliant phrases something much more important than phrases: the promise and proof of victory."

But he provided not only great oratory but also action, because he gave great inspiration by his tireless energy. "In a war of unprecedented magnitude and novelty, he gave the impression of one ready to try everything, bound by no precedent, daunted by no novelty." That mistakes would be made was to be admitted; that disasters would occur was not to be concealed. But the people knew they would not lose, with Sir Winston, through any blind clinging to routine—to repeating the same old mistakes.

And in the darkest hours he always found humor and expression of his natural wit.

The leadership was personal, not merely official, but it was the leadership of a disciplined personality, of a great public servant, writes Mr. Brogan. The contrast between Churchill the leader and the dictator leaders thus is sharp; for the former, "it took a very uncommon man to represent those suffering millions and win their deep and effectionate confidence."

[From the Thermopolis Independent Record, Feb. 11, 1965]

Sir Winston Churchill

"And tell sad stories of the death of kings."

So the fine old line marches down the paths of time. And it comes, at last, to Sir Winston Churchill who wore no crown but lives, in eternity, with all the kings and captains who created, saved, and defended worlds faced with destruction, and with that destruction all that they meant and stood for.

He was many men, was Winston Churchill. He could be arrogant, opinionated, difficult. And he could be gentle, generous, humorous, and responsive. But he was one thing always—the defender of human freedom who would never, desperate as the situation of the movement might be, consider the thought of capitulation or compromise. The cause must be fought through to its finsh, whatever the price and the ultimate payment. And his words were weapons.

He was certainly one of the greatest Englishmen of all time. His place in history is a towering one and will always remain so. And the character of Churchill was perhaps best expressed when he said in Commons, after a disastrous British defeat: "* * * we shall fight on the beaches, we shall fight on the landing grounds, we shall fight in the fields and in the streets, we shall fight in the hills; we shall never surrender, and even if, which I do not for a moment believe, this island or a large part of it were subjugated and starving, then our Empire beyond the seas (armed and guarded by the British Fleet, would carry on the struggle, until, in God's good time, the New World, with all its power and might, steps forth to the rescue and the liberation of the Old."

The world is vastly the richer because he lived in it; the world is the poorer because he is gone.

TRIBUTES BY

REPRESENTATIVE CLAUDE PEPPER

OF FLORIDA

Mr. Speaker, this account by Miss Martin was published in the Washington Evening Star on January 26, 1965. Mr. Speaker, I, myself, had many pleasant visits with Mr. Churchill and I felt that Miss Martin's account was a fine recollection on her part which, in turn, reminded me of my individual visits with him. I felt that this article should be preserved as a part of the heritage of the American people as well as those of the rest of the world. May his memory live on through such fine stories as this.

The article follows:

A NIGHT TO REMEMBER: NEW YEAR'S EVE WITH WINSTON CHURCHILL IN 1942

(By Jackie Martin)

It was New Year's Eve. It is the one New Year's Eve I shall never forget. I'll forget all the other New Year's Eves—but this one I'll remember all my life.

We left Ottawa about 3 p.m. I sat in my compartment by myself and through a diffusing screen of snow, smoke, and steam watched the gray afternoon get grayer. The engine woo-oo-ooed at crossings, and I sat and thought, "Isn't this a swell way to spend New Year's Eve?"

We rounded a sharp curve and I counted the cars—engine, baggage car, club car, four pullmans including the one I was on, the diner, then three more pullmans, and the observation car.

CHURCHILL ABROAD

Somewhere in those cars on the other side of the diner was Winston Churchill.

Maybe he was eating or sleeping or reading or preparing a speech or dictating letters or hearing (through a haze of smoke from his long cigar) that Gibraltar was taking an awful beating or that his boys at Singapore were holding or that somewhere over England Messerschmitts had brought down 20 more youngsters of the RAF.

Or maybe he was sitting by his window like me and thinking that it was, indeed, a dreary New Year's Eve afternoon.

"Bet he's terribly tired," I thought. "You are pretty tired yourself," my feet answered. It was true.

For 2 days I had run after that famous old fellow, and when he moves, he moves fast. And when you are going at an awful clip, I think the follower gets much more worn out than the leader. Maybe I'm wrong—or maybe it was the last assignment that had made me physically cranky: Our bus got to the Uplands Flying Field 5 minutes after the Prime Minister. So in order to get up with him (you can write a story long distance but you can't make a picture that way) I had to run like mad for approximately two blocks—mostly on ice—with an open Grafic camera in one hand, a Rolleiflex around my neck, and a heavy camera case holding bulbs, tripod, holders, and extra batteries over my shoulder.

The loose hand kept the bag and Rolli from flopping up and down, pulled the beret back on, when it threatened to fly off, and kept me nicely balanced.

I looked down at my hands. The veins stood up in open protest of the pace I had been going. I looked out the window again. A crossing bell was clanging. People standing there waving. The train sped on. How did they know it was Churchill's train? Its departure and itinerary were military secrets. We hadn't been allowed to send a wire telling families when we would be home. Strange.

Another crossing, going up an incline, slower. There were more people, very close to the tracks. Anxious eyes, thrilled and glowing faces searched each car as it went by. Women and children. But the one who caught my eye was an old man—maybe 70—white hair. He stood straight and tall—searching, looking. I kept my eyes on him as long and I could and then jumped over to the other seat to watch him for a few seconds longer. Then he must have seen Churchill.

He looked as if he had seen his God. His head went up at a high proud angle. His hat went out in open homage. And the glory and courage that came to his face as Churchill's car flashed by was something that no mere man can ever inspire. I strained against the cold window and watched the lowered hat and proud old head blur from sight.

I sort of collapsed into the seat. I wanted to cry. I wanted to jump off the train and get that old man and let him talk to Churchill. I wanted to say to him, "Look fellow, I don't know how much more time you have, but this afternoon you lent yourself to something. A shinning sword was laid on your shoulder—it was in your face—and I was proud of you—proud that a man of your age still had the spirit and courage and honor that put you apart from all the others as our train rolled by.

He was just an old Canadian at a crossing.

OUT OF OTTAWA

About an hour out of Ottawa, I realized that I was riding backward and that always makes me sick. I moved over, thinking that if I weren't so tired I'd get my woolly bedroom slippers out of my bag.

In the compartments and cars around me there were a bunch of newspapermen and one woman reporter, and three photographers.

And here it was getting on toward New Year's Eve, getting darker and colder. Of course, I'd known the reporters to speak to for years. And the photographers, too. But none of them were my friends, especially. And who wants to spend New Year's Eve with people you just know?

I'd rather read a good book, I thought—but I don't like to read on a train—so I leaned my head against the window—and fell asleep. A fitful unhappy sleep, I heard Winston Churchill call as I raced to get in front of him for a shot, "Watch out for that propeller—watch out." And I had felt ashamed that I had worried him.

At 8 I woke, washed, dressed, and went to the club car for a sherry before dinner. New Year's Eve dinner by myself. I'd rather be working—sitting at my desk with a hamburger and a cup of coffee—with photographers buzzing around.

I sat down next to Pedan of "News of the Day" newsreel. Three or four other newsreel men like Hugo Johnson and Johnny Tondra were there too. Larry Lehrbas of Associated Press with bedroom slippers on his feet, was deep in a book. I don't know, maybe he just wanted to talk, or maybe he just sensed my loneliness, but I'll always be grateful to Pedan. He ordered a cocktail so I wouldn't have my sherry alone. Then he asked if he couldn't go into dinner with me—said he had eaten, but felt like talking.

Just before we left the club car for the diner, Tommy Qualters (the President's personal bodyguard who was on the trip with Mr. Churchill) came through the car with a piece of paper. It was the Prime Minister's New Year's wish for happiness and health to us. It was signed by his naval aide, Comdr. C. M. Thompson.

"Tommy, can I make a picture of you showing this greeting to the boys?"

"Sorry, Jackie, I don't think we better."

So I couldn't even make a picture of New Year's Eve. I thought "What a night." But, of course, I couldn't be expected to anticipate what was coming. None of the reporters had the slightest idea. Some of them even went to bed—and when it happened—they were sound asleep.

So Pedan and I went to the diner, and he ordered up a bottle of champagne for celebration. It was flat. Amid apologies, the attentive steward removed it and brought another bottle. That was flat, too. I looked at Pedan. He looked at me—and we both looked out the window. He had been telling me about his daughter who was home from school. He wasn't going to have much time left to see her. We looked back. "Flat or not," I said, "Let's drink it. It is New Year's Eve—nearly. And there'll be bells at home." We solemnly drank the little bottle of flat champagne.

On the way back to the club car for the last half hour till midnight, I passed a compartment in which sat Doris Fleeson, Walter Thompson, special press representative for the Canadian Government, and a British reporter who had come to this country with Mr. Churchill.

I asked if they had seen the Prime Minister's greeting. They said they had. "Well, has anything been done about it?" I asked. They said not. I allowed as how it seemed plently ungracious of us to receive a greeting from the Prime Minister and not even to send one back. So a greeting was hashed over—and then Doris hurried to her compartment to type it. It was given to the porter, who had exactly 8 minutes to get it back to the Prime Minister's aide.

Then we settled down to wait till the little hand and the big hand of Walter's gold pocket watch got together. It was a forlorn foursome if I've ever seen one. We said nothing for a minute or two. Our train roared through the night and the whistle woo-oo-ooed in a mournful tone. The wheels clicked off the sections of rail. There was silence within the compartment—I guess we were all thinking what a terrible year it had been, what anguish it had brought, what would 1942 be like.

We heard the door at the other end of the car open, and in a voice that got louder at each step, we heard, "Ladies and gentlemen, the Prime Minister will greet you in the dining car. Ladies and gentlemen—" and he was gone into the next car.

JUMPED UP

We jumped up and were out of that compartment as if someone had shot us. Churchill. Finally, we would have an opportunity to see him close by—sort of one of us. New Year's Eve—to bring it in with Winston Churchill. We ran—the train going like mad in one direction—we running the other way and shouting to the others in closed compartments.

As we ran through the cars, afraid that he would get to the diner ahead of us, more people poured out of compartments ahead of us. We all ran—the train going around curves, we being banged from one side to the other. But that wasn't important. Three minutes till we'd all get a new chance at life—and we'd start it off with Winston Churchill.

We burst into the dining car and ran to tables. The four of us had kept pretty well together and we sat down at one of the larger tables—a little over halfway toward the other end of the car. Tommy came by. Maybe it was he who had heralded this historical meeting. I didn't think about that. "Hey, Tommy—Tommy—please I gotta make some pictures."

"Sorry, Jackie, no pictures."

"But Tommy—we can't miss this."

Tommy was gone and out the dining car door—toward the Prime Minister's side of the train.

We all sat down. There was bedlam for a minute. Men in bathrobes and slippers, hair tousled but every one wide awake. And on each face a pleased but slightly strained expression. It was so unexpected. It had happened so quickly. And it was nearly 12. They'd have to hurry if they were going to make it.

Then the door opened and Qualters stepped back. Winston Churchill came through the door toward us. We jumped up and cheered so that the roof could have come off and we'd not have noticed it.

He was wearing his "Siren" suit, sort of a teddybear zipper suit. Blue—but not as light as his eyes. His heavy figure was slightly stooped. His cheeks were ruddy. His cigar was in his hand. And he came on toward us. About 5 feet from our table he stopped. Somehow he seemed to sense us rather than see us. He looked at Qualters who said, "Thirty seconds, Mr. Prime Minister."

There was complete silence in the car. Only the train rushing through the night and the whistle woo-oo-ooing in a mournful tone. I could have touched him, he was so close—this old man. He looked at me for a fleeting half second with those eyes—and the weight of the world was in them. "This is Winston Churchill," I thought, "this is the man whose courage, whose will, whose faith in God and Englishmen has saved the civilized world. It's not us and it's not Roosevelt—we got going too late for it to be us. It's this little guy."

I don't know why I thought of him that second as little. It was the teddybear suit, the ruddy cheeks, the white hair, and the slightly bowed head. His hand was reaching for the glass that sat close to him on the edge of the table. He started to raise it. We cheered lustily for it was midnight. It was 1942. O God—what would this year bring? The cheer died away. Somehow it didn't belong and it was lost in the sound of our engine up front. Silence the click, click of wheels on rail sections—the click, click—what was this man thinking, this man who had given the whole civilized world back its right to live in honor—the glass was being held up high.

"To the New Year," he said slowly, and the words came back from each end of the crowded diner. "A year of struggle and of peril, but a long step forward." Those with glasses in their hands drank. He put his on the table. But before the next cheer broke out, the wheels under us picked up his last phrase and clicked off in ever-increasing tempo—"But a long step forward," and the winter wind against the window whispered, "Ah, yes, ah, yes." "But a long step forward"—the wheels promised and the wind blew, "Ah, yes, ah, yes." "But a long step forward," the wheels pounded—and the wind echoed, "Ah, yes, ah, yes."

CHURCHILL SMILES

The cheer died away. Churchill stuck his cigar in his mouth and gave a puff. "Auld Lange Syne" he said, and crossed his arms. About eight of us were in the circle with him. To one side was Sir Charles Portal, head of the RAF. On the other side of the Prime Minister of England was a corporal—clerk to Sir Charles. And Thompson and the English reporter and Doris and Linkins, the Western Union representative. All through the car little circles were made by men holding crossed hands. The song was started, and Churchill sang: "Should auld acquaintance be forgot?" He smiled at me. I smiled back and tried to sing.

But something stuck in my throat. Should they be forgot indeed. How about Dunkirk? How about London? How about Egypt and on the sands the Englishmen who had died for their country. "And never come to naught." My God! How about Pearl Harbor and our boys? All right, it's 1942 now. This year we're behind you, Winston Churchill. You'll not stand alone any longer. He looked around and smiled, a smile I'll never forget. He was remembering his boys and the Messerschmitts, all right. It was no use. I just couldn't sing any more. I gave it up. But kept on pumping my crossed hands and holding tight to the hands that clasped mine.

The song ended. He stepped back a bit and raised his powerful head. He gave a swift glance around the car. Then he said slowly, and through a mountain-clad silence, "May we all come through safe—and with honor." Then he turned, and with his hand in the air forming the symbolic "V," walked to the door of the car. Every person in the car was holding up his or her hand and forming the "V." And we were singing, "For He's a Jolly Good Fellow."

At the door he waited a second. Then waved—and was gone into the night.

Everyone in the car found a chair as soon as he could. My legs wouldn't hold me any longer. I put my elbows on the table and my face in my hands. I was near crying but that wasn't the important thing. I wanted to remember every little thing about that New Year's Eve—while the last 15 minutes, so strange, so historical, were repeating themselves and surging within me.

I wanted to remember and to keep for always the full glory of those few minutes.

Somebody banged me on the back. "That's all right, Jackie," said the voice belonging to the hand, "nobody got the picture."

But just then that wasn't one of my worries. "Suppose I had gone to bed," I thought—and missed the one New Year's Eve I'll never forget. I wouldn't have had this for me. As we left the dining car I smiled, remembering the old man at the crossing. "This, brother," I said to him, "this makes us kin * * * somehow."

Mr. Speaker, on January 28, 1965, the Honorable Adlai E. Stevenson delivered a magnificent and fitting tribute to the late and great Sir Winston Churchill at the memorial service at the National Cathedral.

This eloquent and moving address will stir and stimulate all who read it as it did those of us who were privileged to hear it. Hence, for my colleagues in the Congress and the citizens of the country who will read this, I take particular pleasure in submitting it.

[From the Washington Post, Jan. 29, 1965]

TEXT OF STEVENSON'S REMARKS

Today we meet in sadness to mourn one of the world's greatest citizens. Sir Winston Churchill is dead. The voice that led nations, raised armies, inspired victories, and blew fresh courage into the hearts of men is silenced. We shall hear no longer the remembered eloquence and wit, the old courage and defiance, the robust serenity of indomitable faith. Our world is thus poorer, our political dialog is diminished, and the sources of public inspiration run more thinly for all of us. There is a lonesome place against the sky.

So we are right to mourn. Yet, in contemplating the life and spirit of Winston Churchill, regrets for the past seem singularly insufficient. One rather feels a sense of thankfulness and encouragement that, throughout so long a life, such a full measure of power, virtuosity, mastery, and zest played over our human scene.

Contemplating this completed career, we feel a sense of enlargement and exhilaration. Like the grandeur and power of this masterpiece of art and music, Churchill's life uplifts our hearts and fills us with fresh revelation of the scale and reach of human achievement. We may be sad; but we rejoice as well, as all must rejoice when they "now praise famous men" and see in their lives the full splendor of our human estate.

And regrets for the past are insufficient for another reason. Churchill, the historian, felt the continuity of past and present, the contribution which mighty men and great events make to the future experience of mankind; history's "flickering lamp" lights up the past and sends its gleams into the future. So, to the truth of Santayana's dictum, "Those who will not learn from the past are destined to repeat it," Churchill's whole life was witness. It was his lonely voice that in the thirties warned Britain and Europe of the follies of playing all over again the tragedy of disbelief and of unpreparedness. And in the time of Britain's greatest trial he mobilized the English language to inspire his people to historic valor to save their beleaguered island. It was his voice again that helped assemble the great coalition that has kept peace steady through the last decades.

He once said: "We cannot say the past is past without surrendering the future." So today the "past" of his life and his achievement are a guide and light to the future. And we can only properly mourn and celebrate this mighty man by heeding him as a living influence in the unfolding dramas of our days ahead.

What does he tell us for this obscure future whose outlines we but dimly discern? First, I believe, he would have us reaffirm his serene faith in human freedom and dignity. The love of freedom was not for him an abstract thing but a deep conviction that the uniqueness of man demands a society that gives his capacities full scope. It was, if you like, an aristocratic sense of the fullness and value of life. But he was a profound Democrat, and the cornerstone of his political faith, inherited from a beloved father, was the simple maxim—"Trust the people." Throughout his long career, he sustained his profound concern for the well-being of his fellow citizens.

Instinctively, profoundly, the people trusted "good old Winnie," the peer's son. He could lead them in war because he had respected them in peace. He could call for their greatest sacrifices for he knew how to express their deepest dignity—citizens of equal value and responsibility in a free and democratic state.

His crucial part in the founding of the United Nations expressed his conviction that the Atlantic Charter he and President Roosevelt audaciously proclaimed at the height of Hitler's victories would have to be protected throughout the world by institutions embodying the ideal of the rule of law and international cooperation.

For him, humanity, its freedom, its survival, towered above pettier interests—national rivalries, old enmities, the bitter disputes of race and creed. "In victory—magnanimity; in peace—good will" were more than slogans. In fact, his determination to continue in politics after his defeat in 1945 and to toil on in office in the 1950's to the limit of health and endurance sprang from his belief that he could still "bring nearer that lasting peace which the masses of people of every race and in every land so fervently desire." The great soldier and strategist was a man of peace—and for the most simple reason—his respect, his faith, his compassion for the family of man.

His career saw headlong success and headlong catastrophe. He was at the height. He was flung to the depths. He saw his worst prophecies realized, his worst forebodings surpassed. Yet throughout it all his zest for living, gallantry of spirit, wry humor, and compassion for human frailties took all firmness out of his fortitude and all pomposity out of his dedication.

Churchill's sense of the incomparable value and worth of human existence never faltered, nor the robust courage with which he lived it to the full. In the darkest hour, the land could still be bright, and for him hopes were not deceivers. It was forever fear that was the dupe. Victory at last would always lie with life and faith, for Churchill saw beyond the repeated miseries of human frailty and larger vision of mankind's "upward ascent toward his distant goal."

He used to say that he was half American and all English. But we put that right when the Congress made him an honorary citizen of his mother's native land and we shall always claim a part of him. I remember once years ago during a long visit at his country house he talked proudly of his American Revolutionary ancestors and happily of his boyhood visits to the United States. As I took my leave I said I was going back to London to speak to the English Speaking Union and asked if he had any message for them. "Yes," he said, "tell them that you bring greeting from an English Speaking Union." And I think that perhaps it was to the relations of the United Kingdom and the United States that he made his finest contribution.

In the last analysis, all the zest and life and confidence of this incomparable man sprang, I believe, not only from the rich endowment of his nature, but also from a profound and simple faith in God. In the prime of his powers, confronted with the apocalyptic risks of annihilation, he said serenely: "I do not believe that God has despaired of his children." In old age, as the honors and excitements faded, his resignation had a touching simplicity: "Only faith in a life after death in a brighter world where dear ones will meet again—only that and the measured tramp of time can give consolation."

The great aristocrat, the beloved leader, the profound historian, the gifted painter, the superb politician, the lord of language, the orator, the wit—yes, and the dedicated bricklayer—behind all of them was the man of simple faith, steadfast in defeat, generous in victory, resigned in age, trusting in a loving providence, and committing his achievements and his triumphs to a higher power.

Like the patriarchs of old, he waited on God's judgment and it could be said of him—as of the immortals that went before him—that God "magnified him in the fear of his enemies and with his words he made prodigies to cease. He glorified him in the sight of kinds and gave him commandments in the sight of his people. He showed him his glory and sanctioned him in his faith * * *."

TRIBUTE BY

SENATOR GEORGE A. SMATHERS

OF FLORIDA

Mr. President, I ask to include an article entitled "The Grand Route to a Simple Grave." The article was written by Jeanne Bellamy, an outstanding editorial writer, and was published on January 29 in the Miami (Fla.) Herald.

This article deals with the solemn ceremony to remind Britons of their glorious past, and yet the simplicity of the final act—the burial of Winston Churchill with his parents, in a simple resting place in a country churchyard in the village of Bladon, England.

The Grand Route to a Simple Grave: Sir Winston's Choice

(By Jeanne Bellamy)

England gains a new place of pilgrimage tomorrow—the grave of Sir Winston Churchill.

Not for him the domed grandeur of St. Paul's Cathedral or the gothic arches of Westminister Abbey. Instead, he chose to have his body buried with his parents in a country churchyard. His only roof will be the English sky.

The spot is almost unknown now. It is St. Martin's Church in the village of Bladon, built against the wall surrounding the grounds of Blenheim Palace, where Sir Winston was born. Bladon is 70 miles northwest of London.

All tomorrow's mournful pomp leads to that simple, resting place.

But Sir Winston did not cheat his countrymen of the solemn ceremony they love. Last rites for him, in line with his wishes, seem intended to remind Britons of their glorious past.

His body has lain in state in Westminster Hall, built by the son of William the Conqueror nearly 900 years ago. For 600 years, the hall was the chief court of English law. Among others, King Charles I was condemned there in 1649.

The hall adjoins the House of Commons, center of Sir Winston's public life for 62 years.

Nearby is Westminister Abbey, dating back 1,200 years. A score of monarchs, including the great Elizabeth, are buried in the abbey. It also holds the tombs or monuments of famous Englishmen from actors and antiquarians to musicians, painters, poets, scientists, and statesmen. Among the last are

Prime Ministers Benjamin Disraeli and William Ewart Gladstone, the last Briton to receive a state funeral 67 years ago.

Queen Elizabeth II and other heads of state will attend the services in St. Paul's Cathedral.

A Christian church stood on the site of St. Paul's as long ago as the year 604. The great fire of 1666 razed the structure then standing. The present church was completed in 1710 by Sir Christopher Wren. His tomb, in the crypt, carries the Latin inscription "Si monumentum requiris, circumspice." ("If you seek his monument, look around you.")

The tombs of Lord Nelson, victor of Trafalgar, and the Duke of Wellington, who conquered Napoleon at Waterloo, are the most conspicuous of many in St. Paul's.

Its high altar was damaged badly by a bomb in World War II. The new altar is a memorial to the fighting men of the British Commonwealth killed in that conflict. Behind the altar is the American Memorial Chapel, built with donations from Britons to honor members of the U.S. Armed Forces who fell while based in England.

Britons will line the streets of London to watch Sir Winston's casket pass by on a naval gun carriage drawn by seamen, to the music of 10 bands. More will line the Thames to see the funeral barge float toward Waterloo Station. Thence the body will go by train to Bladon for private graveside services.

Henceforth, no doubt, endless streams of pilgrims from every corner of the world will make their way to Bladon. Their feet will thread past the large stone cross marking the graves of Lord Randolph Churchill and Jennie Jerome of New York, Sir Winston's parents. They will pause reverently at the burial place of the great statesman-author-orator.

In the distance, visitors will see the towered and turreted bulk of Blenheim Palace, England's largest house. It was a gift of the nation to one of Sir Winston's ancestors, the Duke of Marlborough, who defeated the French and Bavarians, killing 40,000 at Bleinheim in Germany in 1704.

The pilgrims will have much to ponder. Like other English-speaking people, Sir Winston had a goodly heritage, and he ennobled it.

TRIBUTE BY

SENATOR GORDON ALLOTT

OF COLORADO

Mr. President, belatedly I should like to invite the attention of Senators to an article entitled "A Chat With Churchill," which was published in the Denver Post of February 7, 1965. The article was written by that veteran Washington newsman, known and respected by virtually everyone in this city who is connected with Capitol Hill, Barnet Nover, chief of the Denver Post Washington bureau.

In his own inimitable style, as a result of just one short personal association with Sir Winston Churchill, Barney has given each of us a rare insight into the warmth of personality, the fire of principle, and the human qualities of one of the greatest men of the century. Barney's memory, refreshed by a diary he kept that year as president of the Overseas Writers, vividly ushers into contemporary history the strength of Sir Winston as well as his awareness of everything, every event, and everybody around him at all times.

I am grateful to Barney for what I think is a warm, wonderful, and well-told story about a man and a time that nurtured in all the peoples of the world a penchant for greatness and the willingness to make the sacrifices to achieve it.

[From the Denver (Colo.) Post, Feb. 7, 1965]

A Chat With Churchill: Post's Man in Washington Recalls 1943 Luncheon

(By Barnet Nover)

On September 2, 1943, after his arrival in Washington from Quebec where he, President Franklin D. Roosevelt, their civilian advisers, and the combined (Anglo-American) Chiefs of Staff had considered, among other great wartime problems, the impending Italian surrender, I was informed that an invitation I had sent to Prime Minister Winston Churchill to be the guest of the working press of Washington at a luncheon would be accepted.

I need hardly add that I was delighted and gratified. For 8 months, as president of the Overseas Writers, an organization of Washington correspondents who had served as foreign correspondents, I had been trying to get Churchill to come and speak to us but up to then without success.

Nothing happened until September 2. An entry in the diary I kept that year tells of this:

"Friday, September 2.—I had just finished the first page of my column for Saturday—a column on the invasion of Italy—when Jack Winocour (of the British Information Service in Washington) phoned to tell me there was a very good chance Churchill would accept my invitation to address the Overseas Writers and through it the working press. He said that he would call me back, adding that if the answer was 'Yes' the luncheon would have to be held the next day (Saturday). Also, that Churchill first would have to ask President Roosevelt."

That worried me a bit so I phoned Steve Early (Roosevelt's press secretary) and urged him to help us. As it happened, Early hadn't heard about the possibility of a Churchill luncheon with the press. He said he was all for it. (I later discovered that Roosevelt also thought it was a capital idea. The last Churchill press conference had been held in the White House, with Churchill standing on a chair in the President's Office. I was told that neither of the great figures, happy as their relations generally were, liked to perform at a press conference in the presence of the other.)

It must have been shortly before 1 p.m. that Winocour phoned again to say that everything was OK and that Churchill would come to lunch with us at 1:30 p.m. Saturday. I got busy.

There was a room at the hotel to be reserved. There was a list of invited guests to draw up. There was a matter of a cocktail party to precede the luncheon. There was the question of getting out notices. There were, as I later discovered, a thousand other matters to attend to and only 24 hours to take care of them all.

It was soon after Winocour's call that somebody in Churchill's entourage phoned to ask what food would be served. I told him the Statler, where we had tied up the ballroom for the luncheon, planned to serve cold soup, chicken, salad, and ice cream. It was agreed that the Prime Minister would get warm soup, roast beef, salad, and cheese.

The phone rang constantly, and when it wasn't ringing I was busy trying to compose a brief speech of welcome to our illustrious guest.

"Saturday, September 3.—We had engaged a room on the 11th floor to entertain our guests of the speakers' table, and when I got there many already were on hand."

There was Paul Wootton, the secretary of the Overseas Writers, and Eugene Meyer, Ray Swing, Walter Lippmann, Marquis Childs, and Charles G. Ross, representing the Gridiron Club, and Ned Brooks of the standing committee, and Merriman Smith of the White House Correspondents Association, and Felix Cotton of the National Press Club.

Also, Sir Willmott Lewis, of the London Times, and David Bowes-Lyon, brother of the Queen (now the Queen Mother), Sir Ronald Campbell, the British Chargé d'Affaires, and Sir Alexander Cadogan, the permanent Under Secretary of the Foreign Office. Edgar Mowrer arrived but had to be identified by David Bowes-Lyon and myself before the Secret Service men would let him in.

(I later discovered, from the bill sent us by the Statler, that in addition to Churchill and his staff, we also had been hosts to 35 Secret Service men, 32 United States and 3 British. Wartime security was tight, and expensive.)

Soon after 1 p.m., Brendan Bracken (Britain's Minister of Information and a close personal friend of the Prime Minister) arrived, and I had a brief chat with him about the arrangements. Then, around 1:15 in walked Churchill in a cream-colored summer suit, looking very wide of body and face.

I took him around and introduced him to everyone in the room. Later he sat down in a corner with Meyer who tried to dissuade him from publicly denouncing Drew Pearson as apparently Churchill had planned to do for certain "malicious" remarks (the word was Churchill's) Pearson had made about Churchill's second front plans.

Pearson had charged that before invading the Continent, Churchill wanted to wait until the United States could supply 70 percent of the strength because Churchill, realizing that Britain had been bled white in the last war, wanted to keep casualties down in this.

I sat down for a moment with Churchill, and he asked me about the clubs that were participating in the luncheon after I had pointed out to him that this was the first time these clubs had ever joined forces.

It was then time to go downstairs.

Because of wartime precautions we couldn't go down to the mezzanine lobby and on to the ballroom that way. Instead, we took the service elevator to the second floor and through the Statler's huge kitchen to the ballroom.

As soon as we stepped in there was applause, and it continued for some time after we had all taken our places at the head table.

There was one amusing bit of byplay. When we got to the steps leading up to the speaker's table I stepped by to let Churchill precede me.

"The chairman always goes first," he said. So on I went, a little trembly in the knees. But I got to my place and held out the chair on my right for Churchill.

When we sat down Churchill said he didn't want to make a speech but was prepared to answer questions. Written questions, I asked. "No," he said, "let them come from the floor. That will be better."

The waiters brought on the soup. Cold soup for us. Hot soup for the Prime Minister. When the main course came we had chicken. For Churchill, as per orders, there came a large thick slice of roast beef which caused him to whistle—and also to ask for mustard. He then spoke to me again of the Pearson articles and wanted to know if Pearson was in the room. I told him he hadn't come, and he seemed a bit disappointed at getting that information since he was obviously eager to flay Pearson. As it happened, he didn't.

It was a long lunch, and I had an opportunity to talk to Churchill on a variety of subjects. Once I recalled to him his book, "The World Crisis," and said that after reading it I had become fully convinced of the rightness of his Gallipoli plan (to turn the flank of the Central Powers in World War I by a drive through the Dardenelles and establishing contact with Russia).

Pointing to Raymond Swing, the radio broadcaster, who sat on Churchill's right, Churchill said: "He was there on the other (the Turkish side)."

I also mentioned to Churchill that beautiful passage in "The World Crisis" in which he spoke of his visit to Compiègne in June 1918 and how he had taken a walk and thought of the enemy before him.

"Yes," he said, "I remember that very distinctly. And so many of the young men I saw on my visit to the front at that time were destroyed in the (German) drive that followed."

At one point I said: "You won't mind Mr. Prime Minister, if in introducing you I call you a great journalist?"

"Not at all," he replied, obviously pleased.

We talked of Spain.

"You know I changed my mind about that," he said. "At the beginning I was for the rebels. The others had made a mess of it. Besides, I felt that if I had been in Spain, I, as were members of my class, would have been exterminated. But later, after the Germans and Italians began to intervene, I changed my mind. My attitude was determined entirely by considerations of international policy."

"The Spaniards," said Churchill, "are a very bold people."

He said it was his impression that the next stage would be a monarchist restoration and that, at least, would mean the release of political prisoners.

"I'm a royalist, you know," he said.

"Monarchy is all right," I said, "if the monarch does not overstep his limits. That doesn't happen in Britain."

"Yes," said Churchill, grinning, "we know what to do with him if he does, and it can be unpleasant."

At one point Churchill talked to Swing and me about Russia. He said he had got along well with Stalin. Stalin had talked rough, and he had, too, and they understood each other. Swing made some remark about present relations, and Churchill launched into a discussion of the problem. He said he would not and did not hesitate to speak freely on the subject at a secret session of the House of Commons but that, for public consumption, he had to temper his remarks. But the Russians are outspoken, and sometimes it was necessary to be outspoken to them.

When the question of the possibility of the Russians making a separate peace was raised, Churchill said he did not believe they would. He cited a saying that Russia always ends a war on the opposite side from which she begins. That happened in the last war. "And in this war," Churchill noted, "they were on the German side at the beginning, so they'll be on our side at the close."

By this time the moment had arrived to introduce our speaker. I welcomed him not only as a leader of his people but as "one of the ablest practitioners of our craft. We welcome him as a fellow journalist."

I pointed out that before the war, when Churchill was not writing histories, painting pictures, making speeches, and laying bricks, part of his energies were devoted to turning out a fortnightly column on world affairs.

"We think of his speeches," I said, "as inspiring oratory on the road to victory. We newspapermen cannot help but regard them as magnificent reporting. We are even prepared to forgive Mr. Churchill for scooping us from time to time."

I was later told that at this point Churchill turned to Brendan Bracken and asked: "What does scooping mean?"

At another point when I spoke of the ties of blood and language and history and law uniting the British and American peoples, I heard Churchill remark: "Hear, hear."

When I ended, after saying: "Ladies and gentlemen, the Prime Minister of Great Britain, the Right Honorable Winston Churchill," the audience arose and applauded him with great vigor.

He spoke on his feet very briefly. He said he was delighted to find on his desk the invitation to this luncheon since he wanted to meet press members informally and talk to them off the record, and this was a capital way to do it because there was an excellent luncheon thrown in.

He talked of the responsibility of the press and how, in a country which had freedom of the press, discussion of strategic problems, when it takes place at all, should be allsided.

"If we can't have silence," said Churchill, "let us have Babel."

He said he was ready to answer any questions, no holds barred, and as tough as they came he would try to answer them.

Then for more than an hour the questions came. He parried none. He spoke freely and vigorously and with great gusto and high good humor. His words flowed from him in a beautiful flood—well-rounded, eloquent, classic. It was a sheer delight to listen to him, to see the beautiful play of his mind, the precision of his thought, the depth of his feelings. Tense as I was with the responsibilities of the chairmanship I enjoyed every minute of it.

At one point—it was then exactly 3:30 p.m.—I decided we had taken enough of Churchill's time so I announced that there would be just one more question.

"No," said Churchill booming out, "let it go on."

At another point I urged the questioner to speak out loud so he could be heard.

"Loud, but not menacingly," Churchill interjected.

About 10 minutes to 4 he said in a loud stage whisper: "This is the last," after which I closed the meeting.

In the course of the luncheon I had a chance to study Churchill's face. Beautiful skin, smooth and pink like a baby's. No wrinkles. Strong eyes. A strong jaw.

When the photographers came to make pictures he said he would not eat since the photographers have a habit of taking pictures at embarrassing moments, such as when a mouthful of food was suspended in the air at the end of a fork. The photographers—there were four of them—took four pictures each and left.

At the beginning of Churchill's speech the microphone gave out static every time he pounded the table to emphasize a point. He insisted it be taken away.

"What a puny race we've become," he said. "I've spoken in the greatest halls in England and America without such contraptions."

The microphone remained permanently hidden the remainder of the luncheon.

After his introductory remarks Churchill remained seated. That added to the feeling of intimacy of the meeting.

Much of the questioning at the luncheon had to do with immediate issues connected with the war. Some of these issues, such as relations with General Badoglio, of Italy, were ephemeral. Churchill himself in his book on "The Second World War" has given us the authoritative version of those questions. A few of the things Churchill said on that Saturday afternoon in 1943 as he and Roosevelt and the rest of the Allied world waited for the Italian surrender, still have a real point, as reflecting the way Churchill was thinking then.

He made it clear, for instance, that he did not belong to the Morgenthau school (or the English branch headed by Lord Vansittart) that wanted Germany crushed forever. The Germans, he said, have a heavy bill to pay. But he, Churchill, had never attacked anything but Nazi tyranny and Prussian militarism. There had to be tolerance. Who knows what the future will bring?

He defended the Allied deal with Darlan in North Africa which, he said, had saved a lot of lives. He revealed that, contrary to a widespread belief, the Russians, far from disliking the deal, favored it.

"They told me," Churchill said, "that in military affairs it was perfectly all right to walk with the devil and his grandmother."

Churchill also deprecated the idea of forever casting into limbo all those who had been tainted with the Vichy taint. We must have tolerance.

The Prime Minister had arrived at the luncheon minus those big black cigars that had become his hallmark. At one point during the luncheon he turned to me and said: "Cigar?"

That's one thing I had failed to anticipate. But I thought perhaps Eugene Meyer, a cigar addict. would help out. But Meyer revealed that this time he had come without his beloved Belindas and had only picked up a couple of 15-centers at the hotel's cigar counter.

Crestfallen, I went back to tell Churchill the bad news. But the hotel itself came through wonderfully. Having been alerted that Churchill was coming, it had sent a box of Churchill's own favored Havanas down from

New York. So it was with an air of triumph that the maitre d'hotel, who had been hovering in the background, supplied Churchill with the kind of cigar he favored, and in the middle of the press conference he turned to the press and asked permission to light up.

Diary entry, September 4: "At the railroad station I ran into Sir Owen Dixon, the Australian Ambassador (now chief justice of Australia) who wanted to know what Churchill had drunk in the course of the luncheon. I answered: two martinis before lunch, a Scotch with his roast beef, port with his cheese, and a brandy afterward."

Sir Owen revealed that at the Saturday meeting with Churchill at 11 a.m. in the White House (with Churchill still sitting up in bed) the Prime Minister had had two Scotch and sodas with the Dominion representatives.

What a man.

TRIBUTES BY

REPRESENTATIVE W. J. BRYAN DORN

OF SOUTH CAROLINA

Mr. Speaker, Ambassador Adlai Stevenson delivered a magnificent eulogy to Winston Churchill in the Washington National Cathedral on January 28, 1965. I commend Ambassador Stevenson's superb address to the Congress and to the country.

The inspiring address follows:

TEXT OF STEVENSON'S REMARKS

Today we meet in sadness to mourn one of the world's greatest citizens. Sir Winston Churchill is dead. The voice that led nations, raised armies, inspired victories, and blew fresh courage into the hearts of men is silenced. We shall hear no longer the remembered eloquence and wit, the old courage and defiance, the robust serenity of indomitable faith. Our world is thus poorer, our political dialog is diminished, and the sources of public inspiration run more thinly for all of us. There is a lonesome place against the sky.

So we are right to mourn. Yet, in contemplating the life and spirit of Winston Churchill, regrets for the past seem singularly insufficient. One rather feels a sense of thankfulness and encouragement that throughout so long a life, such a full measure of power, virtuosity, mastery, and zest played over our human scene.

Contemplating this completed career, we feel a sense of enlargement and exhilaration. Like a grandeur of power of the masterpieces of art and music, Churchill's life uplifts our hearts and fills us with fresh revelation of the scale and reach of human achievement. We may be sad; but we rejoice as well, as all must rejoice when they "now praise famous men" and see in their lives the full splendor of our human estate.

And regrets for the past are insufficient for another reason. Churchill, the historian, felt the continuity of past and present, the contribution which mighty men and great events make to the future experience of mankind; history's flickering lamp lights up the past and sends its gleams into the future. So the truth of Santayana's dictum, "Those who will not learn from the past are destined to repeat it," Churchill's whole life was witness. It was his lonely voice that in the thirties warned Britain and Europe of the follies of playing all over again the tragedy of disbelief and of unpreparedness. And in the time of Britain's greatest trial he mobilized the English language to inspire his people to historic valor to save their beleaguered island. It was his voice again that helped assemble the great coalition that has kept peace steady through the last decades.

He once said: "We cannot say the past is past without surrendering the future." So today the past of his life and his achievement are a guide and light to the future. And we can only properly mourn and celebrate this mighty man by heeding him as a living influence in the unfolding dramas of our days ahead.

What does he tell us for this obscure future whose outlines we but dimly discern? First, I believe, he would have us reaffirm his serene faith in human freedom and dignity. The love of freedom was not for him an abstract thing but a deep conviction that the uniqueness of man demands a society that gives his capacities full scope. It was, if you like, an aristocratic sense of the fullness and value of life. But he was a profound democrat, and the cornerstone of his political faith, inherited from a beloved father, was the simple maxim—"Trust the people." Throughout his long career, he sustained his profound concern for the well-being of his fellow citizens.

Instinctively, profoundly, the people trusted "good old Winnie," the peer's son. He could lead them in war because he had respected them in peace. He could call for their greatest sacrifices for he knew how to express their deepest dignity—citizens of equal value and responsibility in a free and democratic state.

His crucial part in the founding of the United Nations expressed his conviction that the Atlantic Charter he and President Roosevelt audaciously proclaimed at the height of Hitler's victories would have to be protected throughout the world by institutions embodying the ideal of the rule of law and international cooperation.

For him, humanity, its freedom, its survival, towered above pettier interests—national rivalries, old enmities, the bitter disputes of race and creed. "In victory—magnanimity; in peace—good will" were more than slogans. In fact, his determination to continue in politics after his defeat in 1945, and to toil on in office in the 1950's to the limit of health and endurance, sprang from his belief that he could still "bring nearer that lasting peace which the masses of people of every race and in every land so fervently desire." The great soldier and strategist was a man of peace—and for the most simple reason—his respect, his faith, his compassion for the family of man.

His career saw headlong success and headlong catastrophe. He was at the height. He was flung to the depths. He saw his worst prophecies realized, his worst forebodings surpassed. Yet throughout it all his zest for living, gallantry of spirit, wry humor, and compassion for human frailties took all firmness out of his fortitude and all pomposity out of his dedication.

Churchill's sense of the incomparable value and worth of human existence never faltered, nor the robust courage with which he lived it to the full. In the darkest hour, the land could still be bright, and for him hopes were not deceivers. It was forever fear that was the dupe. Victory at last would always lie with life and faith, for Churchill saw beyond the repeated miseries of human frailty the larger vision of mankind's "upward ascent toward his distant goal."

He used to say that he was half American and all English. But we put that right when the Congress made him an honorary citizen of his mother's native land and we shall always claim a part of him. I remember once years ago during a long visit at his country house he talked proudly of his American Revolutionary ancestors and happily of his boyhood visits to the United States. As I took my leave I said I was going back to London to speak to the English Speaking Union and asked if he had any message for them. "Yes," he said, "tell them that you bring greetings from an English Speaking Union." And I think that perhaps it was to the relations of the United Kingdom and the United States that he made his finest contribution.

In the last analysis, all the zest and life and confidence of this incomparable man sprang, I believe, not only from the rich endowment of his nature, but also from a profound and simple faith in God. In the prime of his powers, confronted with the apocalyptic risks of annihilation, he said serenely: "I do not believe that God has despaired of His children." In old age, as the honors and excitements faded, his resignation had a touching simplicity: "Only faith in a life after death in a brighter world where dear ones will meet again—only that and the measured tramp of time can give consolation."

The great aristocrat, the beloved leader, the profound historian, the gifted painter, the superb politician, the lord of language, the orator, the wit—yes, and the dedicated bricklayer—behind all of them was the man of simple faith, steadfast in defeat, generous in victory, resigned in age, trusting in a loving providence and committing his achievements and his triumphs to a higher power.

Like the patriarchs of old, he waited on God's judgment and it could be said of him—as of the immortals that went before him—that God "magnified him in the fear of his enemies and with his words he made prodigies to cease. He glorified him in the sight of kings and gave him commandments in the sight of his people. He showed him His glory and sanctified him in his faith."

Mr. Speaker, I commend the following very excellent editorial by William Randolph Hearst, Jr., to the attention of my colleagues. This editorial appeared in the Hearst papers throughout the country on January 24, 1965:

THESE REMARKABLE MEN OF HISTORY

(By William Randolph Hearst, Jr., editor in chief, the Hearst newspapers)

The week has been rich in history. We have seen, hopefully and happily, Lyndon Baines Johnson, of Texas, ascend to the pinacle of public office—and then be dramatically whisked to hospital, suffering from a respiratory ailment which his doctors assure us gives no cause for concern.

And we have watched, helplessly and sorrowfully, Winston Spencer Churchill of Britain slip toward the end of life unmatched in greatness.

The origins of these two remarkable men of the 20th century could hardly be more diverse. President Johnson stems from pioneers stock in a harsh and arid region of Texas.

Sir Winston is the product of centuries of aristocracy, steeped in the ancient traditions of Britain—and, we can proudly add, an American mother.

Yet there is no doubt that the two, if history had placed them as contemporaries in office, would have found much in common and a wealth of mutual admiration and respect.

Above all, both would have shared a fierce and identical pride in the parliamentary form of government, common to both our lands, that is the essence of democracy.

The lives of both, in fact, have been greatly influenced by long experience in the deliberative chambers of government. No one has been more inextricably entwined with the British House of Commons than Sir Winston; he is indeed the child of that House, as he has so proudly observed.

And few can compare with Lyndon Johnson as the embodiment of Congress; for years he was the undisputed king of Capitol Hill, transforming the post of Senate majority leader from its hitherto figurehead status to one of unprecedented power and effectiveness.

But what indeed can be said about Sir Winston Churchill to do justice to the man? At the close of two-thirds of the 20th century he so clearly dominates the historical scene as to dwarf his contemporaries and match any of his predecessors.

It is an exceedingly safe bet that no one of his stature will arise, anywhere in the world, during the lifetimes of any of us.

During the past week, moreover, the world watched him wage as valiant a battle as any he has engaged in during his brave and colorful life. Felled by a stroke at the age of 90, his great heart has fought on and on to the astonishment of his doctors and to the fervent prayers of his family and friends.

We venture to guess, however, that this sheer bulldog tenacity comes as little or no surprise to Adolf Hitler's former generals or any other foes he vanquished but a short time ago.

A junior officer always in the thick of combat, a dashing war correspondent—and hair-breadth escape artist—brilliant parliamentary debater, talented painter, patient bricklayer, master politician, visionary statesman, superb historian, mighty war leaders, and a dignified and sentimental gentleman who wept when the ragged, bomb-battered Londoners cheered him during his tours of their devastated streets and homes—all these and more are Winston Churchill.

History rolls inexorably on, but we shall never see his like again.

The story of the Man of the Century has undoubtedly been in President Johnson's thoughts during this past week. L.B.J. has always been influenced by greatness and a sense of purpose in others; hence his devotion to the memories of Andrew Jackson, Abraham Lincoln, Sam Rayburn, and Franklin Roosevelt.

A man so rooted in democratic tradition could not, then, fail to include Sir Winston among his mentors.

Both men elevated the practice of politics to unequaled heights. For Sir Winston, politics meant duty, in the manner of his forebears the Dukes of Marlborough.

Lyndon Johnson has always felt that the art of politics transcends all others; that only through politics can diverse views among factions and nations be reconciled.

We can wonder, though, what else besides the example of Churchill has occupied the President's thoughts during this momentous week. The explosion of an atomic bomb in the remote fastness of Communist China? The enigmas of Kosygin and Brezhnev, and perhaps Charles de Gaulle? or Lee Harvey Oswald and a $12.78 mail-order rifle?

We may never know which formed the President's preoccupation. For this tall, gregarious Texan is now the loneliest American. But there are many things about Lyndon Johnson that we do know—and the time is certainly appropriate to appraise him on the basis of these once again.

First, it is somewhat paradoxical that whereas L.B.J. garnered the greatest electoral majority of any President, he remains a largely unknown quantity to vast numbers of Americans outside Washington, D.C., and Texas.

He does not reflect the youth and magnetism of Jack Kennedy, the military fame of Dwight Eisenhower nor the crispness of Harry Truman. He comes closest, perhaps, to Franklin Roosevelt; but even there the similarity is by no means close.

Yet, in time, I think L.B.J. will become one of the Nation's best known Presidents, not only through communication channels, but through his accomplishments.

For today America is presented with a rare combination: A President with total experience of every nook, cranny, and pitfall of Congress—and with a congressional makeup, in House and Senate, overwhelmingly disposed to favor his programs.

The Congress, moreover, likes Lyndon Johnson. He is privy to its most inner councils; he can be described as a charter member of its establishment.

The congressional system is dominated by the committee chairmen—and this formidable band of Representatives and Senators feel at home with L.B.J. as perhaps with no Chief Executive before him.

As the "master compromiser" L.B.J. has earned the exasperations, admiration, enmity and unswerving loyalty of members of both parties. It is said that no one ever won an argument with him. His secret weapon, it is said, is a total aversion to division and rancor of any kind.

He has sometimes been accused, especially during his Senate tenure, of being too closely allied to Texas oil and gas interests. But L.B.J. shrewdly knew that a politician's first duty is to survive and stay in office—otherwise he is rendered ineffective and his goals of a Great Society or anything else become academic dreams.

He is the middle-of-the-roader who has always had to walk a political tightrope in his home State, a turbulent center of Democratic politics.

For years he was subject to the relentless hostility of the liberal faction of the Texas Democratic Party—yet now that he is in office he is instigating virtually everything that faction has advocated.

He is like his enormous State, both of the South and of the West. Yet few who know Lyndon Johnson will deny his broad sense of national consciousness; and as Senate majority leader the problems he faced and tackled were, of necessity, national rather than regional.

Again those who know him will tell you he is equally at home at a labor union get-together or at an ambassador's salon. "O' Lyndon," an acquaintance once observed, "can talk to you on any level you like." And it is true that L.B.J. has an equal liking for the rough clothes of his ranch country and for Saville Row suits.

He is the Mr. Democrat who for many years loyally supported the foreign policies of President Eisenhower's administration—because he felt it was his duty to do so, because it was essential that the Nation present a unified front to friends and enemies abroad.

He is the former unchallenged leader of the Senate who accepted the Vice-Presidency—against the advice of many closest to him—under the former junior Senator from Masachusetts. L.B.J. did this out of a sense of duty and of loyalty to his party.

Yes, I feel Winston Churchill and Lyndon Johnson would have gotten along well together. The sole holder of honorary American citizenship and the big Texan from the southwest plains would have proved a formidable team.

Thus the curtain rises on a new act in the life of one man and slowly falls on the final, mortal scene of another.

TRIBUTE BY

REPRESENTATIVE JOHN M. MURPHY

OF NEW YORK

Mr. Speaker, I include the following verse composed by Vernon Boyce Hampton of Staten Island, N.Y., on the occasion of the famous Churchill-Roosevelt conference of December 22, 1941. Churchill many times on his secret trips to America stopped on Staten Island, N.Y., and proceeded by train to Washington. With his passing, I feel it is fitting to rekindle these lines at this time:

Churchill Is Here

(By Vernon Boyce Hampton)

The dust of evening softly falls,
On sheltered cot and mansion,
An ending welcomed gratefully,
At close of Yuletide shopping.

Throngs hurry home,
Glad to exchange December night's crisp cold,
For fireside warmth,
An ambered room,
Companionship,
And radio's caroled song.

Peace upon earth and love are mounted here,
In quiet homes:
The season's sanctity is its own blessing,
Veiling the scar of war.
And dimming our bleak questioning,
Since death has struck.
Reality is just beyond the tinsel.

Our programed music stops,
Abruptly,
And a staccato voice,
Sharp as a sword, unsheathed,
Exclaims with scarce a pause excitedly:
"Churchill is here * * *
Arrived in Washington * * *
Tonight."

A thrill that stays our passion,
Holds listeners everywhere transfixed,
Startled amazed,
And cheered:
The wonder and the daring,
Of the dare,
Strike awe in every heart.

Here is a man with rigid rod,
Of upright purpose,
Challenging the womb of time,
To bring to birth,
The vanished freedoms lost awhile.

Facing what other men dared not,
He came alone,
To bind the Anglo-Saxon world in one.
An hour he flew in space,
And spanned the latitudes,
For history to record salvation of a race.

Dunkirk behind.
And London blitzed and burned,
And of the future, no one knows,
What turn the wheel of infirm fortune
May reveal.
Yet here he is,
The man of destiny.

Pearl Harbor but a minute past,
And here is action:
Into this act we read,
The planning of the course,
To Victory:
Now Nations live,
That, moments since, despaired.

His daring quickens,
All the wheels of our great "arsenal,"
And thus,
Foredooms our foes.

Great Winston Churchill,
Here we honor you.
This is your home,
In part,
For Yankee blood courses your veins,
And heart meets heart,
In Freedom's cause anew.

The wild young Eagle of the Stars and Stripes,
Harks to your call, O Man of Britain,
And with spreading wings,
Screams to the fray,
Nothing can cease the battle,
Till the hosts of tyranny,
Are laid,
In vauntless dust,
Defeat and doom.

We fight your fight and guard your home,
In Britain's Isle, as here,
Home of our Freedom's birth.

We stand with thee till death,
These Anglo-Saxon States,
Born in fire of battle,
With our own, * * *
(A family quarrel, that ancient one,
Long healed).
Freemen we stand today,
And none can disunite,
Nations so wed:
We stand with thee!

The thrill of this great hour remains,
As airwaves break the news again: "Churchill is here!"
And we listen, listen, listen,
To the rhythmic repetition:
"Churchill," "Churchill," "Churchill here!"
Anthemed for the world to hear.

The emotion of the moment does not wane;
The buildup to this climax is too strong,
For quick release,
Now we can hope and love and live
As Freedom's pawn,
In spite of war and the unknown:
Churchill is here,
Symbol of Victory!

TRIBUTE BY

REPRESENTATIVE GEORGE P. MILLER

OF CALIFORNIA

Mr. Speaker, the entire world was saddened by the death of Sir Winston Churchill. No man in our lifetime symbolizes both the tenacity and courage of a people struggling against tyranny for the preservation of their democratic way of life.

We Americans certainly join with our English friends in mourning the death of their great hero whom we can also claim as an honorary citizen of our country.

One of my constituents, Mr. John J. Williamson, of Alameda, Calif., was motivated to put his thoughts on this sad occasion into verse. Because I believe that the words of Mr. Williamson appropriately pay tribute to the late Prime Minister of England, I am pleased to insert this poem:

Sir Winnie

(An original unpublished poem dedicated to our English friends and continued good relations between England and the United States of America)

A mighty Warrior, has breathed His very Last!
Like distant Thunder of War Drums, faded with; Reverberations of the Past
No longer Bestires at rumble of Caisson, nor hears; Measured tread of Boot
Those ghostly Echoes of a freedom won, It's Heroes Death; War's "Fruit"!

In Requiem, let not; Bombs speak and Rockets Soar
Stay the Machine Gun's bark, noise of Tank and Jet Plane's Roar!
Count only, stacked Arms of those, That Lie
The rows of countless Dead, Their Living Pray; Often Cry!

Proclaim, that this gallant Soldier/Statesman was; A peaceful Man
True and Righteous Purpose, His simple and singular Plan
Freedom of free People; "Sir Winnie's" cherished and avowed Goal
Determination to lead the Way, to Victory; In steadfast Role!

His "Lethal" Weapons, the timely Gesture and appealing Voice
A friendly Expression, at Time and Place; Not always by Choice!
The "Armor" with which, His body was; So admirably Gird
Were the Promises kept, either in spoken or written Word!

Yet, His was the Strength, Tyrants; Had shunned and forsook
The "Word" Teachings and Truth of; The "Good" Book
With It's Power, to Level; All Armies of the Land
Crush the Forces of Evil, wherever and whatever; The Demand!

This great Man, destined to become Legend, tho' deemed; Essence of Fact
Was quick to Perceive and Comprehend; Quicker to Act!
His Dignity and calm Reserve, exemplified; The Decent and Fine
Be-spoke of Noble Character, "Champagne" 'Midst; Vintage Wine!

Like a Duke of Wellington, Lord Nelson and Kitchener; Rolled into One
Born of American Mother, He proved to be; Britain's finest Son
Displaying the tenacity of a Bull Dog in Prize Ring
He had the Courage of, the English Lion; Historic and Traditional Thing!

As British as, Orange Marmalade; Tea and Kippers
He was "Homespun", liked His "Easy" Chair, Cigar; Robe and Slippers
A Friend of All Who, shunned the "Mean" yet; Knew the "Ing"
A Loyal Subject of His, Benevolent; Queen and King!

Symbol of English speaking Peoples; One Accord
Their Loyalty and undying Friendship toward,
A staunch Ally America; That "Provident" Land
Whose Own "Queen" Lady Liberty, stands guard; Torch in Hand!

Mean't to be the "Floating Log" on a Sea of Depair
The last "Step" left of, a crumbling; Stair!
He, the Twig bent double, an England; That wouldn't Falter or End
Keeping Faith with the Unborn, knowing they'd Live; On His Struggle depend!

Yet, He was but a Catalyst, blending; Simple Hope with Faith of Man
In God's "Scheme" of things, part of; Overall Plan!
Mere Steward, called upon; To Perform and Attain
The Victory, a righteous Cause and good Purpose; Must Gain!

Unshaken and Immovable, in Path of; War's "Hurricane"
He exemplified Forces of Good, that the Evil; Disdain!
Tho' not a God, just Human and; Of Flesh and Blood
A Pawn of Fate, struggling in the Maelstrom of; Battle "Flood"!

He was the "Wallow" and "Steam" of a Jungle; Dense
The "Bee" in Port Moresby's stinging; Island Offense!
The Sweat and Tears, the Drive and "Goad"
Willingness to build, Burma's Hellish tho'; Vital Road!

He was "Tommies", Aussies, Anzacs, Cannucks, and Scots
Nemesis of Hitlers, Mussolinis, Tyrants, and all; Their Plots!
He was the "Silver" of the Thames, London's Fog; Charm of Its Bridge and Tower
He was "Great Britain", through and through; In Its "Finest Hour"!

Yet, He too was a Person, subject to all; Human Ills
Victim of Fevers, Aches and Pains, the Remedys and; Colored Pills
Feeling the Heartaches, Hopes and Longings; Tears and All
Searching for Happiness, hidden in terrible War; Under dismal Pall!

He was the inconvenience of "Queues", Rations and Petrol Stamps
The Smile in "Ducks", Tea and Crumpets; "Light" of Coal Miner's Lamps
Reminder of the Flowers, the Countryside "Scent"; Lush of green Grass too
The "Bat" and "Ball" at Wimbledon's Matches; "Cricket" everyone knew!

He was the "Gleam" from the White Cliffs of Dover
The Siren's "Sound" as Buzz-Bombs; Came over
Westminster's "In" Spire, the tolling Bell's "Chime"
"Refuge" of Air Raid Shelter, to run to, dive in; So little Time!

The living "Fire" of Spitfire Planes; Slowing a Panzer Drive
The "Guts" to take It, and dish It out; In order to Survive!
He was the "Parch and Thirst" of Desert Battle
The "Dimming" Light and dying Gasp of; Death's Rattle!

The "Rock" at Malta "Trial" of Tobruk; Epic of El Alamein!
The Point of Victory's "V", Wings of; Its "Plane"
Both the Failure and the "Save"; In sacrifice of Dunkirk
The Royal Navy's "Miracle", by Fate's; Strange Quirk!

"There" in the Courage and Determination at Coventry
Providing the Will to stay, rebuild; Not Flee!
He was a "Might", in the mightiest Effort to prevail
Strength of a Thousand Armies, all the Fleets; That Sail!

He was the "Die Cast," Delivered and Damned of "D" day's; Normandy Beach
The Drownings and Despair, The Deploy and the Devil; To Breach!
His was the "Wounds" and the Cries; The dying of Men
The Laughter and Shouts of Joy knowing, they'd never Retreat; Nor be defeated again!

He was the "Calm" War's Peace after "Storm," "Sport of Kings" Epsom Downs
Brightest Jewel's "Sparkle" in the Royal Crowns
The "Whimsey" in polished Poetry of a Bard
Grandeur and Precision, in change of, Royal Palace Guard!

His promise of "Blood, Toil, Tears, and Sweat"
Comrades in Arms will long remember, admonishing Sons; Not to Forget!
For He exemplified the inherent "Goodness" of Man
A Desire to Live in Peace, with His Brothers, when and wherever He can!

His Words will Echo loud in History's Halls
As the tolling "Peals" of "Big Ben" falls—
Upon the Youth of future Generations
Calling upon Them, to Emulate great Courage; That saved a Nation!

Tho' future Hitlers, Musso's, and Tojos; Might Rage
While Fortunes of War, They measure and Gauge
His calm Determination, remembered Throughout the Land
Will give Credence to the Conviction and Its Fulfillment:
"There will Always be 'Sir Winnie' and an England" ! !

—JOHN J. WILLIAMSON.

TRIBUTE BY

REPRESENTATIVE COMPTON I. WHITE, JR.

OF IDAHO

Mr. Speaker, the day before yesterday, the world paid its last respects to one of the mighty figures of this century—Sir Winston Leonard Spencer Churchill.

I would like to include an editorial written by William Johnston of the Lewiston, Idaho, Morning Tribune on January 25, 1965, in tribute to this fine English gentleman, honorary citizen of the United States, and certainly man of this century.

The editorial follows:

Churchill: Man of This Century

The inexorable tides of time have brought a whole new generation to manhood since Sir Winston Churchill stood at the summit of his powers as the stirring symbol of freedom's defiance of tyranny.

How can a youth born in that fateful time of Western civilization's darkest peril fully comprehend that he has witnessed now the departure of one of the giants of the earth?

Yet, even the children of this post-Churchillian era do sense that the feeble, fading man, who lingered on to the age of 90 after all his deeds were done, was one whose like they will never see again. They know he was an unrivaled hero of their parents. Their history books are largely his biographies. Even these youngsters know, vaguely but certainly, that Winston Churchill was the dominant figure of the 20th century.

He was perhaps the most multifaceted genius yet produced on this planet. He was a fearless soldier, a superior military strategist, a talented war correspondent, a capable painter, an excellent biographer, an eminent historian, a superb orator, and one of the greatest statesmen in the whole, crowded history of the globe.

This century has hurtled many men to the heights of greatness—Gandhi, Roosevelt, MacArthur, Truman, Kennedy, and many more. Yet, the historians of future generations may chiefly ponder what other mortal besides Albert Einstein, perhaps, can be ranked second in the era's annals of greatness. Even now there can be little doubt as to whom will be ranked first.

What were the secrets of this transcendent personality? How did such a man evolve to lead the Western World, just when he was needed most, to deliverance from the ruthless ambition of totalitarian fanatics?

Fortunately for posterity, the major ingredients of his greatness are posted plainly in his stirring words and astonishing deeds. He was a remarkably direct man, for all his complexities of talents and purposes. He seldom doubted that he knew the route his countrymen and the world should go. He never hesitated to proclaim his conclusions. The story of his life is written plain and clear, and a most instructive and inspiring story it is.

As a child, he was particularly rebellious. "I used to think him the naughtiest little boy in the whole world," one governess related. He had no taste for the rigid discipline or classical orientation of his early school years at Brighton. His boundless energy could never be contained. His instinct for argument constantly exploded into conflict with authority. Arithmetic and Latin baffled and bored him. He survived these subjects chiefly by cramming enough information by rote into his phenomenal memory to carry him precariously through examinations. But he did begin at Brighton and later at Harrow Military School the nourishment of one abiding enthusiasm which sustained him all his life—and which quite possibly saved the Western World from Nazi conquest. He later wrote:

"By being so long in the lowest form I gained an immense advantage over the cleverer boys. They all went on learning Latin and Greek and splendid things like that. But I was taught English. Mr. Somervell—a delightful man, to whom my debt is great—was charged with the duty of teaching the stupidest boys the most disregarded thing; namely, to write mere English. He knew how to do it. He taught it as no one else has ever taught it. As I remained in the third form three times as long as anyone else, I had three times as much of it. I learnt it thoroughly. Thus, I got into my bones the essential structure of the ordinary English sentence—which is a noble thing. And when in after years my schoolfellows who had won prizes and distinction for writing such beautiful Latin poetry and pithy Greek epigrams had to come down again to common English to earn their living or make their way, I did not feel at any disadvantage.

"I would make them all learn English; and then I would let the clever ones learn Latin as an honor, and Greek as a treat. But the only thing I would whip them for would be for not knowing English. I would whip them hard for that"

Churchill left Harrow in 1892. That was a very long time ago as measured in the struggles and concerns of mankind. The passion for English and the love of military strategy he nourished there were considered quite insufficient for a time as a foundation for university training.

But the whole Western World was to listen, anxiously and intently, on June 4, 1940, after France had fallen to the Nazi panzer divisions, as Churchill demonstrated anew that "the ordinary English sentence—is a noble thing":

"Even though large tracts of Europe and many old and famous States have fallen or may fall into the grip of the Gestapo and all the odious apparatus of Nazi rule, we shall not flag or fail. We shall go on to the end, we shall fight in France, we shall fight in the seas and oceans, we shall fight with growing confidence and growing strength in the air, we shall defend our island, whatever the cost may be, we shall fight on the beaches, we shall fight on the landing grounds, we shall fight in the fields and in the streets, we shall fight in the hills; we shall never surrender, and even if, which I do not for a moment believe, this island or a large part of it were subjugated and starving, then our Empire beyond the seas, armed and guarded by the British Fleet, would carry on the struggle until, in God's good time, the New World, with all its power and might, steps forth to the rescue and the liberation of the old."

His majestic words, rolling like distant thunder, convinced England and perhaps America that the British were invincible. Even Adolf Hitler seemed convinced, for he never struck across the English Channel at a virtually defenseless island. Churchill himself was not deluded by his oratory. Years later he chided Hitler for stupidity in waiving his best chance to win the war.

Churchill's unbridled ambition is legendary, of course. His ego was monumental. As a brash young war correspondent, Churchill hesitated not a moment to criticize in detail the military strategies of seasoned generals commanding British battles in Africa. He cheered on troops in battle with the observation that "you are making excellent copy for my paper." Yet, he distinguished himself for bravery on the battlefield, and the annoyance he created always was tinged with respect. One of his early critics observed that Churchill "was born a demagog and happens to know it," and added that "at dinner he talks and talks, and you can hardly tell when he leaves off quoting his one idol, Macaulay, and begins quoting his other, Winston Churchill."

He never indulged himself in modesty and only tolerated those who "shrank from greatness." His successor as Prime Minister, Clement Attlee, was the butt of some of the most scorching Churchillian wit on this score. "He has much to be modest about," said Churchill. And again: "He is a sheep in sheep's clothing."

Yet, there was sympathy and understanding in him that somehow transformed his ambition and egotism into a personification of the aspirations of all the scattered millions he led and inspired. The caustic, dogmatic aristocrat he surely was. Yet, he also was "good old Winnie," the beloved, human, intensely personal leader of the least distinguished fighter for freedom.

Churchill's crowning triumph—the crushing defeat of Germany and Japan in World War II—was shadowed by two keen disappointments. One was that his comrade, confidante and sometimes competitor in arms, President Franklin D. Roosevelt, died shortly before the first atomic bomb brought Japan to its knees. The other was that Churchill himself was voted out of office by his countrymen after Hitler had been defeated but before the war in the Far East had been won.

He later described his premonition of the British election results of July 1945:

"On the whole I accepted the view of the party managers, and went to bed in the belief that the British people would wish me to continue my work. My hope was that it would be possible to reconstitute the national coalition government in the proportions of the new House of Commons. Thus slumber. However, just before dawn I woke suddenly with a sharp stab of almost physical pain. A hitherto subconscious conviction that we were beaten broke forth and dominated my mind. All the pressure of great events, on and against which I had mentally so long maintained my flying speed, would cease and I should fall. The power to shape the future would be denied me. The knowledge and experience I had gathered, the authority and good will I had gained in so many countries would vanish. I was discontented at the prospect, and turned over at once to sleep again."

Churchill was ever discontented with any suggestion that he would lose or fail. Yet, when disappointment or disaster struck, he never whimpered or wavered. His enemies might defeat him, but he never doubted that he would destroy them in the end. His own countrymen might abandon him, but he never regarded this as repudiation—just a temporary aberration. He had studied enough history, forecast enough history, and made enough history to know beyond any deep doubt or posture of humility that his own place in history was secure.

Winston Leonard Spencer Churchill, the only honorary citizen of the United States and the greatest wartime leader who ever led his beloved Britain, is dead. The world cannot expect to see his like again.—B.J.

TRIBUTE BY

SENATOR E. L. BARTLETT

OF ALASKA

Mr. President, on January 28 at Washington Cathedral, there was held a memorial service for Sir Winston Churchill. Some 3,500 foreign diplomats, Government officials, and ordinary citizens attended.

In the course of the service U.S. Ambassador to the United Nations Adlai Stevenson delivered a memorial address. Many of us in the Washington area heard portions of Ambassador Stevenson's remarks replayed over radio last evening. In this morning's Washington Post the full text is printed.

I ask that this deeply moving tribute to the greatest Englishman of the century be included in these tributes, as follows:

Memorial Address by Ambassador Stevenson

Today we meet in sadness to mourn one of the world's greatest citizens. Sir Winston Churchill is dead. The voice that led nations, raised armies, inspired victories, and blew fresh courage into the hearts of men is silenced. We shall hear no longer the remembered eloquence and wit, the old courage and defiance, the robust serenity of indomitable faith. Our world is thus poorer, our political dialog is diminished, and the sources of public inspiration run more thinly for all of us. There is a lonesome place against the sky.

So we are right to mourn. Yet, in contemplating the life and spirit of Sir Winston Churchill, regrets for the past seem singularly insufficient. One rather feels a sense of thankfulness and encouragement that throughout so long a life, such a full measure of power, virtuosity, mastery, and zest played over our human scene.

Contemplating this completed career, we feel a sense of enlargement and exhilaration. Like the grandeur and power of the masterpieces of art and music, Churchill's life uplifts our hearts and fills us with fresh revelation of the scale and reach of human achievement. We may be sad; but we rejoice as well, as all must rejoice when they "now praise famous men" and see in their lives the full splendor of our human estate.

And regrets for the past are insufficient for another reason. Churchill, the historian, felt the continuity of past and present, the contribution which mighty men and great events make to the future experience of mankind; history's "flickering lamp" lights up the past and sends its gleams into the future. So to the truth of Santayana's dictum, "Those who will not learn from the past are destined to repeat it," Churchill's whole life was witness. It was his lonely voice that in the thirties warned Britain and Europe of the follies of playing all over again the tragedy of disbelief and of unpreparedness. And in the time of Britain's greatest trial he mobilized the English language to inspire his people to historic valor to save their beleaguered island. It was his voice again that helped assemble the great coalition that has kept peace steady through the last decades.

He once said: "We cannot say the past is past without surrendering the future." So today the "past" of his life and his achievement are a guide and light to the future. And we can only properly mourn and celebrate this mighty man by heeding him as a living influence in the unfolding dramas of our days ahead.

What does he tell us for this obscure future whose outlines we but dimly discern? First, I believe, he would have us reaffirm his serene faith in human freedom and dignity. The love of freedom was not for him an abstract thing but a deep conviction that the uniqueness of man demands a society that gives his capacities full scope. It was, if you like, an aristocratic sense of the fullness and value of life. But he was a profound democrat, and the cornerstone of his political faith, inherited from a beloved father, was the simple maxim—"Trust the people." Throughout his long career, he sustained his profound concern for the well-being of his fellow citizens.

Instinctively, profoundly, the people trusted "good old Winnie," the peer's son. He could lead them in war because he had respected them in peace. He could call for their greatest sacrifices for he knew how to express their deepest dignity—citizens of equal value and responsibility in a free and democratic state.

His crucial part in the founding of the United Nations expressed his conviction that the Atlantic Charter he and President Roosevelt audaciously proclaimed at the height of Hitler's victories would have to be protected throughout the world by institutions embodying the ideal of the rule of law and international cooperation.

For him, humanity, its freedom, its survival, towered above pettier interests—national rivalries, old enmities, the bitter disputes of race and creed. "In victory—magnanimity; in peace—good will" were more than slogans. In fact, his determination to continue in politics after his defeat in 1945 and to toil on in office in the 1950's to the limit of health and endurance sprang from his belief that he could still "bring nearer that lasting peace which the masses of people of every race and in every land so fervently desire." The great soldier and strategist was a man of peace—and for the most simple reason—his respect, his faith, his compassion for the family man.

His career saw headlong success and headlong catastrophe. He was at the height. He was flung to the depths. He saw his worst prophecies realized, his worst forebodings surpassed. Yet throughout it all his zest for living, gallantry of spirit, wry humor, and compassion for human frailties took all firmness out of his fortitude and all pomposity out of his dedication.

Chuchill's sense of the incomparable value and worth of human existence never faltered, nor the robust courage with which he lived it to the full. In the darkest hour, the land could still be bright, and for him hopes were not deceivers. It was forever fear that was the dupe. Victory at last would always lie with life and faith, for Churchill saw beyond the repeated miseries of human frailty the larger vision of mankind's "upward ascent toward his distant goal."

He used to say that he was half American and all English. But we put that right when the Congress made him an honorary citizen of his mother's native land and we shall always claim a part of him. I remember once years ago during a long visit at his country house he talked proudly of his American Revolutionary ancestors and happily of his boyhood visits to the United States. As I took my leave I said I was going back to London to speak to the English Speaking Union and asked if he had any message for them. "Yes," he said, "tell them that you bring greetings from an English Speaking Union." And I think that perhaps it was to the relations of the United Kingdom and the United States that he made his finest contribution.

In the last analysis, all the zest and life and confidence of this incomparable man sprang, I believe, not only from the rich endowment of his nature, but also from a profound and simple faith in God. In the prime of his powers, confronted with the apocalyptic risks of annihilation, he said serenely: "I do not believe that God has despaired of his children." In old age, as the honors and excitements faded, his resignation had a touching simplicity: "Only faith in a life after death in a brighter world where dear ones will meet again—only that the measured tramp of time can give consolation."

The great aristocrat, the beloved leader, the profound historian, the gifted painter, the superb politician, the lord of language, the orator, the wit—yes, and the dedicated bricklayer—behind all of them was the man of simple faith, steadfast in defeat, generous in victory, resigned in age, trusting in a loving providence, and committing his achievements and his triumphs to a higher power.

Like the patriarch of old, he waited on God's judgment and it could be said of him—as of the immortals that went before him—that God "magnified him in the fear of his enemies and with his words he made prodigies to cease. He glorified him in the sight of kings and gave him commandments in the sight of his people. He showed him his glory and sanctified him in his faith."

TRIBUTE BY

REPRESENTATIVE WILLIAM H. NATCHER

OF KENTUCKY

Mr. Speaker, I include herewith an editorial entitled "A Very Great Man Has Gone to His Reward," which appeared in the January 25, 1965, issue of the Madisonville Messenger, of Madisonville, Ky.

The editorial is as follows:

A Very Great Man Has Gone to His Reward

The stout, courageous heart of Winston Churchill has pumped its last and you can almost see this great man striding up a sunlit avenue to immortality, waving the famous V-for-victory sign to admiring millions.

Seldom is the printed word inadequate to any momentous occasion—solemn or joyful. But only the eloquence and the stirring voice of Winnie himself could adequately portray the emotions of the free world today—the sadness that he is no longer with us, the pride and thanksgiving that he was, indeed, very much with us in one of the world's most perilous hours.

Every American must mourn the passing of the only honorary American citizen, this saucy, tenacious bulldog who singlehandedly turned Britain's despair first into desperation and then into do-or-die spirit when the little isles stood alone against the mighty German war machine.

Who can doubt that it was Prime Minister Churchill, scowling across the narrow English Channel at a mad Hitler, who turned the tide back toward freedom when it seemed that all the lights were going off all over the world?

Here was, precisely and beyond any doubt, the human embodiment of John Bull—as never perhaps there has been a living Uncle Sam. Here was an alternately smiling and glowering countenance and a magnificent voice which lifted the British Isles out of a pit of certain disaster.

To paraphrase his own words: "Never in the field of human conflict have so many owed so much to one man." For it was he who inspired the British people to superhuman efforts in the darkest days of World War II—such miracles as the evacuation of Dunkirk, the Royal Air Force victories in the sky against 7-to-1 odds and the resolution and courage of the British populace in the face of constant bombings.

When France fell, and the Battle of Britain was about to begin, Churchill uttered these prophetic words to his people—and to the world:

"The Battle of France is over, the Battle of Britain is about to begin. Upon this battle depends the survival of Christian civilization. Upon it depends our own British life and the long continuity of our empire.

"The whole fury and might of the enemy must very soon be turned on us. Hitler knows that he will have to break us in these islands or lose the war. If we can stand up to him, all Europe may be free and the life of the world may move forward into broad, sunlit uplands.

"But if we fail, then the whole world—including the United States, including all that we have known and cared for—will sink into the abyss of a new Dark Age. Let us therefore brace ourselves to our duty, so bear ourselves that, if the British Empire and its Commonwealth live for a thousand years, men will still say: 'This was their finest hour'."

And, truly, it was their finest hour. Christian civilization marveled—and took new heart—at the indomitable courage of the British people.

Here, indeed, was the turning point for the powerful German war machine. And none understood it better than "Corporal Hitler"—as Churchill contemptuously called the Nazi dictator. For in the latter period of the war, Hitler literally frothed at the mouth at the mere mention of Sir Winston's name, or the sight of his picture. Adolf was sure that, except for Winston Churchill, the German hordes would have ridden roughshod across all Europe and even the world.

"Blood, tears, toil, and sweat" were all that Churchill promised the British people in their dark days. "We shall fight in the fields, in the streets, and from the rooftops—and we shall never surrender."

But he made their victories more joyful, too, with words like those uttered at the close of the fateful year 1941, recalling that surrendering French generals had predicted that "in 3 weeks England will have her neck wrung like a chicken." Said Winnie:

Some chicken. Some neck. These are words that will ring forever in the history of human greatness and valor.

Here was a man. A cigar-smoking, hard drinking cavalry officer, polo-player, scholar, journalist, foreign correspondent, author, artist, bricklayer, hunter, fisherman—a man who held virtually every important position in the British Government, truly the first statesman of the world. Here, too, was an embodied testimony to the jungle life of politics. For in his hour of victory the people turned him out, not for his own failings but for partisan political reasons.

Here was a man who lived a full life and savored it all, who achieved far more than his allotted three score and ten. It has often been said that man's highest ambition should be to leave the world a little better than he found it. If ever a man exceeded this ambition, certainly Winston Churchill went far beyond such high calling.

His stirring oratory and his inspiring, cigar-crunching countenance, will arouse and encourage freemen so long as there is life on our planet.

We like to believe that there is a Valhalla to which great men—they of uncommon valor and purpose—go when they shuffle off the mortal coil. In this belief, there is no doubt that all that is immortal of Winston Leonard Spencer Churchill dwells now in such a place, in a seat of highest honor.

Grieve not for this great man. Only thank God that such men appear at the times when they are most needed. May it ever be so.

Mr. Speaker, I also include an editorial entitled "Churchill Was Dominant Figure of World War II," which appeared in the January 27, 1965, issue of the Leitchfield Gazette, of Leitchfield, Ky.

The editorial is as follows:

Churchill Was Dominant Figure of World War II

The death of Sir Winston Churchill serves to recall the days of decision after the Nazis and Fascists provoked World War II in 1939. Churchill was one of the few leaders in the free world who saw the danger of totalitarian government and the practical certainty all-out war was unavoidable.

The senselessness and utter tragedy of war was so generally recognized by civilized society during the period prior to the outbreak that many of us refused to believe the signs that pointed inevitably toward another holocaust involving far more casualties than the 1914–18 conflict.

The people and most leaders felt as Neville Chamberlain did in 1938 that war could be avoided by allowing part of the Nazi demands. However, not Winston Churchill who clearly saw and just as clearly enunciated the danger and folly of a policy of appeasement that was leading to a Second World War just two decades after World War I was fought "to end all wars."

When disbelief finally was replaced by realization that another war had come, a fatalistic kind of hopelessness descended on many leaders. After the fall of France, this hopelessness deepened, but most who lived through those times can remember the Churchillian words ringing above the gloom, promising eventual victory for the civilization that was threatened and defeat for the brutal forces that were tormenting Europe.

It was natural for England to turn to Churchill when the war effort appeared to be failing. Immediately after he became Prime Minister, a new spirit permeated the island kingdom. No one in his right mind expected the English to capitulate when days were darkest, but the people needed a lift, and Churchill added his spark to the indomitable will that carried a nation through critical times.

The world has paid tribute to Churchill who was a perfect symbol of the spirit that meets and conquers fear and danger. His oratory would have sounded pompous coming from others, yet coming from him it seemed appropriate and undoubtedly helped rally the strength and steel the fortitude of a people under constant threat of death and destruction.

It is an unforgettable experience for those who lived during a period that saw the drama of the Churchill years. Perhaps never again will such a stand as that made by England be seen, because now all-out wars probably will be measured in minutes or hours at most. The total destruction now possible in all-out war also could preclude any embarkation upon such a suicidal course, and figures of Churchill's stature may never again dominate the scene of nations fighting for existence.

TRIBUTE BY

REPRESENTATIVE JOE L. EVINS

OF TENNESSEE

Mr. Speaker, in a perceptive commentary on "Remarkable Men of History," William Randolph Hearst, Jr., observes that President Lyndon B. Johnson and Sir Winston Churchill shared "a fierce and identical pride in the parliamentary form of government, common to both our lands, that is the essence of democracy."

Important lessons for our time are underlined in this study of America's Chief Executive and the late British statesman by the editor in chief of the Hearst newspapers.

The article follows:

Remarkable Men of History

(By William Randolph Hearst, Jr.)

This week has been rich in history. We have seen, hopefully and happily, Lyndon Baines Johnson, of Texas, ascend to the pinnacle of public office—and then be dramatically whisked to a hospital, suffering from a respiratory ailment which his doctors assure us gives no cause for concern.

And we have watched, helplessly and sorrowfully, Winston Spencer Churchill, of Britain, slip toward the end of a life unmatched in greatness.

The origins of these two remarkable men of the 20th century could hardly be more diverse. President Johnson stems from pioneer stock in a harsh and arid region of Texas.

Sir Winston is the product of centuries of aristocracy, steeped in the ancient traditions of Britain—and, we can proudly add, an American mother.

Yet there is no doubt that the two, if history had placed them as contemporaries in office, would have found much in common and a wealth of mutual admiration and respect.

Above all, both would have shared a fierce and identical pride in the parliamentary form of government, common to both our lands, that is the essence of democracy.

The lives of both, in fact, have been greatly influenced by long experience in the deliberative chambers of government. No one has been more inextricably entwined with the British House of Commons than Sir Winston; he is indeed the child of that House, as he had so proudly observed.

And few can compare with Lyndon Johnson as the embodiment of Congress; for years he was the undisputed king of Capitol Hill, transforming the post of Senate majority leader from its hitherto figurehead status to one of unprecedented power and effectiveness.

But what indeed can be said about Sir Winston Churchill to do justice to the man? At the close of two-thirds of the 20th century he so clearly dominates the historical scene as to dwarf his contemporaries and match any of his predecessors.

It is an exceedingly safe bet that no one of his stature will arise, anywhere in the world, during the lifetime of any of us.

During the past week, moreover, the world watched him wage as valiant a battle as any he has engaged in during his brave and colorful life. Felled by a stroke at the age of 90, his great heart has fought on and on to the astonishment of his doctors and to the fervent prayers of his family and friends.

We venture to guess, however, that this sheer bulldog tenacity comes as little or no surprise to Adolf Hitler's former generals or any other foes he vanquished but a short time ago.

A junior officer always in the thick of combat, a dashing war correspondent—and hairbreadth escape artist—brilliant parliamentary debater, talented painter, patient bricklayer, master politician, visionary statesman, superb historian, mighty war leader, and a dignified and sentimental gentleman who wept when the ragged, bomb-battered Londoners cheered him during his tours of their devastated streets and homes—all these and more are Winston Churchill.

History rolls inexorably on, but we shall never see his like again.

The story of the Man of the Century has undoubtedly been in President Johnson's thoughts during this past week. L.B.J. has always been influenced by greatness and a sense of purpose in others; hence his devotion to the memories of Andrew Jackson, Abraham Lincoln, Sam Rayburn, and Franklin Roosevelt.

A man so rooted in democratic tradition could not, then, fail to include Sir Winston among his mentors.

Both men elevated the practice of politics to unequaled heights. For Sir Winston politics meant duty, in the manner of his forebears the Dukes of Marlborough.

Lyndon Johnson has always felt that the art of politics transcends all others; that only through politics can diverse views among factions and nations be reconciled.

We can wonder, though, what else besides the example of Churchill has occupied the President's thoughts during this momentous week. The explosion of an atomic bomb in the remote fastness of Communist China? The enigmas of Kosygin and Brezhnev and perhaps Charles de Gaulle? or Lee Harvey Oswald and a $12.78 mail-order rifle?

We may never know which formed the President's preoccupation. For this tall, gregarious Texas is now the loneliest American. But there are many things about Lyndon Johnson that we do know—and the time is certainly appropriate to appraise him on the basis of these once again.

First, it is somewhat paradoxical that whereas L.B.J. garnered the greatest electoral majority of any President, he remains a largely unknown quantity to vast numbers of Americans outside Washington, D.C., and Texas.

He does not reflect the youth and magnetism of Jack Kennedy, the military fame of Dwight Eisenhower nor the crispness of Harry Truman. He comes closest, perhaps, to Franklin Roosevelt; but even there the similarity is by no means close.

Yet, in time, I think L.B.J. will become one of the Nation's best known Presidents, not only through communication channels, but through his accomplishments.

For today America is presented with a rare combination: A President with total experience of every nook, cranny, and pitfall of Congress—and with a congressional makeup, in House and Senate, overwhelmingly disposed to favor of his programs.

The Congress, moreover, likes Lyndon Johnson. He is privy to its most inner councils; he can be described as a charter member of its establishment.

The congressional system is dominated by the committee chairmen—and this formidable band of Representatives and Senators feels at home with L.B.J. as perhaps with no Chief Executive before him.

As the "master compromiser" L.B.J. has earned the exasperation, admiration, enmity, and unswerving loyalty of members of both parties. It is said that no one ever won an argument with him. His secret weapon, it is said, is a total aversion to division and rancor of any kind.

He has sometimes been accused, especially during his Senate tenure, of being too closely allied to Texas oil and gas interests. But L.B.J. shrewdly knew that a politician's first duty is to survive and stay in office—otherwise he is rendered ineffective and his goals of a Great Society or anything else become academic dreams.

He is the middle-of-the-roader who has always had to walk a political tightrope in his home State, a turbulent center of Democratic politics.

For years he was subject to the relentless hostility of the liberal faction of the Texas Democratic Party—yet now that he is in office he is instigating virtually everything that faction has advocated.

He is like his enormous State, both of the South and of the West. Yet few who know Lyndon Johnson will deny his broad sense of national consciousness; and as Senate majority leader the problems he faced and tackled were, of necessity, national rather than regional.

Again those who know him will tell you he is equally at home at a labor union get-together or at an Ambassador's salon. "O' Lyndon," an acquaintance one observed, "can talk to you on any level you like." And it is true that L.B.J. has an equal liking for the rough clothes of his ranch country and for Saville Row suits.

He is the Mr. Democrat who for many years loyally supported the foreign policies of President Eisenhower's GOP administration—because he felt it was his duty to do so, because it was essential that the Nation present a unified front to friends and enemies abroad.

He is the former unchallenged leader of the Senate who accepted the Vice-Presidency—against the advice of many closest to him—under the former junior Senator from Massachusetts. L.B.J. did this, again out of a sense of duty and of loyalty to his party.

Yes, I feel Winston Churchill and Lyndon Johnson would have gotten along well together. The sole holder of honorary American citizenship and the big Texan from the southwest plains would have proved a formidable team.

Thus the curtain rises on a new act in the life of one man and slowly falls on the final, mortal scene of another.

TRIBUTE BY

REPRESENTATIVE CHARLES S. GUBSER

OF CALIFORNIA

Mr. Speaker, on Saturday, January 30, many of us sat before our television sets paying final tribute to Sir Winston Churchill, one of the greatest men in the world's history.

As we watched a barge carrying Sir Winston's casket depart from London Tower and make its way along the Thames to Waterloo Station, a familiar voice came through for the world to hear. It was the voice of our own beloved former President, Dwight D. Eisenhower. Although, as he said, he had no charter to speak for the American people, no person more deserved the honor; no person could have more truly represented the deep and personal feeling we, as Americans, have for Sir Winston Churchill.

Along with millions of other Americans I am proud that a man of Dwight D. Eisenhower's stature spoke for me, which indeed he did.

Former President Eisenhower's words of final tribute to Sir Winston Churchill well express the feelings of all Americans:

REMARKS BY GENERAL EISENHOWER

Upon the mighty Thames, a great avenue of history, move at this moment to their final resting place the mortal remains of Sir Winston Churchill. He was a great maker of history, but his work done, the record closed, we can almost hear him, with the poet, say:

> "Sunset and evening star,
> And one clear call for me.
>
> * * * * *
>
> Twilight and evening bell
> And after that the dark.
> And may there be no sadness of farewell
> When I embark."

As I, like all other freemen, pause to pay a personal tribute to the giant who now passes from among us, I have no charter to speak for my countrymen—only for myself. But, if in memory, we journey back two decades to the time when American and Briton stood shoulder to shoulder in global conflct against tyranny, then I can presume—with propriety I think—to act as spokesman for the millions of Americans who served with me and with their British comrades during those 3 years of war on this sector of the earth.

CHURCHILL WAS BRITAIN

To those men, Winston Churchill was Britain—he was the embodiment of British defiance to threat, her courage in adversity, her calmness in danger, her moderation in success. Among the Allies his name was spoken with respect, admiration, and affection. Although they loved to chuckle at this foibles, they knew he was a stanch friend. They felt his inspirational leadership. They counted him a fighter in their ranks.

The loyalty that the fighting forces of many nations here serving gave to him during the war was no less strong, nor less freely given, than he had, in such full measure, from his own countrymen.

An American, I was one of those allies. During those dramatic months, I was privileged to meet, to talk, to plan, and to work with him for common goals.

Out of that association an abiding—and to me precious—friendship was forged; it withstood the trials and frictions inescapable among men of strong convictions, living in the atmosphere of war.

VICTORIES AND DEFEATS

The war ended, our friendship flowered in the later and more subtle tests imposed by international politics. Then, each of us, holding high official post in his own nation, strove together so as to concert the strength of our two peoples that liberty might be preserved among men and the security of the free world wholly sustained.

Through a career during which personal victories alternated with defeats, glittering praise with bitter criticism, intense public activity with periods of semiretirement, Winston Churchill lived out his 4 score and 10 years.

With no thought of the length of the time he might be permitted on earth, he was concerned only with the quality of the service he could render to his nation and to humanity. Though he had no fear of death, he coveted always the opportunity to continue that service.

At this moment, as our hearts stand at attention, we say our affectionate, though sad, goodby to the leader to whom the entire body of freemen owe so much.

CHAMPION OF FREEDOM

In the coming years, many in countless words will strive to interpret the motives, describe the accomplishments, and extol the virtues of Winston Churchill—soldier, statesman, and citizen that two great countries were proud to claim as their own. Among all the things so written or spoken, there will ring out through all the centuries one incontestable refrain: He was a champion of freedom.

May God grant that we—and the generations who will remember him—heed the lessons he taught us; in his deeds, in his words, in his life.

May we carry on his work until no nation lies in captivity; no man is denied opportunity for fulfillment.

And now to you, Sir Winston—my old friend—farewell.

TRIBUTE BY

SENATOR EUGENE J. McCARTHY

OF MINNESOTA

Mr. President, the citizens of the United States share the loss of the people of Great Britain in the death of Winston Churchill, and join them in public acknowledgment of his contributions to our times. His leadership at a time of great danger to the freedom of nations and men is a matter of history and his place in it is secure.

I ask that the New York Times editorial tribute to Winston Churchill, the wartime leader and the man, be included in these tributes.

The editorial is as follows:

[From the New York Times, Jan. 25, 1965]

SIR WINSTON CHURCHILL

The power and the glory are gone, the soaring oratory, the eloquent pen, the cherubic face, the impish twinkle in his eyes, the jaunty cigar, the vitality that sparked a world.

One measure of Churchill's greatness is that no one today, now that the blaze of his genius has subsided into dust and ashes, need explain or describe or grope for words. He is one of those rare figures in history who stand like skyscrapers above the merely great. Usually history waits to recognize its supreme leaders, but there is no need to wait in Churchill's case.

He was Britain's glory in a special way, for he somehow managed to personify what is magnificent in the English race, and what is most appealing—John Bull with imperfections and eccentricities, but with the courage, the doggedness, the loyalty, the strength. Many who sought to isolate the essential quality of his greatness fastened upon the astonishing vitality. Never was there a man so durable, so indefatigable, so indomitable. It is almost incredible that there was a man among us yesterday who rode in the charge of the 21st Lancers at Omdurman and was a Member of Parliament under Queen Victoria, who served as his nation's Prime Minister as late as 1955.

Yet, durability and vitality are not in themselves a guarantee of greatness. They only assured him life and dominance at a moment of history when all his gifts and those of his people could combine to produce the miracle of Britain in the Second World War.

There was some quality of anticlimax about the rest. When the Great War was won, Winston Churchill was rejected as his nation's leader. A few of his military commanders were critical in their memoirs of some of his wartime decisions—as an earlier generation had been critical of his Gallipoli campaign in 1915–16.

A decade ago his work was done, in the sense that he no longer had the strength to carry on in his beloved House of Commons, although he remained a Member of Parliament almost to the end. In some ways the whole of his life was devoted to the House of Commons. He did go on writing and, in fact, the fourth and last volume of his monumental "History of the English-Speaking Peoples" was published only in 1958. Writing for him was always an avocation although for years he had to make a living out of it and wrote superbly.

He was, too, an orator whose speeches were never dull and sometimes reached the most inspiring heights of which our language is capable. Like Shakespeare, he will be "full of quotations" so long as the English language lives. But no one in later generations will ever recapture the thrill that came to us, listening over the radio in moments of glory and agony, as we heard Winston Churchill speak of "blood, toil, tears, and sweat," of "their finest hour," of fighting on the beaches, in the fields, in the streets, of so much being owed by so many to so few.

In the sweet, sad process of looking back we have the consolation of these memories. A man like Winston Churchill makes everyone a part of his life, as if a little of that greatness were shared by each of us. That he should have been half American as well as "all English" was a special source of pleasure to Americans. Nowhere beyond his native land will he be more sincerely mourned than throughout the length and breadth of these United States.

Winston Churchill was the glory of a tremendous era in history encompassed by the two World Wars. He leaves one feeling that an age has gone into history with him. Years ago he wrote that he gave "sincere thanks to the high gods for the gift of existence." We, too, have reason to be thankful for that gift.

One would like to think of his passing in terms jotted down in a notebook by another supremely great human being, Leonardo da Vinci: "Just as a day well spent brings happy sleep, so a life well spent brings happy death."

TRIBUTE BY

SENATOR HARRY FLOOD BYRD

OF VIRGINIA

Mr. President, I submit a most eloquent, timely, and fitting editorial on the late Winston Churchill. The editorial is from the Washington Evening Star as follows:

[From the Washington (D.C.) Evening Star, Jan. 25, 1965]

WINSTON CHURCHILL

Churchill is dead, gone from the world he saved. And the world he saved, distracted still by the flow and eddy of the aftermath, has not yet reckoned its debt to him.

Perhaps that sum cannot be reckoned up, so great it is. Our very troubles of this time derive from that more nearly mortal evil that Churchill fought and ended.

Are the emerging nations irritated and frustrated at what they take to be survivals of the British Raj? Had it not been for Churchill, they would have been spared their hurt feelings, for they would never have emerged at all.

Does Charles de Gaulle grow restive at the failure of the nations to see his glory? The question would not have arisen without Churchill to fight for a France that had been captured.

Are we ourselves troubled with the problems of the alliance? We'd have been spared our troubles had not Churchill stood when all else fell. Is it hard and endless to achieve the unity of Europe? There was a European unity of slavery and depravity designed to last a thousand years. Because of Churchill it is no more.

The Russians themselves may count their debt to that great man. Had England made its peace with evil, the Soviet state would have dropped into the dark of history or have become, in the extension of the Stalin-Hitler pact, the complete political expression of the worst shadows in Stalin's mind.

But Churchill did not fail. He lived and spoke and fought, and so all of us live as we do.

In an age of progressive thought, he seemed an odd man to become a hero. He liked cigars and brandy and high cuisine. He believed deeply in the virtue of royalty. He believed in the British empire, in gallantry, in chivalry. He believed in language and in the golden deeds of the English past. In an age that wrote history in terms of social movements and philosophical evolution, Churchill read history as a glorious record of brave men and the things they did for our country.

He was old fashioned and out of date. But when the hour struck it was his alone. For the evil that rose in Germany was a timeless evil. To meet it required a cast of mind that Churchill had, a dedicated innocence, a belief in battles and in courage. The monstrous German war gods came up from under mountains and brandished again their hammers and axes. Their shadow of death spread through the heart of Europe, north to the polar ice, south to the Sahara, over all of France, and paused for a moment at the little strip of water before England.

In that moment Churchill spoke and his voice was like Roland's horn of Roncesvalles. He broke the spell of the evil magician and roused the world to fight for its freedom. Against the Wehrmacht's mechanical might, he had, for a while, only the gallantry, the courage, the spirit of his people. These old-fashioned virtues held the battle.

He saved the world and his world at home replied by turning him out of office, for a new time had come. He said that he would not preside over the dissolution of the British Empire, but it is dissolved and it had to be dissolved. Yet whatever hope of freedom and dignity all men have today, they owe in part to the last glorious fight of that empire and to the ability of the empire to bring forth, as its last gift, the man, Winston Churchill.

May angels attend him.

Mr. President, I submit a very timely article entitled "Two Incredible Men." The article was written by Mr. Vermont Royster, and was published in the Wall Street Journal of January 25.

Thinking Things Over: Two Incredible Men

(By Vermont Royster)

The year was 1935—it doesn't seem like 30 years ago—and everybody thought that the soldier's course was run. In Washington that autumn day they paraded a guard of honor for him, and the hero who had commanded armies went off in retirement as adviser to a provincial constabulary.

It was the same year, so a date on the book's flyleaf reminds us, that we read the autobiography of another man who had also completed a full life. In his time he, too, had been a soldier, and also a journalist of renown, a historian, a novelist, twice minister to a king, key figure in a great war, and a politician to be reckoned with. Now the old man, as old men will, was rounding it off with the tale of how it all happened.

The first man, of course, was Douglas MacArthur, and the second was Winston Churchill.

What they had done before taxes credulity. Only a hackwriter turning out boys' adventure yarns would spin such derring-do of the handsome young man, first in his class at West Point, mixing with guerrillas in the Philippines, slipping behind enemy lines in Mexico, winning five Silver Stars and the two stars of a general in the trenches of France, all within 15 years of being a schoolboy. Becoming a full general and U.S. Chief of Staff, as MacArthur did in 1930, seemed dreadfully anticlimatic.

Not even a pulpwriter would have dared put Winston Churchill's story in a movie script for Errol Flynn. It would have to come out like a Henty series— "Fighting Afridis in Khyber Pass," "With Kitchener at Khartoum," and "the Escape From the Boers." But G. A. Henty wouldn't dream of casting the same character as First Lord of Admiralty and—of all things—Chancellor of the Exchequer.

What happened to them afterward was patently impossible. You dare recount it only because it happened. The retired general was twice recalled to life, at Bataan and Korea, and twice gained victories for his country; it was left to others to lose them. The discarded minister saved his country from ashes; it was left to others to let its glory fade.

Yet for all the astonishment at such adventures, the most incredible thing is that in the era of common man such men could be.

Each was the son of a father who was himself an uncommon man and in turn the son of an uncommon father. The first Arthur MacArthur was briefly Governor of his State and for years a respected Federal judge. The second one, colonel of a battle regiment as a boy of 20, became a general whose name was as much a household word in his time as the son's in our own. Lord Randolph Churchill, the son of a Duke of Marlboro (name famed by the Battle of Blenheim), was himself a queen's minister and a mover of a nation's affairs.

So both Churchill and MacArthur were born with a heritage, and not the least of which came from their remarkable mothers. Jennie Jerome Churchill and Mary Hardy MacArthur were proud of the men they married, and in a way less now in fashion bequeathed their sons pride in family and a desire to honor it.

A part of their inheritance was an uncommon mind. Churchill won no scholastic prizes as a schoolboy, but to a delight in history he brought incessant curiosity for its meaning and he mastered, as few men do, the structure of the simple English sentence.

MacArthur, as anyone can testify who ever heard him speak, also had the gift to articulate an ordered mind. His rhetoric, as sometimes Churchill's might be a little overblown but whatever the subject the words went to the heart of the matter and, listening, you knew their clarity came from unmuddied thought.

Not the least of their inheritance were the gems of longevity, without which the rest would have been impossible. Both in youth were vigorous in body; in age they kept vigor of mind.

As striking as any of it is that each of these men inherited a 19th century view of man and his destiny and with such a view made themselves towering figures of the 20th.

For each of these men, plainly, was an aristocrat—in birth, breeding, mind, and manner. Toward their fellow man theirs was the attitude of the noblesse oblige; believing themselves superior men, and never deigning to hide their belief, they took it their duty to lead, their destiny to play great roles.

As men conscious of the past as well as the future, they saw the world not as if it were born yesterday but against the sweep of history. Thus Winston Churchill, surrounded by disasters at home, could spend an hour thinking about the Balkans. Thus MacArthur, fleeing Corregidor, was already reflecting on the world after victory.

This way of looking far ahead because they could look far back was noticeably absent in the other leaders, good or bad. Hitler dreamed of a great Reich but had not seriously thought of what he would do with victory if he won it. And much of our present trouble is due to the fact that Roosevelt's postwar planning dealt too much with the immediate, too little with past or future.

For much the same reasons, both MacArthur and Churchill unashamedly used words that today make many people wince—patriotism, duty, honor, loyalty, sacrifice, courage, and self-respect.

You're struck with this reading MacArthur's memoirs recently published in Life magazine; the sentiments sound as old fashioned as McGuffey's Reader. Yet reading them you know why MacArthur would rather be dismissed than fail to urge what he thought Korea required. Churchill sacrified his political career, or so he and everyone thought, because he believed honor and duty to country required him to speak his mind on Hitler, alone if need be.

Men so endowed are likely to have a touch of arrogance. MacArthur, for all his admirers, could probably not have been elected to anything; Churchill would never have been chosen Prime Minister in ordinary days. Yet in each man's case, and several times, when a nation at war had need of uncommon men it turned to them. And every time the people found themselves well served.

Now their story is in the past and other men can only marvel at it.

TRIBUTE BY

REPRESENTATIVE JOHN O. MARSH, JR.

OF VIRGINIA

Mr. Speaker, in recent days, the thoughts of many citizens of the United States, in all walks of life, have turned toward the personality and career of Sir Winston Churchill, whose many distinctions include the award of honorary U.S. citizenship.

Among those who had the high privilege of personal meeting with Sir Winston is State Senator Harry F. Byrd, Jr., of Virginia, who recently wrote for the Winchester, Va., Evening Star an illuminating commentary, which I include, as it appeared on January 16, 1965:

It was in 1929 at the Governor's mansion in Richmond that this writer first met Mr. Churchill; I saw him last in 1951 when Mrs. Byrd and I were his guests at the British Parliament in London.

Between those dates Winston Churchill, British politician and writer, became Prime Minister of England and the man most responsible for the downfall of Hitler and the preservation of England as a free nation.

It was 35 years ago that Mr. Churchill, as author, lecturer and historian, came to Virginia to study the Civil War battlefields around Richmond. His host was Governor Byrd; his battlefield guide was Dr. Douglas Southall Freeman, editor of the Richmond News Leader and perhaps America's foremost authority on Robert E. Lee and Confederate military strategy. Years later Sir Winston was to write that the American Civil War was the "noblest and least avoidable of all the great mass conflicts."

Mr. Churchill, then 54 years of age, spent 10 days in Richmond. He told his host that he regarded his political career behind him.

He had at that time been a member of Parliament for 28 years. He had served in the Cabinets of three Prime Ministers, H. H. Asquith, Lloyd George, and Stanley Baldwin. As such he had served as President of the Board of Trade, Home Secretary, First Lord of the Admiralty, Minister of Munitions, Secretary of State for War and Air, Secretary of the Colonies, and Chancellor of the Exchequer.

But more than a decade was to pass before Winston Churchill was to obtain the political position for which he has now become famous.

Perhaps more than any single factor it was his bulldog tenacity, along with his ability to rally his war-weary people, that saved England during those dark days between 1940 and 1945.

Following the evacuation of the British armies from Dunkirk, Winston Churchill's strong, clear voice hurled a challenge—both to Hitler and to his own people: "We will fight on the beaches, we will fight on the streets, we will fight in the hills."

His tenacity was apparent during his Virginia visit. On the night of his arrival, Governor and Mrs. Byrd entertained at a formal state dinner for the British statesman. During the course of the meal Mr. Churchill asked for mustard. His hostess sent his request to the kitchen only to be informed, to her dismay, that there was none in the house.

Trying to pass it off lightly, Mrs. Byrd told Mr. Churchill of her predicament, but added she would be glad to send someone to the store. He said, yes, that was what he would like. So Mrs. Byrd slowed the dinner down to a snail's pace while this writer was dispatched to the grocery.

Mr. Churchill knew what he wanted and when he wanted it, a characteristic which served him well in war and politics.

As a guest, however, it was a quality that some hostesses did not relish too highly.

During his visit, Mr. Churchill made a habit of specifying the time he would like his meals. And then he began to supervise the menu. My mother would have been happy had the Britisher received an emergency call to return to Parliament.

Winston Churchill was born to statecraft. His father, Lord Randolph Churchill, held posts of importance in the English Government, with the exception of Prime Minister. Winston Churchill was elected to Parliament at the age of 26 and, except for a 2-year period (1922 to 1924), he was reelected until his retirement 64 years later.

Serving for 6 years as a conservative M.P., he shifted to the Liberal Party for the next 16 years. In 1924 he returned to the Conservative Party, where he remained for the rest of his career.

His abilities shone most brilliantly in periods of crisis. He was the first to recognize the potential danger of Adolf Hitler. His was the clearest and most persistent voice against the appeasement policies of the Chamberlain government in the mid-1930's. For years he stood virtually alone—and unheeded.

And then came September 1, 1939. The German armies were on the march, just as Churchill had warned.

It was then that a frightened nation turned to the one amongst them who, for 6 lonely years, had sought without avail to stiffen the policy of his Government toward the German menace.

Winston Churchill overnight became First Lord of the Admiralty in the Chamberlain government. But within a few months Neville Chamberlain was out and Winston Spencer Churchill became in 1940 Prime Minister of England, First Lord of the Treasury, and Minister of National Defense, positions he held until victory was achieved in 1945.

It is perhaps too much to say that Winston Churchill saved England and the British Empire. It is not too much to say, however, that Winston

Churchill did more to that end than any single individual. Mr. Churchill was England's foremost son during "Their Finest Hour."

Having sat at the summit with President Roosevelt and Joseph Stalin, having shared the triumvirate leadership in ridding the world of nazism, having brought his nation from the bitter ignominy of Dunkirk in 1940 to total victory 5 years later, Winston Churchill tuned his thoughts to the rebuilding of England.

The world leaders gathered at Potsdam in the early summer of 1945: An American President who only weeks before had assumed the responsibilities of office, without essential background; the Soviet's determined, crafty Joseph Stalin; and England's resolute, highly experienced Winston Churchill. It was those three, Harry Truman, Stalin, and Churchill, who began the task of reshaping the peacetime world.

And then a bombshell struck.

A supremely confident Churchill had left the German conference site for England, saying he would be back as soon as the election votes were counted.

But the England which turned to Winston Churchill in the darkest period of that Nation's history deserted him still drinking the heady wines of victory.

When the votes were counted that July Winston Churchill no longer was Prime Minister, and his place at the world conference table was taken by Clement Attlee, the leader of the Socialist forces.

In 1940 Churchill had told his people bluntly that if victory were to be achieved he could offer them nothing but "blood, toil, tears, and sweat." The people responded. But in the elections of 1945 they wanted something more comfortable. The war-weary English listened to the siren song of the Socialist. England embraced what Mr. Churchill described as "the philosophy of failure and the gospel of envy."

And Churchill left the role of world leader and went back to his painting, to his bricklaying, to his writing, and to his leadership of the minority party in the House of Commons.

It was in this role that I found Mr. Churchill in the summer of 1951—with elections only a few months away. I met him in his private office at Westminster. We talked for a long time—or rather, Mr. Churchill talked for a long time.

He was interested in Virginia, in the Shenandoah Valley. He told me he had seen most of the Confederate battlefields, but hoped before he died to see firsthand the valley terrain which was the scene of so many of Stonewall Jackson's campaigns.

He told me of some of his great wartime decisions, and then we fell to discussing governmental philosophy.

He spoke of the bombing of the House of Commons; it having been destroyed during the early years of the war (the Commons then met in the House of Lords).

Mr. Churchill said he had had the old Commons restored in exactly its original form. He met much opposition in this, he said, by those who wanted to enlarge and modernize. He opposed this with, to use his own words, "resolution and vigor." One could see that this old chamber where he had spent more than 50 years as the people's representative, was dear to Mr. Churchill's heart.

He gave two pieces of advice on the building of a legislative hall:

One: "Do not make it semicircular like you have in the United States, but rather make it oblong—and put one party on one side and one on the other side, and make them stay there. (He did not mention that he twice had changed parties.)

Two: "Keep it small and compact and do not have enought seats for all the members." (The British House of Commons can seat only 400 of its 600 members.) "It is much better to have a small, compact chamber and make the members sit on the floor and on each other's lap. This is more democratic. And besides, it is much easier to speak to a crowded House than to a sparsely filled one."

In the last assertion was it Churchill the architect speaking, or was it Churchill the orator?

On that interesting occasion we discussed the relative merits of America's constitutional form of government and the British parliamentary system. At one point I mentioned that in some respects the British system had advantage over the American.

Never shall I forget Mr. Churchill's reply:

"Ah, yes, Mr. Byrd, but don't forget this. The basic strength of America, in my judgment, lies in the fact that the 48 States, acting through their own legislative bodies, can to a very considerable degree determine their own local problems. You are not centralized in America like we are in England."

A few months later the British electorate returned Winston Churchill to his wartime position as Prime Minister.

Winston Churchill's leadership was that of an elected leader of a democracy.

He joined battle against, to use his own words, "totalitarian compulsion and the regimentation of our national life." Mr. Churchill had the wisdom, the experience, the character, and the determination to pursue resolutely this goal.

In my judgment, he was without a peer among his contemporaries in three spheres: As a statesman, as orator, and as writer of prose.

He once summed in five words a noble creed for nation or individual:

In war: Resolution.

In defeat: Defiance.

In victory: Magnanimity.

In peace: Good will.

To this may I add, in reference to Mr. Churchill:

In history: Indelible impression.

TRIBUTE BY

REPRESENTATIVE CHARLES McC. MATHIAS, JR.

OF MARYLAND

Mr. Speaker, people throughout the world were warmed by President Eisenhower's tribute to his old comrade, Sir Winston Churchill. I include here this personal tribute delivered by President Eisenhower on January 30, 1965, at St. Paul's Cathedral in London:

A Personal Tribute to Sir Winston Churchill

(By General of the Army Dwight D. Eisenhower, delivered January 30, 1965, at St. Paul's Cathedral, London)

Upon the mighty Thames, a great avenue of history, move at this moment to their final resting place the mortal remains of Sir Winston Churchill. He was a great maker of history, but his work done, the record closed, we can almost hear him, with the poet, say:

"Sunset and evening star,
And one clear call for me.

* * * * *

"Twilight and evening bell
And after that the dark.
And may there be no sadness of farewell,
When I embark."

As I, like all other freemen, pause to pay a personal tribute to the giant who now passes from among us, I have no charter to speak for my countrymen—only for myself. But, if in memory, we journey back two decades to the time when America and Britain stood shoulder to shoulder in global conflict against tyranny, then I can presume—with propriety, I think—to act as spokesman for the millions of Americans who served with me and their British comrades during 3 years of war in this sector of the earth.

To those men Winston Churchill was Britain—he was the embodiment of British defiance to threat, her courage in adversity, her calmness in danger, her moderation in success. Among the Allies his name was spoken with respect, admiration, and affection. Although they loved to chuckle at his foibles, they knew he was a stanch friend. They felt his inspirational leadership. They counted him a fighter in their ranks.

The loyalty that the fighting forces of many nations here serving gave to him during that war was no less strong, no less freely given, than he had, in such full measure, from his own countrymen.

An American, I was one of those Allies. During those dramatic months, I was privileged to meet, to talk, to plan, and to work with him for common goals.

Out of that association an abiding—and to me precious—friendship was forged; it withstood the trials and frictions inescapable among men of strong convictions, living in the atmosphere of war.

The war ended, our friendship flowered in the later and more subtle tests imposed by international politics. Then, each of us, holding high official posts in his own nation, strove together so to concert the strength of our two peoples that liberty might be preserved among men and the security of the free world wholly sustained.

Through a career during which personal victories alternated with defeats, glittering praise with bitter criticism, intense public activity with periods of semiretirement, Winston Churchill lived out his 4 score and 10 years.

With no thought of the length of the time he might be permitted on earth, he was concerned only with the quality of the service he could render to his nation and to humanity. Though he had no fear of death, he coveted always the opportunity to continue that service.

At this moment, as our hearts stand at attention, we say our affectionate, though sad, goodby to the leader to whom the entire body of freemen owes so much.

In the coming years, many in countless words will strive to interpret the motives, describe the accomplishments, and extol the virtues of Winston Churchill—soldier, statesman, and citizen that two great countries were proud to claim as their own. Among all the things so written or spoken, there will ring out through all the centuries one incontestable refrain: Here was a champion of freedom.

May God grant that we—and the generations who will remember him—heed the lessons he taught us: in his deeds, in his words, in his life.

May we carry on his work until no nation lies in captivity; no man is denied opportunity for fulfillment.

And now, to you, Sir Winston—my old friend—farewell.

TRIBUTE BY

REPRESENTATIVE CHARLES S. JOELSON

OF NEW JERSEY

Mr. Speaker, since the Congress of the United States not long ago designated Sir Winston Churchill as an honorary citizen of the United States, I think my colleagues would be interested to know about a moving tribute to him from the city of Paterson, N.J., which is in the congressional district which I have the honor to represent.

Mr. Harry B. Haines, who is the publisher of the Paterson News, originated a type of memorial which directly involved the participation of the schoolchildren of the city, whose world was so greatly shaped by the late and beloved British leader.

Mr. Haines conceived the idea of a condolence message to Lady Clementine Churchill and the people of Britain signed by the schoolchildren of the city.

The response was so great that it became necessary to make a signature book which was ultimately signed by 16,000 boys and girls of the city's public, private, and parochial schools. The book itself was an attractive work of art in royal blue embossed with the seal of the city of Paterson in gold. On its front page it carried the seal of the Churchill family.

The book was delivered to the U.S. Ambassador in London by Brig. Gen. Robert J. Goewey, commander of the Eastern Transport Air Force of the Military Air Transport Service at McGuire Air Force Base, and the Ambassador has transmitted it to Lady Churchill.

In these days when so much is spoken despairingly about juvenile delinquency, it is heartening to witness such a splendid demonstration of juvenile decency. I think that Mr. Haines and the Paterson News are to be congratulated on their worthy project.

The condolence message signed by the 16,000 schoolchildren reads as follows:

To Lady Clementine Churchill and the People of Britain:

As you and your great nation mourn the passing of your beloved husband, world statesman, and honorary citizen of these United States, Sir Winston Churchill, we, the 15,000 students and educators of the public and parochial schools of the city of Paterson, N.J., United States of America, offer our tribute to his memory and a prayer for your comfort and strength.

Over each of the 3,000 miles this message has traveled, our hearts and minds reach out to you and reflect on your wonderful 57-year union in holy marriage to this peerless man whose matchless courage and superb inspiration carried the free world to victory over tyranny.

Your invincible partnership; through peace and war, has helped to make this world a better place for all.

The spirit of your beloved husband has outlived his mortal life. The impact of what he has contributed to Great Britain and to the world will outlast the pyramids.

In every time of crisis, in every age of uncertainty and despair, God has given to mankind one man above all others to guide His people through their trying ordeals.

Such a man was Sir Winston Churchill, whose life and deeds will ever serve as an inspiration to all who follow for centuries.

In grateful salute to his deathless memory and in earnest prayer for your continued good health.

THE SCHOOLCHILDREN OF THE CITY OF PATERSON, N.J.

TRIBUTE BY

SENATOR MIKE MANSFIELD

OF MONTANA

Mr. President, on behalf of the distinguished Senator from Oklahoma [Mr. Monroney], I ask to have printed a brief statement by him, together with the text of an address by Ambassador Adlai E. Stevenson, at the memorial service for Sir Winston Churchill, at the National Cathedral on January 28, 1965.

Statement by Senator Monroney

The American of greatest eloquence has given one of the finest and best biographic reviews of one of the great statesmen of our century. Adlai Stevenson quite properly has spoken, in tune with the sad heart of the Nation, of a leader who led us as well as his own country through the darkest days of World War II.

Text of Stevenson's Remarks

Today we meet in sadness to mourn one of the world's greatest citizens. Sir Winston Churchill is dead. The voice that led nations, raised armies, inspired victories, and blew fresh courage into the hearts of men is silenced. We shall hear no longer the remembered eloquence and wit, the old courage and defiance, the robust serenity of indomitable faith. Our world is thus poorer, our political dialog is diminished, and the sources of public inspiration run more thinly for all of us. There is a lonesome place against the sky.

So we are right to mourn. Yet, in contemplating the life and spirit of Winston Churchill, regrets for the past seem singularly insufficient. One rather feels a sense of thankfulness and encouragement that throughout so long a life, such a full measure of power, virtuosity, mastery, and zest played over our human scene.

Contemplating this completed career, we feel a sense of enlargement and exhilaration. Like the grandeur and power of the masterpieces of art and music, Churchill's life uplifts our hearts and fills us with fresh revelation of the scale and reach of human achievement. We may be sad; but we rejoice as well, as all must rejoice when they now praise famous men and see in their lives the full splendor of our human estate.

And regrets for the past are insufficient for another reason. Churchill, the historian, felt the continuity of past and present, the contribution which mighty men and great events make to the future experience of mankind; history's "flickering lamp" lights up the past and sends its gleams into the future. So to the truth of Santayana's dictum, "Those who will not learn from the past are destined to repeat it," Churchill's whole life was witness. It was his lonely voice that in the thirties warned Britain and Europe of the follies of playing all over again the tragedy of disbelief and of unpreparedness. And in the time of Britain's greatest trial he mobilized the English language to inspire his people to historic valor to save their beleagued island. It was his voice again that helped assemble the great coalition that has kept peace steady through the last decades.

He once said: "We cannot say the past is past without surrendering the future." So today the "past" of his life and his achievement are a guide and light to the future. And we can only properly mourn and celebrate this mighty man by heeding him as a living influence in the unfolding dramas of our days ahead.

What does he tell us for this obscure future whose outlines we but dimly discern? First, I believe, he would have us reaffirm his serene faith in human freedom and dignity. The love of freedom was not for him an abstract thing but a deep conviction that the uniqueness of man demands a society that gives his capacities full scope. It was, if you like, an aristocratic sense of the fullness and value of life. But he was a profound democrat, and the cornerstone of his political faith, inherited from a beloved father, was the simple maxim—"Trust the people." Throughout his long career, he sustained his profound concern for the well-being of his fellow citizens.

Instinctively, profoundly, the people trusted "good old Winnie," the peer's son. He could lead them in war because he had respected them in peace. He could call for their greatest sacrifices for he knew how to express their deepest dignity—citizens of equal value and responsibility in a free and democratic state.

His crucial part in the founding of the United Nations expressed his conviction that the Atlantic Charter he and President Roosevelt audaciously proclaimed at the height of Hitler's victories would have to be protected throughout the world by institutions embodying the ideal of the rule of law and international cooperation.

For him, humanity, its freedom, its survival, towered above pettier interests—national rivalries, old enmities, the bitter disputes of race and creed. "In victory—magnanimity; in peace—good will" were more than slogans. In fact, his determination to continue in politics after his defeat in 1945 and to toil on in office in the 1950's to the limit of health and endurance sprang from his belief that he could still "bring nearer that lasting peace which the masses of people of every race and in every land so fervently desire." The great soldier and strategist was a man of peace—and for the most simple reason—his respect, his faith, his compassion for the family of man.

His career saw headlong success and headlong catastrophe. He was at the height. He was flung to the depths. He saw his worst prophecies realized, his worst foreboding surpassed. Yet throughout it all his zest for living, gallantry of spirit, wry humor, and compassion for human frailties took all firmness out of his fortitude and all pomposity out of his dedication.

Churchill's sense of the incomparable value and worth of human existence never faltered, nor the robust courage with which he lived it to the full. In the darkest hour, the land could still be bright, and for him hopes were not deceivers. It was forever fear that was the dupe. Victory at last would always lie with life and faith, for Churchill saw beyond the repeated miseries of human frailty the larger vision of mankind's "upward ascent toward his distant goal."

He used to say that he was half American and all English. But we put that right when the Congress made him an honorary citizen of his mother's native land and we shall always claim a part of him. I remember once years ago during a long visit at his country house he talked proudly of his American Revolutionary ancestors and happily of his boyhood visits to the United States. As I took my leave I said I was going back to London to speak to the English Speaking Union and asked if he had any message for them. "Yes," he said, "tell them that you bring greetings from an 'English Speaking Union.' " And I think that perhaps it was to the relations of the United Kingdom and the United States that he made his finest contribution.

In the last analysis, all the zest and life and confidence of this incomparable man sprang, I believe, not only from the rich endowment of his nature, but also from a profound and simple faith in God. In the prime of his powers, confronted with the apocalyptic risks of annihilation, he said serenely: "I do not believe that God has despaired of his children." In old age, as the honors and excitements faded, his resignation had a touching simplicity: "Only faith in a life after death in a brighter world where dear ones will meet again—only that and the measured tramp of time can give consolation."

The great aristocrat, the beloved leader, the profound historian, the gifted painter, the superb politician, the lord of language, the orator, the wit—yes, and the dedicated bricklayer—behind all of them was the man of simple faith, steadfast in defeat, generous in victory, resigned in age, trusting in a loving providence, and committing his achievements and his triumphs to a higher power.

Like the patriarchs of old, he waited on God's judgment and it could be said of him—as of the immortals that went before him—that God "magnified him in the fear of his enemies and with his words he made prodigies to cease. He glorified him in the sight of kings and gave him commandments in the sight of his people. He showed him his glory and sanctified him in his faith * * *."

Winston Churchill as Britain's Prime Minister with Marshal Stalin and President Roosevelt at the Teheran Conference in November 1943

Churchill with Gen. Dwight D. Eisenhower, at that time Supreme Commander of the Allied Forces, on a bank of the River Rhine in March 1945

Sir Winston Churchill and President Franklin D. Roosevelt on the Prince of Wales off Newfoundland during their historic Atlantic Charter conference in 1941

Sir Winston Churchill addressing Joint Session of the Congress in 1941

Addresses of
Sir Winston Churchill
Before Joint Sessions of Congress

Address of Right Honorable Winston Churchill, Prime Minister of Great Britain, at a Joint Session of Congress December 26, 1941

Members of the Senate and of the House of Representatives of the United States, I feel greatly honored that you should have invited me to enter the United States Senate Chamber and address the representatives of both branches of Congress.

The fact that my American forebears have for so many generations played their part in the life of the United States, and that here I am, an Englishman, welcomed in your midst, makes this experience one of the most moving and thrilling in my life, which is already long and has not been entirely uneventful. [Laughter.]

I wish indeed that my mother, whose memory I cherish across the vale of years, could have been here to see. By the way, I cannot help reflecting that if my father had been American and my mother British, instead of the other way round, I might have got here on my own. [Laughter and applause.] In that case, this would not have been the first time you would have heard my voice. In that case, I should not have needed any invitation; but, if I had, it is hardly likely that it would have been unanimous. [Laughter.] So perhaps things are better as they are.

I may confess, however, that I do not feel quite like a fish out of water in a legislative assembly where English is spoken. I am a child of the House of Commons. I was brought up in my father's house to believe in democracy. "Trust the people"—that was his message. I used to see him cheered at meetings and in the streets by crowds of workingmen away back in those aristocratic Victorian days when, as Disraeli said, the world was for the few, and for the very few. Therefore I have been in full harmony all my life with the tides which have flowed on both sides of the Atlantic against privilege and monopoly and have steered confidently toward the Gettysburg ideal of "government of the people, by the people, for the people." [Applause.]

I owe my advancement entirely to the House of Commons, whose servant I am. In my country, as in yours, public men are proud to be the servants of the state, and would be ashamed to be its masters. On any day, if they thought the people wanted it, the House of Commons could by a simple vote remove me from my office. But I am not worrying about it at all. [Laughter.] As a matter of fact, I am sure they will approve very highly of my journey here—for which I obtained the King's permission—in order to meet the President of the United States [applause] and to arrange with him for all that mapping out of our military plans, and for all those intimate meetings of the high officers of the armed services of both countries which are indispensable to the successful prosecution of the war.

I should like to say, first of all, how much I have been impressed and encouraged by the breadth of view and sense of proportion which I have found in all quarters over here to which I have had access. Anyone who did not understand the size and solidarity of the foundations of the United States might easily have expected to find an excited, disturbed, self-centered atmosphere, with all minds fixed upon the novel, startling, and painful episodes of sudden war as they hit America. After all, the United States has been attacked and set upon by three most powerfully armed dictator states, the greatest military power in Europe, and the greatest military power in Asia. Japan, Germany, and Italy have all declared and are making war upon you, and a quarrel is opened which can only end in their overthrow or yours. But here in Washington, in these memorable days, I have found an Olympian fortitude which, far from being based upon complacency, is only the mask of an inflexible purpose and the proof of a sure and well-grounded confidence in the final outcome. [Applause.] We in Britain had the same feeling in our darkest days. We, too, were sure that in the end all would be well.

You do not, I am certain, underrate the severity of the ordeal to which you and we have still to be subjected. The forces ranged against us are enormous; they are bitter; they are ruthless. The wicked men and their factions who have launched their peoples on the path of war and conquest know that they will be called to terrible account if they cannot beat down by force of arms the peoples they have assailed. They will stop at nothing. They have a vast accumulation of war weapons of all kinds; they have highly trained and disciplined armies, navies, and air services; they have plans and designs which have long been contrived and matured; they will stop at nothing that violence or treachery can suggest.

It is quite true that on our side our resources in manpower and in materials are far greater than theirs; but only a portion of your resources are as yet mobilized and developed, and we have both of us much to learn in the cruel art of war. We have, therefore, without doubt, a time of tribulation before us. In this time some ground will be lost which it will be hard and costly to regain. Many disappointments and unpleasant surprises await us. Many of them will afflict us before the full marshaling of our latent and total power can be accomplished.

For the best part of 20 years the youth of Britain and America have been taught that war was evil, which is true, and that it would never come again, which has been proved false.

For the best part of 20 years the youth of Germany, Japan, and Italy have been taught that aggressive war is the noblest duty of the citizen, and that it should be begun as soon as the necessary weapons and organization have been made. We have performed the duties and tasks of peace. They have plotted and planned for war. This naturally has placed us in Britain, and now places you in the United States, at a disadvantage which only time, courage, and straining, untiring exertions can correct.

We have, indeed, to be thankful that so much time has been granted to us. If Germany had tried to invade the British Isles after the French collapse in June 1940, and if Japan had declared war on the British Empire and the United States at about the same date, no one can say what disasters and agonies might not have been our lot. But now, at the end of December 1941, our transformation from easygoing peace to total-war efficiency has made very great progress. The broad flow of munitions in Great Britain has already begun. Immense strides have been made in the conversion of American industry to military purposes, and now that the United States is at war, it is possible for orders to be given every day which a year or 18 months hence will produce results in war power beyond anything which has yet been seen or foreseen in the dictator states. Provided that every effort is made, that nothing is kept back, that the whole manpower, brainpower, virility, valor, and civic virtue of the English-speaking world, with all its galaxy of loyal, friendly, or associated communities and states, are bent unremittingly to the simple but supreme task, I think it would be reasonable to hope that the end of 1942 will see us quite definitely in a better position than we are now [applause], and that the year 1943 will enable us to assume the initiative upon an ample scale. [Applause.]

Some people may be startled or momentarily depressed when, like your President, I speak of a long and a hard war. Our peoples would rather know the truth, somber though it be; and, after all, when we are doing the noblest work in the world, not only defending our hearths and homes but the cause of freedom in every land, the question of whether deliverance comes in 1942 or 1943, or 1944, falls into its proper place in the grand proportions of human history. [Applause.] Sure I am that this day, now, we are the masters of our fate; that the task which has been set for us is not above our strength, and that its pangs and toils are not beyond our endurance. As long as we have faith in our cause and unconquerable will power, salvation will not be denied us.. In the words of the Psalmist:

> He shall not be afraid of evil tidings: his heart is fixed, trusting in the Lord.

Not all the tidings will be evil. On the contrary, mighty strokes of war have already been dealt against the enemy. The glorious defense of their native soil by the Russian armies and people have inflicted wounds upon the Nazi tyranny and system which have bitten deep, and will fester and inflame not only in the Nazi body but in the Nazi mind. [Applause.]

The boastful Mussolini [laughter] has crumpled already. He is now but a lackey and serf, the merest utensil of his master's will. [Laughter and applause.] He has inflicted great suffering and wrong upon his own industrious people. He has been stripped of all his African empire. Abyssinia has been liberated. Our armies of the east, which were so weak and ill equipped at the moment of French desertion, now control all the regions from Teheran to

Benghazi, and from Aleppo to Cyprus and the sources of the Nile. [Applause.]

For many months we devoted ourselves to preparing to take the offensive in Libya. The very considerable battle which has been proceeding for the last 6 weeks in the desert has been most fiercely fought on both sides. Owing to the difficulties of supply on the desert flank, we were never able to bring numerically equal forces to bear upon the enemy. Therefore we had to rely upon a superiority in the numbers and quality of tanks and aircraft, British and American. Aided by these, for the first time we have fought the enemy with equal weapons. For the first time we have made the Hun feel the sharp edge of those tools with which he has enslaved Europe. The armed force of the enemy in Cyrenaica amounted to 150,000 men, of whom about a third were Germans. General Auchinleck set out to destroy totally that armed force; and I have every reason to believe that his aim will be fully accomplished. [Applause.]

I am so glad to be able to place before you, Members of the Senate and of the House of Representatives, at this moment when you are entering the war, proof that, with proper weapons and proper organization, we are able to beat the life out of the savage Nazi. [Applause.] What Hitler is suffering in Libya is only a sample and a foretaste of what we must give him and his accomplices wherever this war shall lead us, in every quarter of the globe.

There are good tidings also from blue water. The lifeline of supplies which joins our two nations across the ocean, without which all might fail, is flowing steadily and freely, in spite of all the enemy can do. It is a fact that the British Empire, which many thought 18 months ago was broken and ruined, is now incomparably stronger and is growing stronger with every month. [Applause.]

Lastly, if you will forgive me for saying it, to me the best tiding of all, the United States—united as never before—has drawn the sword for freedom, and cast away the scabbard. [Applause.]

All these tremendous facts have led the subjugated peoples of Europe to lift up their heads again in hope. They have put aside forever the shameful temptation of resigning themselves to the conqueror's will. Hope has returned to the hearts of scores of millions of men and women, and with that hope there burns the flame of anger against the brutal, corrupt invader, and still more fiercely burn the fires of hatred and contempt for the filthy Quislings whom he has suborned. In a dozen famous ancient states, now prostrate under the Nazi yoke, the masses of the people, all classes and creeds, await the hour of liberation, when they, too, will be able once again to play their part and strike their blows like men. That hour will strike, and its solemn peal will proclaim that the night is past and that the dawn has come.

The onslaught upon us, so long and so secretly planned by Japan, has presented both our countries with grievous problems for which we could not be fully prepared. If people ask me, as they have a right to ask me in England, "Why is it that you have not got ample equipment of modern aircraft and army weapons of all kinds in Malaya and in the East Indies?" I can only point to the victories General Auchinleck has gained in the Libyan campaign. Had we diverted and dispersed our gradually growing resources between Libya and Malaya, we should have been found wanting in both theaters. If the United States has been found at a disadvantage at various points in the Pacific Ocean, we know well that it is to no small extent because of the aid which you have been giving to us in munitions for the defense of the British Isles and for the Libyan campaign, and, above all, because of your help in the battle of the Atlantic, upon which all depends, and which has in consequence been successfully and prosperously maintained.

Of course, it would have been much better, I freely admit, if we had had enough resources of all kinds to be at full strength at all threatened points; but, considering how slowly and reluctantly we brought ourselves to large-scale preparations, and how long such preparations take, we had no right to expect to be in such a fortunate position. The choice of how to dispose of our hitherto limited resources had to be made by Britain in time of war, and by the United States in time of peace; and I believe that history will pronounce that upon the whole—and it is upon the whole that these matters must be judged—the choice made was right.

Now that we are together, now that we are linked in a righteous comradeship of arms, now that our two considerable nations, each in perfect unity, have joined all their life energies in a common resolve, a new scene opens upon which a steady light will glow and brighten.

Many people have been astonished that Japan should, in a single day, have plunged into war against the United States and the British Empire. We all wonder why, if this dark design, with all its laborious and intricate preparations, had been so long filling their secret minds, they did not choose our moment of weakness 18 months ago. Viewed quite dispassionately, in spite of the losses we have suffered and the further punishment we shall have to take, it certainly appears to be an irrational act. It is, of course, only prudent to assume that they have made very careful calculation and think they see their way through. Nevertheless, there may be another explanation.

We know that for many years past the policy of Japan has been dominated by secret societies of subaltern and junior officers of the Army and Navy who have enforced their will upon successive Japanese cabinets and parliaments by the assassination of any Japanese statesman who opposed or who did not sufficiently further their aggressive policy. It may be that these societies, dazzled and dizzy with their own schemes of aggression and the prospect of early victories, have forced their country, against its better judgment, into war. They have certainly embarked upon a very considerable undertaking [laughter]; for, after the outrages they have committed upon us at Pearl Harbor, in the Pacific islands, in the Philippines, in Malaya, and the Dutch East Indies, they must now know that the stakes for which they have decided to play are mortal. When we consider the resources of the United States and the British Empire, compared to those of Japan, when we remember those of China, which has so long and valiantly withstood invasion [great applause], and when also we observe the Russian menace which hangs over Japan, it becomes still more difficult to reconcile Japanese action with prudence, or even with sanity. What kind of people do they think we are? Is it possible they do not realize that we shall never cease to persevere against them until they have been taught a lesson which they and the world will never forget? [Prolonged applause.]

Members of the Senate and Members of the House of Representatives, I turn for one moment more from the turmoil and convulsions of the present to the broader spaces of the future.

Here we are together, facing a group of mighty foes who seek our ruin. Here we are together, defending all that to freemen is dear. Twice in a single generation the catastrophe of world war has fallen upon us; twice in our lifetimes has the long arm of Fate reached out across the oceans to bring the United States into the forefront of the battle. If we had kept together after the last war; if we had taken common measures for our safety, this renewal of the curse need never have fallen upon us. [Applause.] Do we not owe it to ourselves, to our children, to tormented mankind, to make sure that these catastrophes do not engulf us for the third time?

It has been proved that pestilences may break out in the Old World which carry their destructive ravages into the New World, from which, once they are afoot, the New World cannot by any means escape. Duty and prudence alike command, first, that the germ centers of hatred and revenge should be constantly and vigilantly surveyed and treated in good time; and, second, that an adequate organization should be set up to make sure that the pestilence can be controlled at its earliest beginnings before it spreads and rages throughout the entire earth. [Applause.]

Five or six years ago it would have been easy, without shedding a drop of blood, for the United States and Great Britain to have insisted on fulfillment of the disarmament clauses of the treaties which Germany signed after the Great War. That also would have been the opportunity for assuring to Germans those raw materials which we declared in the Atlantic Charter should not be denied to any nation, victor or vanquished.

Prodigious hammer strokes have been needed to bring us together today; or, if you will allow me to use other language, I will say that he must, indeed, have a blind soul who cannot see that some great purpose and design is being worked here below, of which we have the honor to be the faithful servants.

It is not given to us to peer into the mysteries of the future; still I avow my hope and faith, sure and inviolate, that in days to come the British and American peoples will for their own safety and for the good of all, walk together side by side in majesty, in justice, and in peace. [Applause, the Members rising.]

Address of Right Honorable Winston Churchill, Prime Minister of Great Britain, at a Joint Session of Congress January 17, 1952

Mr. President, Mr. Speaker, Members of the Congress, this is the third time it has been my fortune to address the Congress of the United States upon our joint affairs. I am honored indeed by these experiences, which I believe are unique for one who is not an American citizen.

It is also of great value to me on again becoming the head of His Majesty's Government to come over here and take counsel with many trusted friends and comrades of former anxious days.

There is a lot for us to talk about together, so that we can understand each other's difficulties, feelings, and thoughts, and do our best for the common cause. Let us therefore survey the field this afternoon with cool eyes, undimmed by hate or passion, guided by righteous inspiration and not uncheered by hope.

I have not come here to ask you for money [laughter and applause]—to ask you for money to make living more comfortable or easier for us in Britain. Our standards of life are our own business, and we can only keep our self-respect and independence by looking after them ourselves.

During the war we bore our share of the burden and fought from first to last unconquered, and for a while alone, to the utmost limit of our resources. [Applause.]

Your majestic obliteration of all you gave us under lend-lease will never be forgotten by this generation of Britons or by history.

After the war, unwisely as I contended and certainly contrary to American advice, we accepted as normal debts nearly four thousand million pounds sterling of claims by countries we had protected from invasion or had otherwise aided, instead of making counterclaims which would at least have reduced the bill to reasonable proportions.

The thousand million loan we borrowed from you in 1946 and which we are now repaying was spent not on ourselves, but mainly in helping others. In all, since the war, as the late government affirmed, we have lent or given to European or Asiatic countries thirty hundred million pounds in the form of unrequited exports. This, added to the cost of turning over our industry from war to peace and rebuilding homes shattered by bombardment, was more than we could manage without an undue strain upon our life energies from which we shall require both time and self-discipline to recover.

Why do I say all this? Not to compare our financial resources with yours, for we are but a third of your numbers and have much less than a third of your wealth; not to claim praise or reward but to convince you of our native and enduring strength and that our true position is not to be judged by the present state of the dollar exchange or by sterling area finance.

Our production is half as great again as it was before the war; our exports are up by two-thirds; recovery while being retarded has been continuous and we are determined that it shall go on. [Applause.]

As I said at Fulton, in Missouri, 6 years ago, under the auspices of President Truman, let no man underrate the abiding power of the British Commonwealth and Empire. Do not suppose we shall not come through these dark years of privation as we came through the glorious years of agony, or that half a century from now you will not see seventy or eighty millions of Britons spread about the world and united in defense of our traditions and way of life and of the world causes which you and we espouse.

If the population of the English-speaking Commonwealths be added to that of the United States we will all have such cooperation with all that such cooperation implies, in the air, on the sea, and all over the globe, and in science, industry and moral force, there will be no quivering precarious balance of power to offer its temptation to ambition or adventure. I am very glad to be able to say the same to you here today. [Applause.]

It is upon this basis of recovery in spite of burdens, that the formidable problem of the new rearmament has fallen upon us.

It is the policy of the United States to help forward in many countries the process of rearmament. In this we who contribute ourselves two-thirds as much as the rest of Europe put together require your aid if we are to realize in good time the very high level of military strength which the Labor government boldly aimed at and to which they committed us. It is for you to judge to what extent the United States interests are involved. Whether you aid us much or little, we shall continue to do our utmost in the common cause. But, Members of the Congress, our contribution with perforce be limited by our own physical resources and thus the combined strength of our two countries and also of the free world will be somewhat less than it might be.

That is why I have come here to ask, not for gold but for steel, not for favors but equipment, and that is why many of our requests have been so well and generously met.

At this point I will venture, if I may, to make a digression. After a lot of experience I have learned that it is not a good thing to dabble in the internal politics of another country. It is hard enough to understand one's own. But I will tell you something about our British politics all the same.

In our island we indulge from time to time in having elections. I believe you sometimes have them over here. [Laughter.] We have had a couple in 20 months, which is quite a lot and quite enough for the time being. [Laughter.] We now look forward to a steady period of administration in accordance with the mandate we have received. Like you we tend to work on the two-party system. The differences between parties on our side of the Atlantic, and perhaps elsewhere between British parties, are often less than they appear to outsiders. In modern Britain the dispute is between a form of socialism which has hitherto respected political liberty on the one hand, and, on the other, free enterprise regulated by law and custom. These two systems of thought, whose differences, I assure you, give plenty of room for argument between political opponents, fortunately overlap quite a lot in practice.

Our complicated society would be deeply injured if we did not practice and develop what is called in the United States the bipartisan habit of mind, which divides, so far as possible, what is done to make a party win and bear in their turn the responsibility of office and what is done to make the Nation live and serve high causes.

I hope here, Members of Congress, you will allow me to pay a tribute to the late Senator Vandenberg. [Applause.] I had the honor to meet him on several occasions. His final message in these anxious years gave the feeling that in this period of United States leadership and responsibility all great Americans should work together for all the things that matter most. That, at least, is the spirit which we shall try to maintain among British leaders in our own country and that was the spirit which alone enabled us to survive the perils of the late war.

But now let me return to my theme of the many changes that have taken place since I was last here. There is a jocular saying: To improve is to change, to be perfect is to have changed often. I had to use that once or twice in my long career; but if that were true, everyone ought to be getting on very well. The changes that have happened since I last spoke to Congress are indeed astounding. It is hard to believe we are living in the same world. Former allies have become foes; former foes have become allies; conquered countries have been liberated; liberated nations have been enslaved by communism. Russia, 8 years ago our brave ally, has cast away the admiration and good will her soldiers had gained for her by their valiant defense of their own country. It is not the fault of the Western Powers if an immense gulf has opened between us. It took a long succession of deliberate and unceasing words and acts of hostility to convince our peoples, as they are now convinced, that they have another tremendous danger to face and that they are now confronted with a new form of tyranny and aggression as dangerous and as hateful as that which we overthrew.

When I visited Washington during the war I used to be told that China would be one of the Big Four Powers among the nations and most friendly to the United States. I was always a bit skeptical, and I think it is now generally admitted that this hopeful dream has not yet come true, but I am by no means sure that China will remain for generations in the Communist group. The Chinese said of themselves several thousand years ago: "China is a sea that salts all the waters that flow into it." There is another Chinese saying about their country which is much more modern. It dates only from the fourth century. This is the saying: "The tail of China is large and will not be wagged." I like that one. [Laughter.]

The British democracy approves the principle of movable party heads and unwaggable national tails. It is due to the working of these important forces that I have the honor to be addressing you at this moment. You have rightly been resolute, Members of the Congress, in confronting Chinese Communist aggression. We take our stand at your side. [Applause.] We are grateful to the United States for bearing nine-tenths or more of the burden in Korea which the United Nations have morally assumed. I am very glad, but whatever diplomatic divergencies there may be from time to time about procedure, you do not allow the Chinese anti-Communists on Formosa to be invaded and massacred from the mainland. [Applause.] We welcome your patience in the armistice negotiations and our two countries are agreed that if the truce we seek is reached only to be broken, our response will be prompt, resolute, and effective. What I have learned over here convinces me that British and United States policy in the Far East will be marked by increasing harmony. I can assure you that our British hearts go out in sympathy to the families of the 100,000 Americans who have given their lives or shed their blood in Korea. We also suffer these pangs for the loss of our own men there, and not only there, but in other parts of Asia as well under the attack by the same enemy.

Whatever course events in Korea may take in the near future, and prophecy will be difficult, much too difficult for me to embark upon it, I am sure our soldiers and your soldiers have not made their sacrifice in vain.

The cause of world law has found strong and invaluable defense, and the foundations of the world instruments for preserving peace, justice, and freedom among the nations have been deepened and strengthened. They stand now not on paper but on rock.

Moreover, the action which President Truman took in your name and with your full support in his stroke against aggression in Korea has produced consequences far beyond Korea, consequences which may well affect the destiny of mankind. The vast process of American rearmament, in which the British Commonwealth and Empire and the growing power of united Europe will play their part to the utmost of their strength, this vast process has already altered the balance of the world and may well, if we all persevere steadfastly and loyally together, avert the danger of a third world war or the horror of defeat and subjugation should one come upon us. [Applause.]

Mr. President and Mr. Speaker, I hope the mourning families throughout the great Republic will find some comfort and some pride in these thoughts.

Another extraordinary change has taken place in the Far East since I last addressed you. Peace has been made with Japan. There, indeed, I congratulate you upon the policy which in wise and skillful hands has brought the Japanese nation from the woe and shame of defeat in their wicked war back to that association with the Western democracies upon which the revival of their traditions, dignity, and happiness can alone be regained and the stability of the Far East assured. [Applause.]

In the anxious and confused expanses of southeast Asia, there is another sphere where our aims and interests and those of the French, who are fighting bravely at heavy cost to their strength in Europe, may find a fertile field for agreement on policy. I feel sure that the conversations we have had between our two Foreign Secretaries, Mr. Eden and Mr. Acheson, men whose names and experience are outstanding throughout the world, will help to place the problems of southeast Asia in their right setting.

It would not be helpful to the common cause—for our evils all spring from one center—if an effective truce in Korea led only to aa transference of Communist aggression to these other fields. Our problems will not be solved unless they are steadily viewed and acted upon as a whole in their integrity as a whole. [Applause.]

In the Middle East enormous changes have also taken place since I was last in power in my own country. When the war ended, the Western nations were respected and predominant throughout these ancient lands, and there were quite a lot of people who had a good word to say about Great Britain. Today it is a somber and confusing scene. Yet there is still sunshine as well as shadow.

From the days of the Balfour Declaration, I have desired that the Jews should have a national home, and I have worked for that end. I rejoice to pay my tribute here to the achievements of those who have founded the Israelite state, who have defended themselves with tenacity, and who offer asylum to great numbers of Jewish refugees. [Applause.]

I hope that with their aid they may convert deserts into gardens. But if they are to enjoy peace and prosperity, they must strive to renew and preserve their friendly relations with the Arab world, without which widespread misery might swallow all.

Britain's power to influence the fortunes of the Middle East and guard it from aggression is far less today, now that we have laid aside our imperial responsibility for India and its armies. It is no longer for us alone to bear the whole burden of maintaining the freedom of the famous waterway of the Suez Canal. That has become an international rather than a national responsibility. I welcome the statesmanlike conception of a four-power approach toward Egypt announced by the late British Government, in which Britain, United States, France, and Turkey may share with Egypt in the protection of the world interest involved, among which Egypt's own interests are paramount. [Applause.]

Such a policy is urgent. Britain is maintaining over 50,000 troops in the Suez Canal Zone who again might be well employed elsewhere—not for national vainglory or self-seeking advantage, but in the common interest of all nations. We do not seek to be masters of Egypt. We are there only as the servants and guardians of the commerce of the world. It would enormously aid us in our task if even token forces of the other partners in the four-power proposal were stationed in the canal zone as a symbol of the unity of purpose which inspires us. I believe it is no exaggeration to state that such token forces would probably bring into harmony all that movement by which the four-power policy may be made to play a decisive part by peaceful measures, and bring to an end the wide disorders of the Middle East, in which, let me assure you, there lurk dangers not less great than those which the United States have stemmed in Korea.

Now I come to Europe, where the greatest of all our problems and dangers lie. I have long worked for the cause of a united

Europe, and even of a United States of Europe, which would enable that continent, the source of so much of our culture, ancient and modern, and the parent of the New World, to resume and revive its former splendors. It is my sure hope and conviction that European unity will be achieved and that it will not ultimately be limited only to the countries at present composing Western Europe. I said at Zurich in 1946 that France should take Germany by the hand and lead her back into the family of nations, and thus end the thousand-year quarrel which has torn Europe to pieces, and finally plunged the whole world twice over into slaughter, and havoc.

Real and rapid progress is being made toward European unity, and it is both the duty and the policy of both Great Britain and our Commonwealth, and of the United States, to do our utmost—all of us—to help and speed it. As a forerunner of a united Europe there is the European army which could never achieve its necessary strength without the inclusion of Germany. If this necessary and urgent object is being achieved by the fusion of the forces of the continental nations outside what I have called, in former times, the Iron Curtain, that great operation deserves our fullest support. But, Members of Congress, fusion is not the only way in which the defense of Western Europe can be built. The system of a grand alliance, such as has been created by the North Atlantic Treaty Organization, is no bar to the fusion of as many of its members as wish for this closer unity; and the United States, British, and Canadian troops will stand, indeed are already standing, shoulder to shoulder, with their European comrades in defense of the civilization and freedom of the West. We stand together under General Eisenhower to defend the common cause from violent aggression. What matters most is not the form of fusion or melding—a word I learned over here—but the numbers of divisions and of armored divisions, and the power of the air forces and their weapons available for unified action under the supreme commander.

We in Britain have denuded our island of military formations to an extent I have never seen before; and I cannot accept the slightest reproach from any quarter that we are not doing our full duty, because the British Commonwealth of Nations, spread all over the world, is not prepared to become a state or group of states in any continental Federal system on either side of the Atlantic.

The sooner strong enough forces can be assembled in Europe under united command, the more effective will be the deterrents against a third world war. The sooner also will our sense of security and the fact of our security be seen to reside in valiant, resolute, and well-armed manhood, rather than in the awful secrets which science has wrested from nature. These are at present, it must be recognized, the secrets, the supreme deterrent against a third world war and the most effective guarantee of victory in it.

If I may say this, Member of the Congress, be careful above all things, therefore, not to let go of the atomic weapon until you are sure, and more than sure, that other means of preserving peace are in your hands. [Applause.]

It is my belief that by accumulating deterrents of all kinds against aggression we shall in fact ward off the fearful catastrophe, the fears of which darken the life and mar the progress of all the peoples of the globe. We must persevere steadfastly and faithfully in the task unto which, under United States leadership, we have solemnly bound ourselves. Any weakening of our purpose, any disruption of our organization will bring about the very evils which we all dread, from which we all suffer and from which many of us would perish.

We must not lose patience and we must not lose hope. It may be that presently a new mood will reign behind the Iron Curtain; if so, it will be easy for them to show it, but the democracies must be on their guard against being deceived by a false dawn.

We seek or covet no one's territory; we plan no forestalling war; we trust and pray that all will come right. Even during these years of what is called the cold war material production in every land is continually improving through the use of new machinery and better organization, and the advance of peaceful science. But the great bound forward in progress and prosperity for which mankind is longing cannot come until the shadow of war has passed away. There are, however, historic compensations for the stresses which we suffer in the cold war. Under the pressure and menace of Communist aggression the fraternal association of the United States with Britain and the British Commonwealths and the new unity growing up in Europe, nowhere more hopeful than between France and Germany, all these harmonies are being brought forward perhaps by several generations in the destiny of the world. If this proves true, and it has certainly proved true up to date, the architects in the Kremlin may be found to have built a different and a far better world structure than what they planned. [Applause.]

Members of the Congress, I have dwelt today repeatedly upon many of the changes that have happened throughout the world since you last invited me to address you here, and I am sure you will agree that it is hardly possible to recognize the scene or believe it can truly have come to pass. But there is one thing that is exactly the same as when I was here last: Britain and the United States are working together and working for the same high cause. [Applause.]

Bismarck once said that the supreme fact of the 19th century was that Britain and the United States spoke the same language. Let us make sure that the supreme fact of the 20th century is that they tread the same path. [Applause, the Members rising.]

U.S. GOVERNMENT PRINTING OFFICE: 1965 O—49-390